THE
BROKER'S
EDGE

HOW TO SELL SECURITIES
IN *ANY* MARKET

STEVEN R. DROZDECK / KARL F. GRETZ

NEW YORK INSTITUTE OF FINANCE

NEW YORK • TORONTO • SYDNEY • TOKYO • SINGAPORE

10 9 8 7 6 5 4 3 2 1

This publication is designed to provide accurate and authoritative information in regard
to the subject matter covered. It is sold with the understanding that the publisher is not engaged in
rendering legal, accounting, or other professional service. If legal advice or other expert assistance is
required, ther services of a competent professional person
should be sought.

*—From a Declaration of Principles jointly adopted by a Committee of the
American Bar Association and a Committee of Publishers and Associations.*

Library of Congress Cataloging-in-Publication Data

Drozdeck, Steven R.
The broker's edge : how to sell securities in any market / Steven
Drozdeck and Karl Gretz.
p.   cm.
Includes bibliographical references and index.
ISBN 0-13-311044-3 :
1. Selling—Securities.   2. Stockbrokers.   I. Gretz, Karl F.
II. Title.
HG4621.D76   1995
332.63'2'0688—dc20

94-37830
CIP

ISBN 0-13-311044-3

 NEW YORK INSTITUTE OF FINANCE
Englewood Cliffs, NJ 07632

Simon & Schuster, A Paramount Communications Company

Printed in the United States of America

DEDICATION

The Broker's Edge is gratefully dedicated to those giants of the industry who have done so much to move securities sales away from a strictly transactional base to true customer financial service:

Daniel P. Tully, Chairman & CEO of Merrill Lynch & Co.

John L. Steffens, Executive Vice President, Merrill Lynch & Co.

Alan Levitt, Chairman of the Securities and Exchange Commission

John Phelan, Jr., former Chairman of the New York Stock Exchange

In 1975, Merrill Lynch commissioned the first serious studies to determine what services customers really wanted from their brokers in the 1980s. Dan Tully took this important information and used it to move Merrill Lynch into a marketing orientation. John Steffens was the first to recognize the importance of asset gathering and financial planning, rather than straight commission sales, as the key to success in financial services. From these important steps came Merrill Lynch's, and then the entire industry's, move toward true customer-based selling and true customer service. In addition, Alan Levitt (as Chairman of the SEC) and John Phelan (as President of NYSE) have gone above and beyond to not only protect investors, but also to convince the financial industry to take a "customer first" approach.

This book is also dedicated to the hundreds of others within each area of the financial services industry who have worked tirelessly to build and support a customer-based sales orientation.

ACKNOWLEDGMENTS

We wish to express our thanks to numerous people that we contacted for advice and assistance in writing this book. All of the following provided advice and valuable ideas: Jeff Bouchard, Ann Marie Brancato, Paul Calendrillo, Jeff Champlin, Sandy Drozdeck, Ed Folk, Mike Golden, Pattie Goldfarb, Bob Gulick, William Hobing, George Janos, Bob Kurtz, Chris Maloney, Art Mortell, Tom Muller, Stephen Murray, Tom O'Neill, David Phelps, Sherrie Rhoads, Sheri Russell, James Seitz, and Debbie Wachsmuth. Unfortunately, due to the length of the book and the topics addressed, not every suggestion, technique, and piece of advice could be included within these pages. However, they will be incorporated into future works, as well as our courses and workshops.

The following people deserve an extra measure of appreciation based upon the ideas and materials we were able to include: Anita Andrews, Jim Fridl, Michael Gayed, S. Randy Gretz, Gene Ingargiola, Alex Jacobson, Frank McAuliffee, Kathryn Napier, Jack O'Neill, Jerry Rosenstrach, Joseph Ross, Dick Thornblad, Paul Weisman. Their thoughts helped shape this work, and while we may not have quoted all of them directly, we did learn from them. We thank you all.

Randy Gretz and Kathryn Napier went far beyond the call of duty and provided a great deal of assistance in terms of ideas, and in Kat's case, conducting a few interviews for us, hence, a big "meow" to her.

A special thank you to Drew Dreeland for getting this book off the ground, to Caroline Carney who kept it going, and Barry Richardson who brought it home.

Over the years we have had the fortune of meeting numerous industry "stars" who have influenced our thinking. Although too numerous to mention, they include: Joseph Ross, Michael Gayed, Richard Bondler, Linda Sommer, Robert Dilts, Joseph Yeager, John Charlesworth, John L. Steffens, Roger Birk, Dan Tully, Bill Keogh, Tom Muller, Jim Lusk, Jim O'Donnell, Bill Schreyer, Stu Gamerov, Art Mortell, Tom Hallett, Bob Cohn, Randy Gretz, Bob Farrell, Arthur Zeikel, Arthur Levitt, "Wick" Simmons.

CONTENTS

PREFACE

The *Broker's Edge* shows how to become a leading producer within your firm—whether brokerage, bank, insurance company, or mutual fund. Success in this business depends on numerous factors including: being able to effectively motivate and persuade your clients to make appropriate investment decisions; a thorough knowledge of their financial needs and goals, including their understanding of and ability to assume risk; knowledge of market and portfolio strategies; and maintenance of long term motivation necessary to keep up the daily efforts. These key factors, plus a host of others, are explored within this book.

The authors have trained many of the leading brokers in the business, as well as over 30,000 financial professionals and managers at such firms as Merrill Lynch, NationsBank, Barnett Bank, Prudential Securities, Wood Gundy and for the Securities Industry Association. The ideas and techniques presented here are pragmatic and will increase your long term relationships with your clients; your ability to assist your clients to achieve their financial goals; the power of your presentations; and, your overall production. Consultative selling techniques work.

Certain segments of the *The Broker's Edge* are designed for senior brokers, while other segments are designed with the new broker in mind. The book provides in-depth explanations and examples of powerful profiling and selling techniques which cannot be found in other works, as well as overviews of certain basic information. In essence, regardless of your current level of expertise, you will find a lot of value within these pages.

After you've finished reading this book you'll know "the differences that make the difference" between being an average producer and a star producer. Furthermore, you'll know what steps to take to become the latter. Undoubtedly, you will see much of yourself within these pages; you will also learn much about yourself and others; and, finally, you will increase your profits and professionalism by incorporating these methods.

I

THE DIFFERENCE THAT MAKES THE DIFFERENCE

Over the last 25 years, numerous formal and informal studies have focused on the star performers in our business. Whether these brokers are members of a "Chairman's Club," "President's Council," or "Executive Committee," they represent the top producers of their firm and of the industry. There are certain characteristics that most, if not all, share with respect to how they work, what they do, their investment philosophy, and their approaches to the business. It's interesting to note that these brokers (the top 20 percent) generate about 80 percent of the firm's/industry's commission revenue. Think about the ramifications of these numbers.

Group	Percentage of Brokers	Percentage Revenue
Top producers	20%	80%
Everyone else	80	20

On average then, *a typical top producer generates 16 times more commission revenue for the firm than an average broker—16 times more!* Certainly, these brokers are not 16× more efficient; they're not 1,600 percent more intelligent or better looking, nor are they 16× better than anyone else. Since we know that one person is not 1,600 percent better, the question is, "What's the difference that makes the difference?" We call it "The 2 percent differential." This 2 percent represents minute, yet significant, differences in how these leading brokers conduct their business, they think and believe, how they act, and what they do. An overview of these characteristics is presented in this section and explored in greater detail throughout the book.

The differences that make the difference can be divided into the following categories:

- *Concern for the client's well-being.* They care about their clients and are able to communicate that care.
- *Professional ethics.* They consistently try to do the right thing for their clientele.
- *Diversification.* Top performers tend to work with a broad range of products and services as possible to (1) meet the needs of their clients and (2) then be able to respond to changing market conditions.
- *Investment philosophy.* A systematic, consistent, objective approach to investments is taken. Their clients are aware of this approach and generally follow their broker's recommendations.
- *Maintain consistent work effort and personal motivation.* They continue to maintain their efforts through good and bad times. They get paid accordingly (1,600 percent more than others.)
- *They use the "consultative selling" approach.*
- *They have "success habits."*

The following poem addresses a key characteristic of the top performers.

I am your constant companion.
I am your greatest helper or heaviest burden.

I will push you onward or drag you down to failure. I am completely at your command.

Half the things you do you might just as well turn over to me and I will do them—quickly and correctly.

I am easily managed—you must merely be firm with me.
Show me exactly how you want something done and, after a few lessons, I will do it automatically.

I am the servant of all great people; and, alas, of all failures as well.

Those who are great, I have made great.
Those who are failures, I have made failures.

I am not a machine, though I work with all the precision of a machine,
plus the intelligence of a person.

You may run me for profit or run me for ruin
—it makes no difference to me.

Take me, train me, be firm with me, and
I will place the world at your feet.

Be easy with me and
I will destroy you.

Who am I?
I am Habit.

Anonymous

Success habits are the thought processes, beliefs, ways of doing business, levels of enthusiasm that make all the difference in the world.

This book offers a lot of information and pragmatic techniques to help you achieve and maximize your potential. Many of the ideas are taken from the author's sales and management training courses and represent a few of the approaches we teach. All our techniques are carefully integrated to provide a comprehensive, effective approach to doing well by placing your clients first in the financial services business. This systematic approach to success is internally consistent and proven effective.

While we make a strong case for certain things, such as consultative selling, we are not attempting to be dogmatic. There are different approaches that we have not presented and numerous techniques that can and should be employed.

1

Consultative Selling Is "the Broker's Edge"

Consultative selling is the new standard of the brokerage industry. Various regulatory agencies as well as the leading firms are endorsing the consultative sales approach. It's interesting to note that the leading producers within the financial services industry have been employing variations of this approach for years. As you will discover, the fact that they have been using these techniques is one of the reasons that they have achieved "stardom" and the material of most of this book. This chapter presents four critical aspects of consultative selling that will determine your success as a financial professional. Those critical aspects are:

1. Your attitude toward your customer and your work
2. Your professional knowledge
3. Your ability to effectively communicate your attitude and knowledge
4. Continuous personal and professional development

#1: THE ATTITUDE THAT YOU WANT TO HELP YOUR CUSTOMERS

By more than any other single factor, the broker's "edge" can be defined as *your attitude toward your customer and your work*. That may sound pretty basic, but it's the basics, rather than the "razzle-dazzle," that determine just how successful the real stars are in any profession. Ask yourself one simple question, and be completely honest with yourself when you answer: "What are you doing in this business?" Or "Why did you decide to become a broker?" Was it the money? The challenge? Perhaps the excitement? Or to help people achieve *their* financial goals/dreams? If you're like most financial professionals, you had several reasons for becoming a broker, including, perhaps, all of the above. There is nothing wrong with that. They're all good reasons.

However, take a moment, now, and prioritize those reasons. Without realizing it, you will communicate the reason most important to you in everything you do or say (or fail to do or say) in your relationship with your customer. That is, *if your first priority is to help your customers achieve their financial goals, you will unconsciously communicate that to your customers, and they will quickly trust you.* However, if your first priority is making money for yourself, you will also communicate that, and you will find yourself facing increased resistance, stalls, and objections both when you prospect for new customers and when you try to sell something to existing customers. This is true no matter how polished and professional your communications and sales skills.

Thousands of experienced brokers, to whom we have provided advanced training in consultative selling techniques, have told us that they often waste up to 80 percent of their presentation time trying to overcome customer resistance. Once they finished our course, they told us that they finally realized that not only was most of that resistance unnecessary, but also that they had caused it, themselves, when they made their goal the individual "sale," instead of their customer's need. At that moment, they had unwittingly identified themselves as salespeople whose agenda was to sell a financial product instead of a professional whose sole agenda was to help their client. The result—stalls, suspicion, and instant sales resistance.

Both our own experience as brokers, as well as that of thousands of professionals whom we have trained, has been that when you put the needs of your customer (rather than the sale/commission) first; not only will you earn more commissions, but you will also gain several other very positive side effects, such as:

- Being given a greater percentage of your clients investment assets to manage
- Making more sales, ultimately, to each client

- Facing less resistance from customers
- Receiving more referrals
- Developing a loyal client base
- Having fewer compliance problems
- Experiencing considerably less stress when you prospect or sell

In traditional selling approaches, your goal, your reason for existence, is to move as much product as possible within the guidelines established by industry regulations. Unfortunately, such systems almost force you into a client-professional relationship in which your job is to tell the client what to do so you can both make money. Thus, even the most professional, traditional broker constantly searches for ways to make additional money for his or her clients and additional commission for himself (or herself). Sounds reasonable, doesn't it? Unfortunately, in the process, several potential problems become inevitable:

- The broker accepts virtually full responsibility for each recommendation and sale, including its suitability. Later, if the client feels that the sale was inappropriate—or if they don't like the results—they can always sue, or at the very least, take their business elsewhere. After all, you're the expert who told them you could make money for them if they would trust you with their assets. Thus, brokers are held accountable and blamed for things over which they have no control (e.g., sudden, large swings in the market). During good markets, clients are loyal, sales are relatively easy, and referrals are good. However, during bad markets, clients leave, sales are difficult and referrals are nonexistent.
- Since the broker acts as an outside expert, each recommendation made faces the automatic resistance each of us gives anything that is imposed upon us from the outside. Thus, every sales call faces automatic sales resistance.
- Finally, because each broker acts as a source of investment tips, rather than as a comprehensive financial advisor, most good customers divided their assets among several. After all, no broker was right all the time, and just as the broker preaches diversification of assets among different investments, it makes sense to also diversify among brokers. Thus, few brokers ever receive more than a tiny portion of any customer's investment assets with which to work.

The whole idea behind consultative selling is to "consult" with your clients to help them; that is, you work with them as a partner. When you prospect, present yourself as a helping *professional* rather than as just another financial *salesperson* out to help them make money. Make the effort to meet with your prospects and profile them to determine not only the nature of their financial goals, but also the parameters of each other those goals.

Meeting with each prospective client may seem like a waste of valuable time when you could be selling. However, keep the following in mind:

- On average, it takes six calls to a prospect to obtain the first small trade. If the average call takes only 5 minutes, that's 30 minutes to make the first small trade. With a little practice, it is possible to professionally profile someone in that same 30-minute period and set up the next three to five sales calls at the same time.

- Most brokers obtain 80 percent of their business from just 20 percent of their customers. Obviously, this is because those 20 percent not only represent their largest clients (interestingly, this is not always true), and it is with these clients that they have the best relationship. The most successful brokers in the entire financial services industry try to meet all their clients. The key to any relationship, especially one in which you are asking someone to place a large portion of their finances in your hands, is *trust*. How much would you trust a faceless voice over the phone?

- It is easier to obtain and maintain your prospect's undivided attention during the all important task of profiling their needs if they are with you in your office rather than speaking to you from their office. Constant interruptions by their secretary and others can make such an important information-gathering and relationship-building task that much more difficult.

Finally, in addition to your attitude and treatment of your customer, what is your attitude toward your work and your career? There is no other profession in which an individual with a basic college education (and, sometimes, less) can make as much money helping others as that of being a broker. However, as with all great opportunities, there is also a cost in terms of hard work and personal and professional development. Are you willing to pay that cost in terms of working extra nights each week to build up and service a client base, to study your profession from one to three hours each and every day to really learn your profession and then keep up with the changes, to improve your interpersonal skills? If not, you will never rise above mediocrity. The importance of a helping, positive, and motivating attitude will be emphasized throughout this book.

#2: YOUR PROFESSIONAL KNOWLEDGE

As a financial professional, your clients will look to you for the same kind of guidance in their financial matters as they do their doctor in matters of their health. They will expect you to know not only how to diagnose and solve their financial needs, but also how to explain both their situation and the solutions you recommend in ways that they will understand. Today, more than ever before, your role as a financial professional will require you to educate your clients about the investment decisions you ask them to make so that they are "informed" decisions. Not only are more clients making this demand, but more regulatory bodies as well.

Both the National Association of Security Dealers (NASD) and the Securities and Exchange Commission (SEC) are rapidly moving toward requirements for the continuing education of brokers (something the insurance industry has required for years). Within the next few years, it is probable that every broker will be required not only to take so many hours of professional training each year, but professionally recertify every few years.

As a professional, your knowledge of this industry should include not only that part of it which you serve, but the strengths and weakness of the other parts as well. What client needs can you service and what needs can you not service? Who can? You must know not only your own products and services and how they work, but also how to explain them to your clients. And you must know and understand what changes are occurring in the industry and how they will affect you, your clients, and your firm in both the near and long term. Otherwise, you are likely to be caught unprepared when those changes occur. Chapter 3 discusses changes occurring within the industry that will give you a better idea of some of the things for which you will need to prepare.

#3: EFFECTIVE COMMUNICATION SKILLS

Yours is a career based squarely upon the ability to communicate effectively with your clients, your peers and superiors, and the support staff on which you depend to accomplish your job. However, communication occurs beyond the simple definitions of the words we choose when speaking or writing. In fact, psychologists tell us that up to 93 percent of the meaning of any communication is transmitted nonverbally, through everything from which words we emphasize, their context, their private meaning, and the speed and level of energy with which they are spoken. Even our posture and breathing can have a tremendous effect on both how and what we communicate. For example, it is appropriate to introduce here a sign you will see again, which says:

> I know you think you understood what you thought I said. But I'm not sure you realize that what you heard is not what I meant.

While humorous as a sign in someone's office, this thought is not funny when you have to "bust" a trade because you misheard your client or when you have to explain that you really weren't guaranteeing that the stock you recommended would never go down in value. Such difficulties in communication can be expensive and difficult to repair.

Communication also includes both your ability to establish rapport and trust as well as to listen for important information regarding how your client makes decisions and how they are motivated. If you know how to listen for it, your clients will literally tell you everything you need to know to match their hidden emotional agendas as well as their thinking and decision-making patterns. Think what a difference such information could make in the effectiveness of any sales presentation. Sections II and III will introduce these skills.

#4: YOUR PERSONAL AND PROFESSIONAL DEVELOPMENT

Last, yet no less important, is the need for continuous personal and career development. Most people never rise above mediocrity in any profession because they never establish goals to guide them in important areas of their life. By goals, we don't mean just idle thoughts about how nice it would be to someday be elected CEO of your firm or make a million dollars. While admirable, these are no more than adolescent fantasies unless you sit down and develop them fully, including a plan of how you will obtain them. At that point, your goals can become powerful motivating forces that can propel you to the heights of excellence in any area you choose.

When you think about it, there are three areas where you must establish goals: your character, your personal development, and your career. These three areas will determine your ultimate success.

During management training sessions, we often ask senior executives what they want to be when they grow up. Of course, some find such a question insulting at first. But after they think about it, we usually get an interesting discussion about the kind of person each wants to be and what they are going to do about it beginning that day. As you read through the pages of this book, think about the kind of character you will need to achieve your goals and become the kind of man or woman you want to be; then establish a set of character goals and a plan to achieve that character.

Having decided what you want to be "when you grow up," think about your career goals and their place within your overall development. According to Ken Dychwald, author of *Agewave*, you'll be productive at least 10 to 20 years longer than your parents. Besides a certain level of income and quality of life, what do you want to achieve in your career(s)? According to Dychwald, many people will begin entire new careers in their midforties to midfifties because they will be seeking new challenges or their industry has changed too much. What knowledge and skills will you need to reach your goal? What obstacles will you face and what resources will you need to overcome them?

What are your personal goals? Beyond character, what do you want your life and the lives of your family to be like? How do you want to interact with them? How much, and what kind of time do you want to spend with them? How will you handle the high stresses traditionally associated with the investment industry?

Our previous book, *Consultative Selling Techniques for Financial Professionals*, provides information and guidance on how to establish character, personal, and career goals as well as ways to manage your time efficiently and deal with stress. Whether you are a brand-new broker or an old hand, this book is a useful resource.

2

The 2 Percent Differential

Leading brokers have certain success characteristics that form "the 2 percent differential." While many average producers have some or all of the components, it is the way they are combined and the underlying consultative selling attitude that makes all the difference in the world.

Chapter 1 explored four aspects of consultative selling: your (1) attitude, (2) professional knowledge, (3) communications ability, and (4) personal and professional development. This chapter takes a slightly different approach by introducing the following keys to success:

- Understanding your client
- Creating the right environment
- Maintaining your motivation

Each key to success has numerous aspects that are briefly explained in this chapter and more fully explained in other book chapters.

KEY 1 TO SUCCESS: UNDERSTANDING YOUR CLIENT

Top producers within our business recognize the vital importance of client satisfaction. It is only through earning the client's confidence and trust that you may develop a loyal group of people who have entrusted you with substantial portions of their net worth and who are therefore helping your business grow.

If a client knows that her broker has her best interests at heart, there is a very high probability that she will stay with that financial advisor over many years. She will seriously consider anything that is recommended to her because the advisor has earned her trust. There are few higher honors than to be deemed a "trusted advisor." To become a trusted advisor there are a number of things that must be done, including

- Establishing an atmosphere of confidence and trust
- Truly understanding your client's financial goals and aspirations
- Knowing what makes that person "tick" as an individual
- Becoming an asset gatherer so the client can place a large portion of her assets under your management
- Tailoring presentations to the "individual" client, taking into account background, sophistication, learning styles, and predispositions
- Keeping track of the client's investments and realizing the economic and psychological effects of his or her financial situation
- Learning about your clients' personal life. Although it is unnecessary to become their closest friend, you should learn what most friends would know about significant changes in their life situation
- Be willing to recommend strategies that may be difficult for the client to hear, such as identifying a financial asset as an error or telling them they may not be able to achieve all of their current financial goals
- Ensuring ongoing client education
- Making recommendations because it is the right thing to do, rather than recommending something to make a commission
- Developing a diversified client base and diversified portfolios

Establishing an Atmosphere of Confidence and Trust

The adage "People don't care how much you know, until they know how much you care," remains consistently true. Because leading producers do care, and because their concern for the client's financial well-being is evident, they radiate a series of unconscious signals that indicate this caring attitude to their clients. Such brokers listen very carefully; they verify their understanding of what the client actually said, as well as the implications or inferences of what they said; they check and cross-check to make sure that they have as complete an understanding of the client's needs as possible.

Asking numerous astute questions allows these brokers to uncover needs that many other brokers might miss. Being a leading producer, they've gone through this questioning process perhaps thousands of times before and therefore have confidence in their own abilities—generating, of course, confidence on the part of the client. (Unfortunately, many newer brokers try to portray confidence by becoming pushy and arrogant. Some of these people may be confident, but are not necessarily competent.) Real leading producers are both confident and competent. They also know enough to comfortably say, "I don't know. But I will find out."

Clients feel comfortable with certain brokers for reasons previously stated, as well as the fact that these brokers quickly gain rapport. These competencies were attained to a large degree, over time via hit-or-miss methods. We identify and teach specific competencies within the book so that readers can "streamline their own learning" by emulating characteristics and behaviors that have proven themselves successful, and so that senior people can become both more highly successful and more consistently successful by bringing these characteristics and behaviors to their conscious attention. Topics in the book—such as generating rapport, the client's unconscious thinking processes, identifying key buying motivations, and identifying personality traits and needs—identify and teach these key characteristics and behaviors.

Truly Understanding the Client's Financial Goals and Aspirations

The statement "I want a growth stock" might cause many brokers to respond with the latest stock of the hour/day/month. Even if they ask a couple of questions, such as, "What stock did you have in mind?" and "What time frame are you interested in?" the typical broker still responds with the equivalent of, "OK, have I got a stock for you. Let me tell you about it. It's the greatest stock in the world."

Leading brokers or those becoming leading brokers, on the other hand, respond with such questions as, "What does 'growth' mean to you?" "What higher goal are you trying to accomplish with a growth stock?" "What are your other financial goals and how are they integrated?" "How does this fit within your overall financial plan?" Thus, you will uncover a series of needs, aspirations, goals, and criteria that would otherwise never be discovered. The possibilities for multiple sales (integrated account transactions) to achieve financial objectives, plus attaining significantly greater account penetration and assets under management, allow you to do a better job for your clients than the financial salespeople who merely do a series of individual transactions.

What questions to ask, and how to penetrate accounts more fully, are presented within the "profiling" and the "money management" sections (Sections IV and VI).

Understanding What Makes Clients "Tick" as Individuals

There is no such thing as a "generic" client. Each person we meet has independent motivations and criteria for decision making. You must adapt your sales presentations to the individual, and you may have to explain the benefit of diversification, for example, a dozen different ways, depending upon the client's personal motivations. What is exciting and motivating to one person is humdrum or demotivating to another.

Many of the million-dollar producers that we've interviewed over the years did not know how they knew what to do. They just did it. Of course! They were employing the success patterns on an intuitive basis. In Chapter 11, you'll learn how to discover a person's conscious *and* unconscious buying criteria (motivations) and how to use that information within the consultative sales process.

Become an Asset Gatherer

The more assets you have under management for a client, the better you can help the client, as well as yourself. Over the years, numerous industry surveys have validated (+ or −) the following conclusions: If a client has only one product/service with you, the chance of keeping the client for one year is only 33 percent. If the client has two products/services with you, the chances of keeping the client jumps to 67 percent. However, if the client has three or more products/services, there is an 83 percent probability of client retention after one year. Furthermore, if you actively gather assets, the clients place more than just their stocks and bonds with you. The Security Industry Association's Jack O'Neill said that most successful brokers of the next decade will be those who gather and actively manage assets.

Make a Presentation to "Individual" Clients Taking into Account Their Background, Sophistication, Learning Styles, and Predisposition

This concept extends the psychological buying motivations previously referenced and includes a host of other pragmatic techniques. For example, over the years more sales have been lost by giving too much information than not enough information. Of course, it is important to provide the essential information so the client can make an informed buying decision, but overwhelming the individual with "facts and figures" often loses the sale and can be counterproductive to the consultative selling process.

Even the best brokers on "the Street" must present their ideas to the rest of their clients and their prospects in a convincing manner. They keep it short and simple, and they employ a technique which we call "KISS and the three-level presentation." Chapter 16 presents this technique to help insure that you only provide the "appropriate amount" of information, at the correct sophistication level, while simultaneously determining the client's hot buttons.

Keep Track of the Client's Investments and Realize the Economic and Psychological Effects of Their Financial Situation

If there is one constant in life, it is that things are changing. Each investment made is designed to fulfill a specific financial need. However, because of changes in the economy, the market, the underlying creditworthiness, and so on, of the security, adaptations must be made. Yet, most people find it difficult to take a loss or reevaluate their situation based upon the changing circumstances. You must help your clients through this process.

This can be done in a variety of ways, including periodic portfolio reviews, regular monitoring of investments, ongoing updating of any strategies employed, as well as constant learning. Since change is the only constant, it is irrational to hold onto a position, that was once logical, but which is no longer appropriate at this juncture or for the foreseeable future. An essential ingredient of successful investing is the ability to change your opinion when the circumstances warrant it. However, this should not done by the seat of your pants; rather you must have logical, precise reasons for these strategic shifts. Section VI deals with these issues and the establishment of an integrated, coordinated, and comprehensive investment philosophy.

Learn Something About Your Client's Personal Life

Although it is unnecessary to become their closest friend, you should learn what most friends would know about significant changes in their life situation. The birth of a child, the death of a loved one, the changing of a job, and so on are all times when a change in financial posture may be warranted. While certain events happen unexpectedly, there are many situations where planning ahead allows the client to make the correct financial decisions rather than accepting the only financial decision available. In other words, they can become proactive rather than reactive.

Contact your clients regularly and make sure that you know what is going on. Your clients will understand this as concern for their financial well-being (and then provide you with even more referrals.)

Be Willing to Recommend Strategies That May Be Difficult for the Client to Hear, Such as Identifying a Financial Asset as an Error

Nobody is perfect and everyone makes mistakes. Yet very few people are willing to admit their mistakes. Fewer still are willing to take corrective action. Those who do tend to come out ahead.

Nobody likes saying, "I was wrong." However, leading brokers have their clients follow a predetermined, logical investment strategy that forces a periodic, objective look at their entire portfolio, and if something isn't performing to expectations, the logic of maintaining the situation is seriously reviewed. If there is no compelling logic to maintain the position, it is changed to something that has a higher probability of success.

"Probabilities of success" are what brokers deal in. There is no such thing as a riskless transaction, and no one can take everything into consideration. You can only do your best based upon the information that you have available to you at the moment. Too many uncontrollable factors can occur. A perfectly logical strategy can become illogical with a major change in Federal Reserve Bank policy or the passage of certain legislation. "When circumstances change, change your investment posture." Again, Section VI deals with this issue.

Provide Ongoing Client Education

It is important to teach clients enough so that they understand what you are recommending and don't have to put blind trust in you. This is important from both a legal and moral perspective. Top brokers want their clients to achieve a type of educational independence so that if the broker were to leave the business) or die, those clients can go forward and intelligently work with other financial advisors. Again, the concern is for the client's well-being. This concern permeates everything and is the basis of consultative selling.

Make Recommendations Because It Is the Right Thing to Do, Rather than Recommending Something to Make a Commission

This is often "easier said than done." Yet it is partly because of this that the real professionals became top producers in the first place. "Maybe *they* can afford to do it," is a typical comment from newer brokers. Throughout the book, it will be demonstrated that "you cannot afford not to do the right thing for your client."

Develop a Diversified Client Base and Diversified Portfolios

A diversified client base, with the vast majority of clients having a diversified portfolio, allows you to offset various risks effectively and to respond appropriately to changes within the financial markets.

Leading producers also realize that regardless of how good they are, upwards of 20 percent of their client base will disappear every year for a variety of reasons. Thus, these producers are constantly seeking newer, often larger, clients. Many ways to prospect as well as highly effective ways to obtain referrals are presented within the book.

In summary, all the previously discussed attributes of the leading producers of the financial services industry are incorporated within the Consultative Selling umbrella. The desire to truly assist others to achieve their financial goals automatically leads to the development of the attributes presented thus far. In order to help, you must ask astute questions, regularly update your information, make clients more knowledgeable, gather assets, etc. It is by doing these things that you create a win-win-win situation for the client, yourself, and your firm.

KEY 2 TO SUCCESS: CREATING THE RIGHT ENVIRONMENT

The right environment is essential if you are to succeed in consultative selling. You may *want* to do a good job, you may know *how* to do the job, but if you don't have a *chance* to do it, your efforts may be in vain and potentially self-defeating. Despite the environment, leading brokers tend to prevail. They may switch their marketing strategies and work with different financial products, but they prevail. The right environment includes

- What John Q. Public believes
- The economic/market environment
- The corporate culture
- The office environment
- Leveraging your time and effort
- The available product line

"John Q. Public's" Attitudes and Beliefs

As you read in the introduction, the entire financial services industry is moving toward the consultative selling approach. Consultative selling is being endorsed by the regulatory authorities and by most leading firms. The brokerage industry has incurred an unfortunate bad reputation due to the abuses of a few "burn 'em and churn 'em" brokers. The popular press has certainly had numerous field days at the industry's expense, and the word spread that brokerage firms may be a dangerous place for small investors. Of course, this is not true. The overwhelming majority of brokers were (and are) competent, dedicated professionals who realized that if their clients did well, they did well. However, publicized abuses bring about unrealistic, and unfair, expectations, which may affect your ability to help people.

Unfortunately, there remain some transaction-oriented firms whose sales people employ "hard sell" techniques—for whom a long-term relationship is settlement day. These tactics have hurt the entire financial services industry, especially stockbrokers. Banks have traditionally derived benefit from negative brokerage publicity. However, similar abuses (real or enhanced by the media) are occurring within the banking industry. Bank representatives occasionally neglect to mention that the mutual funds and annuities they recommend are not FDIC insured. Industry surveys show that the majority of bank customers automatically assume FDIC coverage for any product the bank offers. Again, the media is having a field day. (A typical news report appears in Chapter 24.)

When faced with such "negativity," many brokers tend to give up and stop prospecting. They may then leave their firms or the business. But leading brokers tend to prevail despite all the "hardships." They continue to do well (perhaps less well than before, but substantially better than others) because they follow many of the principles of business success, their clients know that the negative remarks and attributions do not apply to *their* "trusted advisor," clients will refer their friends and associates to their "quality broker" more forcefully, and the leading producers realize that "this, too, shall pass." Because they have diversified, both their clients and their holdings can survive, continue to grow slowly, and prosper.

The Economic/Market Environment

Whether you call it an "aberration," a "market retrenchment," "a cosmic joke," or a "Democratic plot to defeat the Republicans," the "Crash of 1987" had a significant impact on the financial services industry. Investor confidence was shaken, making it significantly more difficult to sell financial products. Or did it?

Leading producers continued to sell financial products. They, shaken like everyone else, changed tactics. They, and their clients, continued to take advantage of the emerging trends. It's also interesting to note how many leading brokers and top money managers were already out of the market. While no one expected such a disastrous day, many had been expecting a major market decline for a long time. The more sophisticated brokers had already pulled out of the market and were in the "preservation of capital" or "flight to quality" mode.

It's interesting that in a bull market, the leading brokers do not make substantially more money (on a percentage basis) than anyone else. In a bull market most people (including members the dart board school of security selection) tend to ride the rising averages and do relatively well. This is to be expected. In a bear market, however, leading brokers tend to lose substantially less money (on a percentage basis) than other brokers do. Perhaps it is because they learned the hard way by making mistakes in the past, perhaps they are more sophisticated, perhaps they learned from the mistakes of others. After analyzing the investment tactics of numerous top producers (both those we've talked to over the years and those we've read about), we've found that they have a systematic approach to getting into *and out of* the markets. Their investment philosophy (addressed in Section VI) takes into account not only what they would like to happen (i.e., make money), but also what *can* happen (i.e., lose money). In essence, they have downside contingency plans.

The Corporate Culture

The core beliefs of senior management directly affect the way most of a firm's brokers do business. People do what they are rewarded for doing. To implement consultative selling and obtain its many long-term benefits on a firm-wide basis, it needs the active support of upper management as well as the endorsement of the firm's leading brokers—only then will the rest follow.

Many firms have been headed toward consultative selling for quite some time. The visionaries of Wall Street had a strong profit motivation and the realization that you can only help yourself by helping others. Consider the following:

> Memorandum to the Organization[1]
>
> The most valuable asset of an investment firm is its good name. Let us do everything we can to protect it and let us not allow profit to distort our judgment. We have a sacred trust to protect our customers.
>
> In the long run those firms which survive and prosper are those who maintain conservative policies and put their customer's interests first.

Scott & Stringfellow, Inc., has the following mission statement: "Since 1893 our mission has been to put our clients' interests first and foremost by providing superior investment products and service." We know, from our personal experience, that the managers and brokers at Scott & Stringfellow fulfill their stated purpose.

The Office Environment

There are two aspects of the office environment that we will briefly mention: the prevailing attitude, and the work ethic.

Each office has its own culture which is directly affected by the office management and senior brokers. The attitude and work ethic employed by the leader filters down to every member of the office. If you are entering the business, be careful to choose an office environment that will help, rather than hurt, you. Even the most honest broker will be negatively affected if surrounded by people who are decidedly unprofessional, if for no other reason than his office will have a bad reputation. Our reputation is affected by the reputation of those around us—otherwise known as "guilt by association."

While it is not always possible to change a negative office environment, you can choose not to be part of it or affected by it. Leading producers are usually not part of the coffee crowd—they don't have time for it.

[1]Internal memorandum to the organization by Dean Witter on December 17, 1967.

Leveraging Your Time and Effort

Leading producers leverage their time as much as possible. Most have excellent sales assistants (although a surprising number of leading producers do virtually everything themselves). Because "time is money" and because their income is directly dependent upon their sales-oriented activities, the leading producers

- Work both hard and smart
- Use effective time management
- Are highly organized

To maximize your potential as a broker, you must have enough products to meet different financial needs and to address various market environments. No one mutual fund can be all things to all people. Neither can one fund be appropriate for all economic scenarios. A family of funds may meet the need for a flexible approach. As reviewed in Section VI, asset allocation is an important ingredient to success. You cannot allocate a client's assets if you don't have an adequate product line.

KEY 3 TO SUCCESS: MAINTAINING YOUR MOTIVATION

The third key to success consists of maintaining your personal motivation. This is sometimes a difficult task, but it is absolutely essential. To do well in the financial services business, you must be persistent:

> Press on. Nothing in the world can take the place of persistence. Talent will not: Nothing is more common than unsuccessful men with talent. Genius will not: Unrewarded genius is almost a proverb. Education alone will not: The world is full of educated derelicts. Persistence and determination alone are omnipotent.
>
> Calvin Coolidge

While persistence is essential, it is partly dependent upon a series of other factors, including

- Realistic goal setting
- Having a personal mission

- Effective stress management
- Ongoing professional development

Realistic Goal Setting

Too often, brokers set goals that are difficult, if not impossible, to reach. The result is usually frustration and the setting of new goals that are ridiculously easy to reach. The other option is to just go through life on a day-by-day basis without any real goals or direction. Having realistic goals will allow you to maintain your motivation while going through the day-to-day efforts.

Too many people set wonderful-sounding goals only to discover that the goals are too difficult or are not motivating. The goals often get dropped or substantially reduced. If you can't measure it, you can't manage it. Within our previous works and referenced in this book, we've provided numerous, easy-to-use tools to allow you to measure your progress.

Personal Mission

You will make an important difference in the lives of most people. In many cases, your advice will determine whether or not your clients attain their financial goals. Realizing that most people retire essentially destitute—having to rely on the government, their family, or charity to survive—leading producers throughout the industry assume almost a personal responsibility to motivate people to take care of themselves appropriately.

The following story represents a typical would-be investor giving excuses why an investment program cannot be started—going from why investing has to wait till sometime in the future to how investments are no longer a possibility. Consider how many times you've heard the equivalent.

"I CAN'T INVEST *NOW.*"

Age 18 to 25: Picture a college student saying, "Why invest right now? I'm still getting my education. I don't have the money for any investments. I want to have a good time. After awhile, I'll get out of college and begin earning some real money. Then, I'll be able to invest."

Age 25 to 35: That same person in a good business suit, saying, "I've only been working for a few years and am at the beginning of my career. I have to dress well to make a good impression. I haven't had a chance to accumulate any excess cash. Besides, there's plenty of time."

Age 35 to 45: The person holding children's toys in both hands, saying, "I'm married, have children to care for…there are a lot of expenses. I really can't invest right now but intend to once the kids get a bit older."

Age 45 to 55: The person has empty pockets: "I really wish that I could invest now, but I just can't do it. With the kids in college, I'm spending every penny that I have. In fact, we've had to go into debt to help them pay for the education. Once they're out of college, then I'll be able to invest."

Age 55 to 65: The person with a worried look: "Of course I should be investing right now, but money is very tight. I just can't switch jobs at my age. I'm happy to be hanging on. I wish I had started investing 20 years ago. I wouldn't be in this situation now. Well, I'll just hope for the best."

Age over 65: The person with slightly hunched back, looking dejected, saying: "It's too late. We're living with our children. It's not great but what can we do? Social Security isn't enough to live on. If only I had invested years ago when I had the money. There's no way to invest after there is no income."

"I *CAN'T* INVEST NOW"

Adapted from the original
Author unknown

As a broker, you should develop a personal mission statement indicating why you are in business and the value that you bring to the lives of the people you are able to help. This helps maintain long-term motivation.

Stress Management

Being a broker can be among the most stressful jobs in the world. Too often we get into the mode of working harder and harder with less productivity. If continued for too long, burnout may occur, and you, your clients, and your firm lose. To maintain a strong work effort, you must learn how to manage stress. Studies in all industries have repeatedly demonstrated that efficiency and effectiveness increase when you take periodic breaks, handle conflicts appropriately, and deal with the day-to-day pressures.

3

The Wave of the Future

There have always been two approaches to doing business: the *marketing approach* and the *sales approach*. Under the marketing approach, you find out what customers want/need, produce it, and they'll buy it. Under the sales approach (basically a manufacturing mindset) you sell as much as you can of whatever you can produce. *Consultative selling is a logical extension of the marketing approach in which you try to find out what your customer needs, and then fill that need—if possible, with one of your products or services.* If you can't fill it yourself, you send them to someone who can. The benefits of consultative selling are numerous. They include increases in

- Assets under management and account penetration
- Customer retention and satisfaction
- Broker productivity, retention, and satisfaction

However, to be truly effective, consultative selling transcends the mere process of eliciting customers' needs and trying to fill them with appropriate products. It is an attitude that begins in the board room and cascades down through every level of management to the most junior investment reps and their support staff. At its most basic level, consultative selling is an integral part of the quality movement and begins with the realization that *we are in business for one purpose and one purpose only: to service our customers financial needs—to help them achieve their financial goals.*

THE PROBLEM AND THE COST

The failure to recognize our reason for existence is an example of "marketing myopia," that is, the tendency, once you have something that "works," to stay with it and move into a sales mentality. For some banks, such a mind-set might be exemplified by, "Since our customers like the security of FDIC-insured accounts, we will continue to provide *ONLY* products and accounts offering FDIC insurance." They may continue to promote such accounts actively even when rates on traditional FDIC insured items are so low they are not only unattractive, they can actually be disadvantageous. For brokerage firms, this same mind-set can be seen in the continued emphasis on selling stocks as the primary vehicle for achieving most/all of their customers' needs.

The classic example of marketing myopia is represented by the railroad industry, whose leaders thought they were in the railroad business instead of the transportation industry. As a result, they were bypassed by the trucking, airline, busing, and the shipping industries. Has they recognized earlier that their purpose was the transportation of people and goods, they would have diversified their efforts to include trucking, bus and airlines, and shipping lines, participating in the growth and development of these industries. Instead, they focused only on competing with each other.

Another classic example is Hollywood, whose leaders thought they were in the motion picture business instead of the entertainment industry. As a result, they have been bypassed by television, cable (MTV, HBO, CNN, ESPN, etc.), and video games and largely taken over by conglomerates that are prepared to cater to all aspects of entertainment, from publishing to television and movies to games and theme parks (the only exception has been a late-comer, Disney, with its own syndicated television programs, children's clothing and toy lines, and theme parks).

For years following the Glass-Steagall Act, banks thought they were in the "banking business" while brokers thought they were in the "stock and bond business." Some of the larger brokers woke up first to the fact that they were in the *financial services* industry. Up until the 1960s and 1970s, if you wanted to buy stocks and bonds, you went to a brokerage house. They were the only ones allowed to sell them, and that's basically all they sold. However, two events occurred in 1975 that provided this wake-up call. First, on May 1, 1975, the commission structure of the brokerage industry was deregulated. Prior to that, there was little internal competition (between brokerage firms) and no external competition. Second, Merrill Lynch commissioned the Stanford Research Institute to find out what consumers would want in terms of financial services in the 1980s. The two most important findings were

1. Customers wanted total access to their assets.
2. Customers wanted financial planning.

As a result, Merrill created the first Cash Management Accounts (CMA™) and, later, The Equity Access Account™ and became the first major firm to broadly offer total financial management to affluent Americans. Others followed until, in the late 1980s, the other large firms became more like financial "supermarkets" than just sellers of stock and bonds. "All things to some people," as Merrill Lynch's John Steffens once put it.

At this time, brokerage firms began to think beyond stocks and bonds. In 1983, Merrill Lynch was the first to recognize the importance of holding customers' assets. They had come to realize that clients will usually conduct any transaction related to an asset at the firm at which the asset is held. Merrill's CMA, which was created in response to the 1975 SRI customer needs survey then became the primary asset-gathering tool that catapulted Merrill ahead of its competitors with over $550 billion in customer assets as of 1994. As these assets have grown, so have revenues and the distance between Merrill and its more traditional competitors. (Note: Merrill's larger competitors later followed suit, creating their own versions of central asset accounts.)

The idea was to capture larger portions of customers' assets by providing for almost all their financial needs. Beginning with central asset accounts, the major firms offered everything from insurance to mortgages, to college and retirement planning, to unit investment trusts. It was hoped, even then, that each new product would bind customers closer to the firm, making it harder for them to leave when tempted by a competitor or when their broker left for a competitor firm. This was the beginning of the idea of formally establishing a firmwide strategy to maintain long-term relationships with clients.

At this time, many of the larger firms spent fortunes developing and strengthening training programs to produce the kind of professional financial consultants that would attract and keep valuable clients. Unfortunately, the continuing proliferation of products and services also meant that selling and appropriately mixing them in some kind of balanced portfolio became increasingly complex. Brokers who once needed only to call clients with the latest buy or sell recommendation from their firm's analysts now had to be concerned with how the purchase or sale of any single product would affect the overall portfolio. A daunting task for even an experienced professional, this was virtually impossible for newly licensed brokers. This difficult responsibility was further complicated by two other factors: first, brokers were still urged and paid to move product, measuring success on daily sales rather than long-term customer relationships; and second, most sales training, especially at the branch level, focused on increasing transactional selling.

The problem faced by brokers today who have been trained in consultative selling is that when they return to their branch office, there are few, if any, consultatively oriented models for them to emulate. Sales managers rarely remain with any branch longer than two years and are both paid and promoted based on the short-term results of those two years. They have little or no incentive to emphasize the development of asset-gathering and long-term relationships over short-term sales. As a result, they tend to hire, praise, and hold up as models those brokers who produce large amounts of commission by selling even larger amounts of product. Unfortunately, selling is viewed as transactional, while the long-term benefits to the firm of consultative selling are played down.

The danger of losing customers from pushing sales is particularly large for banks entering the securities arena at this time, because the typical client of the bank investment rep is *already* a customer of the bank. If a bank broker (investment rep) loses a client because of "pushing" product or poor service, there is every chance that the bank will also lose the rest of their business with that customer.

LIGHT AT THE END OF THE TUNNEL

The problems of both compensation and expertise are already being addressed by several of the more visionary firms. Citibank is experimenting with a program that compensates investment reps based upon items such as client satisfaction, portfolio performance, and total assets gathered. This is a complex program that will, undoubtedly, go through several changes before it is perfected. But it is a step in the right direction. Several large brokerage firms are making increased use of "wrap" accounts and other packaged products while exploring ways to compensate brokers based on assets under management and customer satisfaction, rather than just straight commission.

To those brokers whose income has depended upon constantly trading large volumes of stocks, these programs may have mixed appeal. However, for newer brokers, they offer a more consistent income with less month-to-month performance anxiety by enabling the brokers to focus the majority of their attention on servicing the clients instead of watching for minute-to-minute changes in the market. Financial planning, whether full service or limited to college or retirement planning, also provides great value in the information and guidance such plans provide reps in their efforts to meet clients' needs. In a way, the financial plan can be said to provide the definitive embodiment of consultative selling (that's why most financial institutions—from insurance companies to brokers and banks—are offering some form of financial planning to their clients). In reality, the time will come when the compensation earned by an investment rep will be determined, at least partially, by whether or not he has established some kind of financial plan with his customer *and* how any given investment relates to that financial plan. This is true because, even if an investment performs "well"; if the client doesn't understand why he owns it and how it works, versus something else, his satisfaction has not been maximized. Thus, an 8 percent rate of return from an insured certificate of deposit (which the client understands) may be preferable to a 9 percent rate of return from a fixed annuity, which he does not understand and may worry about.

An important aspect of the trend toward financial planning can be seen in the way it often allows investment reps to act in concert and build relationships with their client's other financial advisors (e.g., lawyer, CPA, insurance agent) as revealed in the plan. Its often not surprising, in a consumer-oriented country/economy, to find that most people don't really have enough money to meet all their financial goals. At this point, consultative selling begins with helping the client to define and prioritize their goals and finding ways to achieve them. However, this kind of expertise requires training. To help with this, many banks are beginning to follow in the footsteps of larger securities firms such as Merrill Lynch, Prudential, and Smith Barney to roll out financial planning software to help their brokers understand their customers' assets. By definition, some feel this will help them boost fee income dramatically.

Traditionally, new brokers have been expensive investments that have often been frittered away with little thought to the cost of replacing them. With the exception of the best firms, little time or money has been dedicated to the expensive proposition of continuously training new, and even experienced, brokers. As a result, up to 75 percent of all new brokers leave the industry within the first three years.[1] The constant message of "perform today" places investment reps under high stress and a great deal of pressure to sell something, *anything* (possibly with little regard for suitability), just to survive. For them, consultative selling becomes a nice buzzword that they may someday be able to employ.

The brokerage branch manager is a key person in establishing the sales attitude of investment reps. Efforts to help new brokers transition from a transactional to a consultative selling approach can be hampered by branch managers who are transaction oriented. Reports of newly trained consultatively oriented brokers being told to forget everything they had been taught in training school and to get on the phone and start selling the latest product have been legend. Branch managers must also be committed to the consultative approach because that's how they are compensated, or even the best investment reps will become transaction oriented under their direction.

It is ironic that just as the brokerage industry is trying to move increasingly toward a consultative approach, many banks are turning toward the traditional sales techniques to promote proprietary funds. The dangers inherent in such an approach have already been explored in *Bank Investment Representative*.[2] According to Jeff Champlin (the publisher), in the past bankers enjoyed a large advantage over brokers in attracting customers' assets because of the significant difference in levels of trust associated with banks verses brokers. Banks were seen as conservative, nonsales oriented, whereas brokers were perceived as interested primarily in quick trades and quicker profits. Today, many banks are risking a loss of that "trust" by encouraging their investment reps to sell primarily, or exclusively, the bank's own proprietary funds (often, with woefully inadequate product knowledge). Many new bank program managers are often ex-transaction-oriented stockbrokers who only know the hard sell method and who must show immediate productivity increases for the program. Hence, the short-term orientation is inadvertently reinforced.

Moving aggressively into a sales orientation places banks at risk of appearing no different from brokers in their customers' eyes. Areas where this can be seen are "compensation policies, emphasis on the platform versus dedicated delivery methods, and efforts to severely limit approved products list." Champlin feels that the net result of such policies will be to lose the

---

[1]"Sins of Commission," *Worth*, April/May 1992.

[2]Jeff Champlin, "Off Course," *Bank Investment Representative*, April 1993, p. 4.

customer's trust. Before running blindly into these pitfalls, banks must review all policies and procedures—from compensation to delivery methods—to determine whether they are consistent with the bank's overall philosophy of service.

STEPS TO ESTABLISHING CONSULTATIVE SELLING

Establishing a program of consultative selling for investment reps is far more complex than merely telling them to put the customer first, or even changing the way they are compensated. If a firm adopts the consultative selling approach, the entire corporate culture, from the CEO and board room and all support personnel, must move from the traditional, short-term profit orientation to a genuine recognition that they are in the financial services industry, and *their only reason for existence is to serve their customers, by helping them meet their financial needs and goals on a long-term basis.* Those that don't will be taken over or eliminated by the first serious institution that does.

Banks face a confusing array of choices as they try to determine their direction in dealing with this same problem. Traditionally nonsales oriented with long-term deposits in mind, many banks see themselves as playing catch-up with the brokerage industry. To accomplish this, many have tried to expand rapidly into the securities area by offering a variety of products and services from annuities and mutual funds to full-service brokerage in affiliation with a securities firm. There has also been a continuous dialogue in terms of whether it is better to train bank personnel to sell securities or hire trained/experienced brokers instead. To date, most banks appear to have preferred the quicker process of hiring experienced brokers to sell for them. This has been particularly effective in situations where banks have encouraged investment reps to emphasize proprietary funds. However, it also carries the inherent dangers previously discussed. As a result, whether the investment rep is bank grown or hired because of prior brokerage experience, there are several important steps that can be taken to improve the quality of consultative selling provided.

- Branch managers and investment reps need to be brought into the bank philosophy and mentality of "customer first." This may require the implementation of cultural change training to bring the attitude and sales mentality of the investment reps into line with that of the bank as a whole.

- Compensation for both managers and reps can be structured to reward consultative selling and discourage transactional selling, perhaps by following the examples of some of the larger firms.

- Branch managers and investment reps can only benefit from both elementary and advanced training in communications, relationship, and motivational skills to enable them to establish trust and long-term relationships with their customers. Managers must be trained in ways to encourage investment reps to sell consultatively and discourage transactional selling. Note: According to a 1991 report by the Council on Financial Competition on "Upgrading the Quality of Branch Management,"[3] "top-notch training can make a substantial contribution to managerial quality of branch manager corps; effective training is a 'necessary condition' for top performance in bank branch setting, no matter what the 'raw material.' "[3]

- Depending upon the type and depth of their experience, both managers and investment reps will benefit from additional training in *customer profiling* and *consultative selling techniques*. Effective customer profiling not only uncovers a customer's assets and financial goals/needs, it also sets up the first few sales as a form of informed, partner-based operation between the customer and the investment rep.

- Depending upon whether the investment reps are selling only mutual funds and annuities or providing full-service brokerage, they may benefit from training in securities selection and portfolio management. According to Malcolm B. Chancy, Jr., chairman of Liberty National, training 450 branch managers in how to sell mutual funds has been very productive, helping the bank to reach its mutual fund sales goal of $1 million a week well ahead of schedule.[4]

In the increasing competition for customers' loyalty as expressed by custody of their assets, banks still hold a tenuous advantage in terms of customers' trust. However, many leading brokerage firms have committed themselves to developing a sales culture in which the customer truly is king. Thus, for this temporary gap in perception to be of real value, banks must both protect it and use it as they roll out new investment programs and products for their customers. *Consultative selling, as both a technique and a way of thinking, can be a tremendous resource for any firm, and any individual*

[3]*Council on Financial Competition*, "Upgrading the Quality of Branch Management," 1991.

[4]"For Liberty National, sales training pays off," *American Banker*, 6/9/93.

professional, in their efforts to capture new customers while maintaining those they already have. Unfortunately, traditional transaction selling can easily cost anyone not only years of customer trust, but also their business.

Customers are tired of being taken for granted by financial institutions and, according to Jack O'Neill of the Securities Industry Association, "will gravitate to those firms which have their interests at heart." Consultative selling provides a powerful tool for discovering, defining, and meeting customers' financial goals. However, consultative selling cannot succeed in a vacuum and must be supported with effective training in product knowledge and financial strategies, and even financial planning. In addition, compensation plans must be placed in effect that provide a clear message from management that sales reps and their managers will be compensated for servicing customers needs, building long-term relationships, and gathering assets. Otherwise, even the best intentioned efforts to develop a consultative selling program will fail. After all, sales reps and sales managers will do what they are paid to do. If they are compensated and promoted for gathering assets and serving their customers, they will do so. However, if they are compensated and promoted for short-term sales, even the best will focus on selling rather than servicing their customers. They are not paid to be ideological.

The customer is king! There are too many firms ready and willing to meet their needs to dare take them for granted. Only the recognition that you are in business solely to serve this individual, on an individual basis, will enable you, as a financial professional, to obtain and hold this customer's trust, not to mention his business. In addition, you must constantly strive to improve your personal and technical skills through constant training in everything from customer profiling to financial planning and security selection. In a word, if you are to be a "financial physician" to your customers, you must be prepared to commit yourself to serious training and constant improvement. It is the logical extension of the "Know Your Customer" and "Suitability" rules. The SEC, NASD, NYSE, OCC and other regulatory agencies are actively promoting further efforts in this direction.

II

TECHNIQUES OF GREAT COMMUNICATORS

When you think about it, your credibility as a financial professional depends upon several things: your professional knowledge (i.e., how well you understand both the products and services you offer as well as the consultative selling process), how much you actually care about your customers and their needs, and your ability to communicate that professional knowledge and caring attitude. In this section we will provide a series of advanced communications skills that will increase your confidence when working with any customer. One area where this will become extremely important is in "overcoming customer resistance."

Did you know that the average financial professional wastes over 80 percent of her sales presentation time trying to overcome unnecessary resistance she herself unwittingly caused the moment she opened her mouth? Perhaps that's why there are so many books and articles written on how to overcome or overwhelm that resistance. The advanced communications techniques provided in this section offer highly effective ways to establish, maintain, and enhance the trust and confidence of your clients, as well as communicate with them more precisely. In our experience (we have both been brokers and have trained over 30,000 financial professionals in brokerage, banking and insurance), over 90 percent of all resistance arises from three sources:

1. *The customer's perception that you are a saleperson.* This causes automatic "sales resistance" to almost any offer of help or suggested course of action. For example, think of your response the last time you were in a store and a clerk offered to help. If you're like most people, you said, "No thanks, just looking." This will be dealt with in more detail, later.

2. *Your inability to communicate clearly from the customer's point of view.* We all "speak the same language," but it doesn't always mean the same to each of us. The art of helping others depends upon the ability to understand them and be understood by them.

3. *Your ability to establish a deep level of rapport and trust with your customer.* Lack of trust is the single greatest barrier to any sale. (This will be discussed in the next chapter.)

The art of selling is the art of communicating, of convincing others of your point of view. Indeed, you could say that the best test of your effectiveness is whether or not your customers change their behavior or points of view to match your own. If you can't convince your customers to purchase what's truly appropriate for them, you'll go out of business.

To an extent, you might say that whenever we communicate something, we are acting as a salesperson in some way and that our listeners are our customers. For that reason, we will use the terms "customer," "client," and "investor" throughout this book to represent your listener, whether that person is a customer, a subordinate, an associate or peer, or a superior. After all, we have to "sell" our "bosses" as well as our traditional customers on our ideas if we are to get anything accomplished. The same could also be said to apply to our friends and family.

Many people feel threatened by "salesmen." Once a customer perceives you as a "salesman" they may actually avoid you. Why? We've already discussed how you responded when a sales clerk offered to help you. Instant sales resistance! Even though you went into the store with the intent to buy something, the minute someone offered to help sell it to you, you backed away. Why? Because most of us seem to have an unconscious image of a salesman as someone who is interested only in commission, and not in us. We may even feel that they see us as objects to be used or manipulated to obtain their end, sales. In the next chapter, you'll learn to develop immediate rapport.

This feeling of being an object instead of a person may well be the reason that more and more professionals are moving toward a customer-centered approach to selling financial services. In the customer-centered approach, you treat the customer as a person with financial needs that you, the professional, are here to meet. Our experience has been that customers respond with loyalty in good markets *and* bad. In addition, you are perceived as a professional who is a resource to help solve their problems instead of an adversary who causes them.

We like people who listen to us. Yet the biggest complaint directed toward many financial consultants is that they rarely listen and call only to sell something. Customers complain that, instead of trying to find out their needs, too many reps don't take enough time to really try to hear what their customers try to tell them. You know your industry, your products and services, and how they fit into the current economic and market environments. As a result, it can become very easy to think that only you know what's best for your clients.

Just as each of us has our own way of looking at things, we also each have our own "private language." This private language consists of the special meanings we assign to words (their connotations) as well as the way we process information. To the extent that you can recognize and communicate from your customers' point of view and in their language, you will be that much more effective. Remember the sign that says

I know you think you understood what you thought I said. But I'm not sure you realize that what you heard is not what I meant.

The purpose of this section is to help you to better understand your customers' needs and to hold on to them in good markets and bad by working from *their* point of view.

4

Becoming a Professional Communicator

As a financial advisor to your customers, you are a professional communicator who must both understand and be understood if you are to be effective. Even the most brilliant market strategist will be unable to help a client solve a problem if she cannot understand the problem or effectively communicate her solution. You know your products and services and you understand how they can help meet your customer's needs. Thus, you have considerable impact upon your customers' opinions regarding the quality of your products and their need to purchase them.

A CARING MIND-SET

Someone once said, "People don't care how much you know until they know how much you care." When you get right down to it, this is the basis of all trust. If your customers believe that you are a only "salesman" out to make a commission, or even just a glorified "clerk" going through the motions, they will never develop the level of trust needed to take the risks involved in making investment decisions. Whenever you make a recommendation, they may be second-guessing your motives instead of examining it on its merits.

Thus, one of the most important factors in communications is the "mind-set" of those involved. Your mind-set, or attitude, about your business, yourself and your customer is communicated clearly to virtually everyone with whom you deal. When you first meet a customer, his first impression creates a mental image of you which will strongly influence his expectations of you in the relationship.

Books such as *Megatrends* and *In Search of Excellence* have clearly shown that to be successful in sales you will have to put your customer first and the sale second. This is the key to consultative selling.

We all know how important first impressions are. Once set, they frequently stay with us for the rest of the relationship. Unfortunately, "bad" first impressions have a way of ending even the most profitable relationships before they begin. It has been suggested that an initial impression—good or bad—is made within the first three seconds. Thus, when you meet someone for the first time, everything you do, what you are wearing, and everything you say (or fail to say) communicates important information about your attitudes and mind-set to your customers. This, in turn, establishes a mind-set in them. Whether or not this is fair is immaterial. How you look, talk, and act all contribute to your customer's feeling that you are or are not someone with whom they are comfortable.

Fortunately, you can make sure that your appearance and behavior are consistent with what people expect of their financial advisors. This initial appearance and behavior provide the first opportunity to set customers at ease and develop a relationship (for those interested, see Malloy's *Dress for Success* or Thorolby's *You Are What You Wear.* The next opportunity to reinforce that positive first impression will be when you begin to communicate. How do you communicate a caring mind-set?

In his famous book, *How to Win Friends and Influence People,* Dale Carnegie offers "six ways to make people like you" that any sales professional should know and use:

1. *Become genuinely interested in other people.* You will have more influence and make more friends in two months of showing interest in others than you will in two years of trying to make others interested in you (or your products). However, to be effective, any show of interest must be sincere. that is, it must benefit you as well as your customer. Fortunately, your interest in your customer always benefits you because it helps you to better serve them and results in greater customer loyalty and sales. Simply learn to say, "Tell me about yourself." Then listen closely.

2. *Smile.* Smile at people and show them you are *genuinely* happy to see them. This goes far beyond an insincere grin and must grow naturally from an authentic interest in people. Carnegie points out how powerful a

smile can be even when it is unseen, with the example that telephone companies throughout the United States have a program called "Phone Power" which they offer to people who use the telephone in sales. They strongly suggest that you smile when using the phone because your smile comes through in your voice. Blind people can almost always tell when someone is smiling at them, and they return that smile.

3. *Remember that a person's name is to that person the sweetest and most important sound in any language.* Learn your customers' names, and use them. The famous department store Lord & Taylor has a policy in which all sales professionals are to look for their customers' names on their checks or charge cards and use their name when thanking them for an order. Harry Lorayne and Jerry Lucas have several excellent books out on how to memorize anyone's name, using simple association techniques (e.g., *The Memory Book*). The highest-paid bank tellers in the world work for Morgan Bank and Trust in New York, where each customer must have over $1 million to open an account. One of the reasons those tellers are paid so much is the requirement that they know every customer by name.

4. *Be a good listener. It encourages others to talk about themselves.* The key to discovering your customers' needs and how you can meet those needs is to be an effective listener. Obviously, speaking is one of them. There's an old saying that "God gave us two ears and only one mouth for a reason."

5. *Talk in terms of the other person's interests.* The key to consultative selling is to sell from the customer's point of view in an effort to meet their needs. What do they need? *Not,* what do you want to sell?

6. *Make the other person feel important—and do it sincerely.* This should be easy for any financial professional who realizes that their customer is important. *"Anyone who feels that the customer is not important should try doing without one for ninety days"* (Anonymous). Since your very survival depends upon your customers, let them know that they, and their needs, are important to you. Far from making you vulnerable to them, it shows your sincere interest and concern for them.

These simple rules of thumb may seem basic or even unimportant. However, a remarkable number of very successful brokers tell us not only that they practice them, but also require junior brokers assigned to them in a "mentor programs" to do the same. Making others feel valued/important is the key to almost any relationship.

While most people feel they can be very effective in person, many of your initial contacts as a broker will be made over the phone, where all that you are and all that you hope to be to your customer must be communicated in your voice. What you say and how you say it will establish in their mind whether you are just another "salesman" or a *professional financial advisor!*

Thus, according to Jeffrey Jacobi, director of Jacobi Voice Development, your voice can make or break you before you even meet your prospect face to face. "If a sales person speaks badly—mumbles, whines, [or] talks, too fast—it can turn people off." He mentions that one of his clients lost a sale because he spoke too quickly, making his customer feel uneasy. This customer distrusted such a "fast talker." Jacobi offers the following suggestions to counter voice problems:

JEFFREY JACOBI'S TIPS FOR THE TELEPHONE

"*If you speak with a nasal or whining tone,* open your mouth wider when speaking to get more chest resonance and reduce the nasal quality."

"*If you mumble,* a client may wonder what you're hiding. Take the time to enunciate your words."

"*If you're a 'fast talker,'* you're cramming too many words in one breath. Slow down; punctuate your speech using phrases and pauses."

"*If you have a breathy or weak voice,* you may sound like you lack confidence. A 'vocal workout' using long, sustained sounds and vowel exercises (saying words that are vowel-heavy, such as alibi and agenda, with emphasis on the vowels) will add power to your voice."

Jacobi says using these techniques will improve voice quality. But don't force the voice. Build gradually to achieve a natural, powerful voice that will call attention to what you are saying and make clients want to listen to you longer."[1]

If your voice sounds flat or monotonous, you may put clients or prospects to sleep. Your vocal range is too limited, so use inflection—change pitch on key words in your presentation—to develop an attention-grabbing voice. Try taping yourself or ask some friends to listen to you and give you feedback.

CLAP

Sometimes prospects or clients will bring up questions or concerns about something you are discussing. To deal with such issues, there are four easy steps you should take before attempting to respond to their concern. Only

[1]Ginger Trumfio, "The Voice Connection," *Sales & Marketing Management*, December 1993, p. 54.

after these steps have been followed can you respond to your customer's question and, if appropriate, return to your agenda. The four key steps, known as CLAP,[2] are

1. Clarify
2. Legitimize
3. Acknowledge
4. Probe

Step 1: Clarify

Before attempting to handle a customer's resistance, it is important to be sure you are dealing with the real source of their concern. It is easy to respond to what we *think* the customer wants without checking first to see if we are on track. Doing this can complicate your efforts to deal with their concern by trying to deal with something other than the real problem. This can happen in one of two ways:

1. Sometimes customers will resist you because they are uncomfortable with an aspect of your presentation without being entirely sure why (they may wish additional information, feel that you are being "too pushy," or not understand some of the technical jargon being used). In such cases, it is important to help them explore the cause of their discomfort until it is clearly identified and it can be usefully discussed. Attempting to overcome resistance without identifying the cause of that resistance invariably leads to resentment on their part.

2. Sometimes the real cause of their discomfort is not the one the customer first gives (e.g., they may claim to be uninterested in an idea when, in reality, they are too embarrassed to admit that they haven't taken the time to read the product literature you sent them). For this reason, it is very important to persist in your efforts to clarify and not to quit until all the causes of the customer's resistance have been uncovered and dealt with. For example, "If I'm hearing you correctly, you're concerned that the money manager may not have enough flexibility to meet your future needs. Is that correct?"

[2]Originally introduced in *Consultative Selling Techniques for Financial Professionals*, by Karl F. Gretz and Steven R. Drozdeck (New York: Simon & Schuster, 1990).

By clarifying, you will verify that you have correctly understood your customer's concern while deepening your level of rapport with them.

Once you have *clarified* the nature of the resistance, you must communicate to the customer that you both *acknowledge* and understand their concern and also accept it as *legitimate* (a customer's concerns are always legitimate, even when unfounded). *Remember: Your failure to convey that you regard a customer's question or concern as legitimate is equivalent to telling her that you don't consider it (or her) to be very important.*

Steps 2 and 3: Legitimize and Acknowledge

When customers resist committing to our suggested solutions to their needs, it is frequently because they have concerns, or anxieties, that the presentation has not relieved or addressed. Unfortunately, before we can respond to customers' objections, we must successfully communicate to them that we understand their concerns and that it is all right for them to be open about those concerns (i.e., that we are not threatened by their questions or concerns). Continuing from previous example, "That's an appropriate concern for any business owner. It's wise to think about your company's future requirements at this stage."

Legitimizing and acknowledging a customer's concerns does not mean you agree with them, only that you respect and understand them. Many financial salespeople *tell* their clients that they understand their concerns but fail to demonstrate that understanding. Therefore, they often appear condescending and defensive and cause their customer to become resistant. Always remember that, as a professional, you will never need to be defensive because you are always doing the best possible job for your customers. Hence, if a customer resists or becomes upset, it won't be because of your performance; it will be because either they don't appreciate/understand something you said, or you don't understand the entire situation. Also remember that you have to show someone that you understand before you can provide an explanation. Otherwise, they won't believe you. CLAPing demonstrates your understanding.

Step 4: Probe

Having communicated your understanding and acceptance of your customer's concern, you must probe to determine if your assessment is accurate. This step accomplishes two things:

1. It demonstrates your interest to the customer.
2. If you find out that you are on the wrong track, you will be able to go back and try again until your assessment is confirmed by the customer. The entire **CLAP** process is designed to get to this point. This will prevent the frustration that comes from trying to solve the wrong problem. Most customers will appreciate your efforts to understand them and be willing to try again.

If you are correct in your assessment of the problem, you not only improve your level of rapport with your customer, but also lower their resistance. In addition, you will know that you are on the right track in meeting their needs. Even if the nature of their concern is such that you cannot complete your presentation at the first meeting, you have at least improved your relationship with the customer and paved the way for your next meeting.

Paraphrasing (Summary Probe)

One of the easiest ways to CLAP is through the use of paraphrasing. When a customer states a concern, paraphrase that concern in your own words and probe to see if you are correct. In so doing, you will simultaneously clarify the nature of their concern, acknowledge and legitimize it, and demonstrate your understanding—or at least your desire to understand—and verify the correctness of your assessment. Then probe for acceptance. For example, "You're saying that financial protection for your family is your primary concern. Is that correct?"

Once you are sure that you understand the question or concern, you should briefly respond to the concern by providing the information they need. Finally, probe once again to insure that you and your client on the same wavelength. Continuing the previous example, "I can certainly appreciate your desire to protect your family. That's why this annuity would be so good for your particular situation."

SPEAKING THEIR "PRIVATE LANGUAGE"

Each of us has our own private way of "looking at things," of thinking, and of expressing our thoughts. In some cases, individual words will mean one thing to us, and something completely different to someone else (e.g., ask several investors what the word "safe" or "service" mean to them and you'll get several different answers). We also tend to emphasize certain aspects of our experiences that affect the way we remember and discuss them. For example, have you ever heard someone say, "It *looks* good to me" or "It *sounds* good to me" or "It *feels* good to me." Phrases like these, as well as others like them, provide important information about how individuals think or process information. By learning to recognize and use the clues people give you about how they think, you can literally communicate in a way that they will perceive you as being "just like them."

Some of us think by *seeing* images in our mind, others by *discussing* a concept with ourselves to *hear* how it sounds, while still others of us need to determine how something *feels*. Regardless of how we process information (via the visual, auditory, or kinesthetic/feeling mode), we tend to verbalize our thoughts using words and phrases which most closely match how we think.

The Three Houses

We have conducted the following *experiment with over 20,000 people* and have found the results staggering. Each group was to imagine themselves in the market for a house. Each person is told that he or she can choose *only one* of the three houses based upon the descriptions that follow. The houses are identical (size, location, rooms, etc.) in every other aspect. As you read the descriptions, determine which house you like the most and the least.

There is a house which I'm sure you would like to see. The first house is in a beautiful neighborhood and is very picturesque. Even the doorbell has a unique design. You'll certainly see for yourself that the rooms appear large and have the right colors. If you go to the balcony, you can see some really nice scenery. I'm sure you'll perceive this as an excellent choice.

Yet, there is another house that I'm sure you would like to hear about. This second house is in a quiet neighborhood and is of very sound construction. Even the doorbell has a nice tone. You'll certainly say to yourself that the rooms are large and have the right tones. If you go to the balcony, you can hear the birds chirping and the sound of the breeze. I'm sure you'll tell yourself that this is an excellent choice.

There is one more house that I'm sure you would find satisfying. This third house is in a warm neighborhood and is very solidly built. Even the doorbell gives a welcome feeling. You'll certainly sense that the rooms are spacious and have the right touch. If you go to the balcony, you can feel the warm sun and a light breeze. I'm sure you'll feel that this is an excellent choice.

Analysis Which house did you like the most? the least? As you undoubtedly realize, the same house was described using visual, then auditory, then kinesthetic/feelings terms. On average, one-third of any audience chose each of the three houses—which is in line with population norms. What was both surprising and enlightening to the members of our audiences was that 50 percent of any group either actively disliked one of the houses or became confused due to the description. They could then more fully appreciate the need to "package" their messages appropriately.

Variations of this experiment have been applied to product descriptions, advertising approaches, persuasive communications, and informal meetings with similar results; that is, we have found that if a person's preferred thinking mode is mismatched, miscommunication, confusion, distrust and an occasional complete disregard for the message can occur. Remember, these are unconscious responses. Therefore, if you wish to be an effective communicator, you must *match the person's preferred thinking modality.* While not guaranteeing success, it does substantially increase the probability that the message will be understood and accepted.

As indicated before, people think using visual, auditory, or feelings terms. One of the most important reasons we do this deals with our five senses and our experiences as we mature. Although we are born with five senses, as we mature we begin to rely upon one or two more than the others. One result of this is a tendency to remember that aspect of an experience more completely than the others. Hence, if we tend to rely upon our sight, we are more likely to remember the visual aspects of an experience more distinctly than the sound or other sensory aspects. As a result, when we relate our experience to someone else, we will tend to emphasize visual terms to describe it. The same would be true of the other senses. Of course, some experiences naturally dominate a specific sense regardless of which one we tend to rely upon. For example, a cold shower would dominate the kinesthetic sense, while a symphony would compel the auditory and a rainbow, the visual. Because of that, even people who rely primarily upon their sight will sometimes use auditory and kinesthetic terms.

Once we begin to rely upon one sense over the others, the data received through that sense tend to dominate our thought processes. As a result, we may even begin to "specialize" in that sensory mode when we think. What this means is that if you tend think by making pictures, you are probably someone who also tends to rely upon your sight and to be most aware of the visual aspects of your experiences. Of course, this doesn't mean you aren't capable of remembering the sounds and feelings associated with an experience. They probably just aren't remembered as being as "obvious" as what you see. This can result in our using some of the other senses so infrequently that we can actually become confused when we receive too much information through them. Psychologists refer to this as *sensory overload*.

Since we understand the familiar more quickly than the unfamiliar, we "understand" words and phrases that most closely correspond to those that we use in our thinking process. In short, something as simple as our choice of words can make the difference between whether or not we are understood by others. For example, if a customer uses words and phrases that are primarily visual (sight-oriented), and you make an annuity presentation using phrases that are primarily auditory (sound oriented), you may actually confuse them. In fact, they may tell you that they "just can't *see* an annuity in their future." We call these sensory-oriented words *predicates*.

Similarly, if you want to communicate clearly with someone who uses a particular sensory orientation in their thinking, you will be most successful if you use predicates that match the way they process information. Try it! You'll be amazed at the improvement in understanding that occurs when you match predicates compared to the difficulty created when they are mismatched. For example,

- If you have a visually oriented client, use pictures and graphs in your presentations to help them get a *clear picture*. Use visually oriented words and phrases to describe your product or service. For example, "Mrs. Alexander, I'm confident that as you *look* at this chart, you will *see* just how strongly this Putnam fund has performed over the last ten years."

- However, if they are sound oriented, be prepared to discuss it with them and give them a brochure on the product that they can read as a form of review (most people subvocalize—hear their own voice in their head—as they read). Use terms and phrases that are sound oriented in your presentation. For example, "Mr. Johnson, why don't we take a moment to *discuss* the ways in which this wrap account will help you manage your investments. I'm confident you'll like the *sound* of the program and *tell* yourself its just what you need."

- Finally, if they are kinesthetic based, be sure to give them something tangible to remind them of what they are purchasing. For example, when limited partnerships sold railroad cars as a way to reduce taxes, investors were each given a toy railroad box car to help them understand and identify with the product they were buying. This was particularly helpful for individuals who just couldn't *grasp* the idea. When making a presentation, use kinesthetic terms and phrases. For example, "Mrs. Smythe, we feel that Reebok Athletic Shoes represents a *solid* investment for your future. You mentioned that you like to jog. I'm confident you'll feel that Reebok is as *comfortable* a *fit* for your portfolio as it is on your feet."

Read the following scripts, and after you finish them, determine which broker you think has the best chance of continuing the conversation with this customer.

Reading I

Broker #1: "I just came across a report on a stock, the XYZ Company, that looks interesting, and, if you have a moment, I'd like to show it to you."

Customer: "Sounds interesting. I'd like to hear some more."

Broker #1: "Well, I just saw something that shows that their earnings have really improved in the last few months."

Customer: "What do you mean? I've heard that XYZ is in really bad shape."

Broker #1: "Yet, this financial report clearly shows that it has really improved, which is why you..."

(Customer interrupts.)

Customer: "My gut reaction tells me that it hasn't changed at all."

Broker #1: "What have you seen to make you think that way? I perceive the change as very positive."

Customer: "Well, I've been hearing just the opposite."

Broker #1: "Look, I want to show you a few things that should give you a better picture."

What was your gut feeling as you read this dialogue? Were you comfortable, or did you feel that, somehow, the broker and the customer just weren't on the same wavelength? Go back and read it again, then go on to Reading II.

Reading II

Broker #2: "I just came across a report on a stock, the XYZ Company, that looks interesting and, if you have a moment, I'd like to show it to you."

Customer: "Sounds interesting. I'd like to hear some more."

Broker #2: "Well, I just heard something that states that their earnings have really improved in the last few months."

Customer: "What do you mean? I've heard that it's in really bad shape."

Broker #2: "Yet, this financial report clearly states that it has really improved, which is why you..."

(Customer interrupts.)

Customer: "My gut reaction tells me that it hasn't changed at all."

Broker #2: "What have you heard to make you think that way? I feel the change is very positive."

Customer: "Well, I've been hearing just the opposite."

Broker #2: "Listen, I want to tell you a few things that should give you a better feeling.

Which broker do you think has the better chance to continue the conversation? We like to present these dialogues as an introduction to our training sessions (before we've discussed the concept). In fact, we've presented these scripts with over 15,000 financial professionals and most of them think that broker #2 has the better chance. Ninety-five percent comment that broker #1 was more "confrontive," aggressive, uncaring, and didn't listen and that broker #2 is usually labeled as being more supportive, understanding, and responsive. Let's look at them again and compare them word for word.

Broker #1: "I just came across a report on a stock, the XYZ Company, that looks interesting, and, if you have a moment, I'd like to show it to you."

Broker #2: "I just came across a report on a stock, the XYZ Company, that looks interesting, and, if you have a moment, I'd like to show it to you."

Customer: "*Sounds* interesting. I'd like to *hear* some more."

Broker #1: "Well, I just *saw* something that *shows* that their earnings have really improved in the last few months."

Broker #2: "Well, I just *heard* something that *states* that their earnings have really improved in the last few months."

Customer: "What do you mean? I've *heard* that it's in really *bad shape*."

Broker #1: "Yet, this financial report clearly *shows* that it has really improved, which is why you..."

Broker #2: "Yet, this financial report clearly *states* that it has really improved, which is why you..."

(Customer interrupts.)

Customer: "My *gut reaction* is that it hasn't changed at all."

Broker #1: "What have you *seen* to make you think that way? I *perceive* the change as very positive."

Broker #2: "What have you *heard* to make you think that way? I *feel* the change is very positive."

Customer: "Well, I've been *hearing* just the opposite."

Broker #1: "*Look*, I want to *show* you a few things that should give you a better *picture*."

Broker #2: "*Listen*, I want to *tell* you a few things that should give you a better *feeling*."

If you're like most people, after a second reading you're amazed that the mere change of predicates (mismatched by broker #1and matched by broker #2) makes all of the difference. As we've said before, we've given this exercise to thousands of participants, and found that the vast majority label the first broker as aggressive, uncaring, not listening, and so on. Broker #2 is usually labeled by over 95 percent of any audience as more caring, willing to listen, and helpful.

The change in response occurs outside of conscious awareness. You can see for yourself the difference that matching someone's predicates can make in a sales situation. For example, a customer approaches you to discuss a new mutual fund she's heard about, and says, "I've been *looking over* this new mutual fund and I'm sure that you'll agree that it *shows* excellent potential. How about *seeing* if you can get me some." You might respond in any one of several ways:

- "It certainly *looks* interesting to me. Let's *see* if it fits your investment goals." or

- "It certainly *sounds* interesting to me. Let's *discuss* it and determine if it fits your investment goals." or

- "It certainly *feels* good to me. Let's *take it apart* to find out if it fits your investment goals."

All three responses *mean* essentially the same thing, don't they? But note the difference. Which response most closely matches the way that the sales campaign was presented? The first response. The other two responses mismatch the speaker and may actually result in a misunderstanding or in confusing him. You might say that the last two responses might convince the speaker that you just can't *see* what he's getting at.

If you've ever tried to learn a foreign language, you can probably recall how you had to mentally translate into English whatever someone spoke in that language. Pretty frustrating, wasn't it? Whenever someone speaks to you using a sensory style different from your own (e.g., if you're speaking in *visual* terms and they say something in *auditory* or *kinesthetic* terms), you have to unconsciously translate what they are saying into your terms. This takes a moment and can be confusing. They're not "speaking your language." At this point, you can either attempt to shift gears and speak in their terms or allow yourself to become frustrated and annoyed. Which you choose will depend upon how important it is to make that person comfortable. For example,

Have you ever explained something very "clearly" to a client only to have them respond with confusion? Did their understanding improve the second or third time you "explained"? If not, it may not be a case of their being stupid. Rather, it is possible that the two of you were "speaking" different languages and that they just weren't "grasping" what you were "saying." (Notice the predicates placed in quotes in the previous sentences.) If you were using one set of predicates (perhaps visual), while they were using another set (such as auditory), your visual concepts may have caused their confusion.

Success consists of convincing your customer to follow your advice as they attempt to meet their financial needs. Matching predicates allows even more effective communication and is really worth utilizing to improve your relationship with your customers. Literally and figuratively, matching predicates allows you to speak their language. Hence, if you want to lead someone to commit to a solution to their need, speaking their language will greatly increase your effectiveness. Listen for the predicate system an individual uses (*simply note which words they use the most*) before giving directions or answering a question. Then match it. You'll probably get a much more satisfying response. Note: This skill takes some practice. Listen to conversations around you, to television and radio and make note of the patterns you hear. After a while, it will become second nature.

Since mismatching someone's predicates can lead to confusion and misunderstanding, how do you open a conversation before you know their sensory preference? Just as there are predicates that match a particular sensory orientation, there are others that are neutral and that can be used with any orientation. We call these words "unspecified," and they can be very useful when opening a conversation with someone new. For example,

"Mr. Daniels, we *anticipate* that Disney will successfully *weather* their difficulties with Euro-Disney in France and *experience* significant long-term growth over the next year. As you *contemplate* this, I hope you'll *consider* Disney as an addition to your long-term investments."

For your convenience, we have provided a brief listing of predicate words and phrases:

Sensory-Oriented Words (Predicates)

Visual	Auditory	Kinesthetic	Unspecified
Aim	Announce	Active	Accept
Angle	Articulate	Affective	Activate
Appear	Audible	Bearable	Admonish
Aspect	Boisterous	Callous	Advise
Clarity	Communicate	Charge	Allow
Clear	Converse	Concrete	Anticipate
Cognizant	Discuss	Dull	Assume
Conspicuous	Dissonant	Emotional	Believe
Examine	Divulge	Feel	Cogitate
Focus	Earful	Firm	Communicate
Foresee	Earshot	Flow	Comprehend
Glance	Enunciate	Foundation	Conceive
Hindsight	Inquire	Grasp	Conceptualize
Horizon	Interview	Grip	Consider
Illusion	Hear	Handle	Contemplate
Illustrate	Listen	Hanging	Create
Image	Loud	Hassle	Decide
Imagine	Mention	Heated	Deliberate
Inspect	Noise	Hold	Depend
Looks	Oral	Hot	Determine
Notice	Proclaim	Hunch	Develop
Obscure	Pronounce	Hustle	Direct
Observe	Remark	Intuition	Discover
Obvious	Report	Lukewarm	Evaluate
Outlook	Resonate	Motion	Help
Perception	Ring	Moves	Imagine
Perspective	Roar	Muddled	Indicate
Picture	Rumor	Numb	Influence
Pinpoint	Say	Panicky	Judge
Regard	Scream	Pressure	Know
Scope	Screech	Rush	Manage
Scrutinize	Silence	Sensitive	Mediate
Scene	Shrill	Set	Motivate
See	Sound	Shallow	Permit
Show	Speak	Shift	Plan

Visual	Auditory	Kinesthetic	Unspecified
Sight	Speech	Soft	Ponder
Sketchy	Squeal	Softly	Prepare
Survey	State	Solid	Prove
Vague	Tell	Stir	Reckon
View	Tone	Stress	Repeat
Vision	Tune	Structured	Resolve
Vista	Vocal	Touch	Think
Watch	Volume	Warm	Understand

Sensory Word-Oriented (Predicate) Phrases

Visual	Auditory	Kinesthetic
An eyeful	Blabber mouth	All washed up
Appears to be	Clear as a bell	Boils down to
Bird's eye view	Clearly expressed	Chip off the old block
Catch a glimpse of	Call on	Come to grips with
Clear-cut	Describe in detail	Cool/Calm/Collected
Dim view	Earful	Firm foundation
Eye to eye	Express yourself	Floating on thin air
Flashed on	Give an account of	Get a handle on
Get a perspective on	Give me your ear	Get a load of this
Get a scope on	Heard voices	Get the drift of
Hazy idea	Hidden message	Get your goat
In light of	Hold your tongue	Hand-in-hand
In person	Idle talk	Hang in there
In view of	Idle tongue	Heated argument
Looks like	Inquire into	Hold it
Make a scene	Keynote speaker	Hold on
Mental image/picture	Loud and clear	Hot-head
Mind's eye	Power of speech	Keep your shirt on
Naked eye	Purrs like a kitten	Lay cards on the table
Paint a picture	Outspoken	Light-headed
Photographic memory	Rap session	Moment of panic
Plainly see	Rings a bell	Not following you
Pretty as a picture	State your purpose	Pull some strings
See to it	Tattletale	Sharp as a tack

Visual	Auditory	Kinesthetic
Short-sighted	To tell the truth	Slipped my mind
Showing off	Tongue-tied	Smooth operator
Sight for sore eyes	Tuned in/out	So-so
Staring off in space	Unheard of	Start from scratch
Take a peek	Utterly	Stiff upper lip
Tunnel vision	Voiced an opinion	Stuffed shirt
Up front	Within hearing range	Topsy-turvy
Well defined	Word for Word	Underhanded

Being able to "speak their language" by matching predicates is valuable in virtually every situation in which it is important for you to relate to another person. Do have a customer who has previously been difficult to communicate with? Perhaps someone who doesn't seem to *see* what you're *showing* him, or someone who doesn't *hear* what you're *saying*, or someone who doesn't *grasp* your *point*. Try matching their predicates and see what a difference it makes, not only in your sales presentations, but also in your relationship. Note: To gain real proficiency, prepare your presentations in each mode.

Everything we do or say (or fail to do or say) communicates something about us. From the first time someone sees us or hears our voice they are forming an impression of us that will affect our relationship for years to come. This impression will also determine whether they will do business with us and entrust us with their assets. Be sure that your appearance, your speaking voice and the language you use convey the impression you wish to your prospects and customers.

In summary, each of us speaks our own private language. An important source of that language comes from the predominant sense(s) we use to process information. Some of us think by making mental pictures, others by discussing something internally, or with someone else and still others "go with their gut" response, before making a decision. In addition, many words have different meanings for different people (e.g., "good service" may mean ten things to ten people).

In Chapter 5, we'll explore ways to make sure that the words you use mean the same thing to your customer as they do to you. You'll see how something as simple as positive versus negative speech patterns make a huge difference in what you communicate, and how the words you emphasize can change the entire meaning of something you say.

Special Note to Readers

Key verbal and listening skills such as open and closed probes, bridging, building and acknowledging techniques must also be artfully employed. These skills are briefly reviewed in Chapter 9.

5

What Did You Say?

Have you ever felt that you and your customer were speaking two different languages? Although the words were all English, they just didn't seem to mean the same thing to you as they did to your customer? Frustrating, isn't it? Yet, this happens to all of us sometimes. Because of past experiences, the *personal* meaning of a word may not be the same for everyone. Remember our saying from the beginning of the section:

> I know you think you understood what you thought I said. But I'm not sure you realize that what you heard is not what I meant.

That can happen to anyone in any conversation. Here is a just such a conversation between a job applicant and an interviewer:

Interviewer: "We're looking for someone who is absolutely honest and can be trusted around important data."

Applicant: "That's me. I've always been known for my absolute honesty. You can ask any of my previous employers. There have been many times when confidential matters were discussed. I can assure you that I'm the soul of discretion."

Interviewer: "You do look honest. However, the position that I'm trying to fill requires a person who can work alone and who is a self-starter. There are times when little or no direction can be offered, so the ideal candidate would also have to take the initiative to solve any unusual problems that may occur."

Applicant: "I also appreciate those qualities in others because I've always prided myself on having them and, unfortunately, find that relatively few people have them. I've spent the majority of time in positions where working alone was normal. If it were not for a high degree of self-motivation and a personal desire for excellence, some of my tasks would not have been completed otherwise. I can assure you that I am a self-starter and highly motivated to succeed.

"As for the ability to take the initiative, let me respond by letting you know that I once received a company commendation for handling an unexpected problem in an expeditious manner. I know how to follow the rules, and I also know when to make exceptions."

Interviewer: "Well, enough for now. Please send us a completed resume. You are certainly a strong candidate for this position."

Applicant: "Thank you very much. It will be in the mail tomorrow. I am definitely interested in being associated with this corporation."

Interviewer to Sales Director: "I think I've found our candidate for that opening as an investment rep."

Applicant to Spouse: "Honey, I think I got the job as night watchman!"

"I know that you think you understood what you thought I said. But I'm not sure you realize that what you heard is not what I meant." If this interview weren't so common, it would be funny. However, situations like this occur all of the time.

There are times when precise communication is imperative, when a misunderstanding can be costly or even cause a compliance problem. At these times, you must insure that the message was both transmitted and received clearly and concisely. To assure this, it is useful to have a series of specific tools to insure more precise communication. While these techniques, associated with effective questioning, are important to anyone, they are particularly critical for you as a financial professional.

The ability to communicate effectively presupposes that we have a relatively good understanding of what the other person is trying to say. Yet, many studies on communication have suggested that as much as 90 percent of all communication problems occur because brokers "assume" that they and their customer know what each other is talking about.

Assuming that people understand you is a common error made in everyday language that may come back to haunt you. In this chapter we will provide a number of very effective tools to deal with this problem. While these techniques are not something that you would normally use in day-to-day conversations, you'll be able to employ them during conversations with your customers, friends, and family whenever you absolutely have to have clear communication. Their purpose is to both impart and receive exact information when it is necessary to clarify what is being said. To accomplish this, it is important to know both *how* and *what* to clarify.

Some language patterns are so pervasive that we fail to hear them simply because they are so common. One such pattern can be seen in assumption that the words we use mean the same thing to our customer as they do to us. We opened the chapter with an example of the use of such an assumption and its possible results. Here is another example that has significant applications for financial professionals:

> "Service" is one of the most overused words in business. "I want good service," says the customer. The broker, of course, replies, "I'll give you great service." The customer may expect him to return her calls within five minutes while he may think that one hour is exemplary. The customer service department may be happy, given their volume, with a one-day turnaround. Each individual could literally do their absolute best and be thoroughly proud of how well they had done, while the other two parties in the transaction end up being totally dissatisfied. Unless you know what your client wants, you can't win. Unless you know what your customer service department can deliver, neither you nor your client can win. "Little things" like this can ruin a relationship.

"Service" is one of those vague words that has a different meaning for each person who uses it. Words that are equally vague include "comfortable," "satisfaction," "safety," and "risk."

The typical response to the comment, "I feel satisfied," is, "I know what you mean." That's impossible! We can only have a vague idea of what someone means, because the word "satisfied" represents an internal state. It is interesting to realize that many people automatically assume that you have the same meaning for words, or connotation, that they do.

Its important to understand the difference between a word's denotations (dictionary definition[s]) and its connotations (the emotional meaning[s] we each assign to it). For example, the word "family" has the same denotation for everyone. The dictionary defines a "family" as "a social unit consisting of parents and the children that they rear" or "a group of people related by ancestry or marriage." However, the *emotional meaning (connotation)* of the word "family" will depend upon one's experience within one's own family. For example, what might "family" mean to one who was raised

- In a warm, nurturing, environment
- In a situation where they have been abused
- In an orphanage
- In a single-parent environment
- As a "latch-key" child, where they must spend long hours alone because both parents work.

Obviously, depending upon the experience of your customer, using the word "family" in an effort to communicate something might provoke a very unexpected response.

Without realizing it, people often naturally delete, distort, or even overgeneralize information. While this is immaterial most of the time, there are some occasions when failure to obtain complete and accurate information can cause serious problems. You'll undoubtedly find that you already employ many of the techniques listed here. These techniques will help you

- Resolve organizational problems more quickly
- Deal with interpersonal conflict
- Understand and deal with customer problems
- Clear up confusion (muddied thinking)
- Deal with distraught clients (when combined with other techniques not yet introduced)
- Clarify legal issues
- Conduct effective profiling interviews

As we mentioned before, people often delete, distort, or overgeneralize information. This is true of everyone and occurs on an unconscious level. For instance, if sales assistant told you "They told me that I had better get it resolved to his satisfaction," your response might be, "Huh?" After your initial reaction you would still have to determine

- Who are "they"? customer? office manager? the IRS?
- What is "it" that needs to be resolved?
- What needs to happen for them to be "satisfied"?
- What is the meaning of the implied threat behind better get it resolved.
- Who is the "he" who must be satisfied?
- Is "he" a part of "they"?

In this example your sales assistant deleted information you needed to understand what was really going on. She needs to provide you with more explicit information on the meaning of some of the key words.

We also know, intuitively, that "satisfaction" for one customer is not necessary "satisfaction" for another. One person may merely desire an apology (an older, but still used, definition of satisfaction), while another may need specific operational action(s) to be taken, and still others may require some combination of both of these and more. Given the example, we also know that it will be important learn the specific criteria to satisfy this customer. After all, what a customer wants may or may not be possible (or even reasonable). However, until the issue is addressed, we may have an angry customer who has implied an undesirable next step. The nature of that next step has yet to be determined. Following are examples of language patterns that are so pervasive that you will hear them regularly from both your customers and your peers. They are among the dozen or so that we address in our advanced sales and management classes.

ONE CAUSE OF BURNOUT

Have you ever seen people burn themselves out? Work so hard that they seemingly can't see straight? Work so hard that they become both inefficient and ineffective? Such individuals are "driven" by some internal motivation that is literally getting in their way.

"I *have to* get this done by tomorrow." "If this doesn't get done there will be trouble." "We need to do this." These are statements that are commonly found both inside and out of the brokerage office. They represent a *psychological imperative* that is driving the behavior or thought. It has created a need that *must* or *ought to* or *should* be fulfilled. The consequences of not performing the action are intimidating. But are they really?

So, what? What's the problem? Often, people give something a significantly higher priority than it actually deserves. They "have to" do something, even if its to the detriment of something else. You may someday have a customer who "must," for instance, invest only in FDIC-insured vehicles such as CDs, insured savings accounts, and bank IRAs. Or you may obtain another customer who is only willing to buy computer stocks. At such times, such individuals tend to become very narrow-minded and very focused. Sometimes that can be good, but it often isn't.

The situation just described is not uncommon and drives most brokers crazy wondering what is wrong with this customer's priorities. You might ask her what she is doing and why. Then, depending upon the answer (there may be contingencies of which you are unaware), you might ask her the equivalent of, "What would happen if you invested in something that wasn't FDIC insured?" Or "What would happen if you bought a stock that wasn't a computer company?" Usually, nothing. This can enable you and them to discover what, if any, consequences they fear for investing against their "rule." For example, the first customer may be concerned with safety and believe that only FDIC-insured investments are really safe. If she buys anything else she may lose everything. Similarly, the second customer may only be willing to invest in computer stocks because his father told her that they were the best possible buy before he died 15 years ago.

Consider brokers you know who spend all of their time "organizing" and "getting ready" to do production. Others spend substantial amounts of time on customer service problems (paying credit balances, checking on operational issues, etc.). While these things need to get done, it is obvious that some people use them to procrastinate. If you find yourself involved in this kind of behavior, it may be necessary to confront yourself and bring your lack of prioritizing into the forefront. You may honestly believe that you are doing what is required. One way to give yourself a useful "reality check" is to ask yourself a few questions regarding the natural consequences of doing or not doing certain things.

If a customer comes to you with a complaint, or if you are involved in any sort of difficulty, you'll find that a good part of the problem is muddied thinking. They may not understand why you recommended a certain course of action, or why the firm changed a policy or "buy" recommendation on a security. "They can't see the forest because of the trees" is a common situation. They are focused on what is happening to them and may not understand the larger picture. The fact is, that it is hard for anyone to be objective when he is too close to a problem. However, this lack of objectivity is reflected in people's communication and often leads to misunderstandings and destructive feelings. Hence, it is easy to get into arguments and get off the track of solving their problem.

When a customer has a problem or complaint, you must assume that it is real (at least to them). Almost by definition, if a customer is upset, their problem is real to them. This is true for anyone. For example, have you ever gone to your friend, spouse, or boss and inquired, "What did you do that for?" Once they gave you the answer, you may not have agreed, but you were probably at least satisfied. However, before they gave you their answer, an important piece of information was missing: the rationale for their behavior.

That's true for your customers as well. They also have issues, conflicts, problems, areas of confusion, frustrations, and so on that result from missing information or muddied thinking. Thus, make it a habit to keep your customers fully informed, not only about changes in policy or recommended courses of action, but also the reasons behind the changes. Customers who don't understand what is happening with their money can become very anxious *and* stubborn. Each questioning category that follows is presented so that you can easily recognize it and use it with others. You'll find them very effective in reducing or avoiding the normal, day-to-day miscommunications and conflicts.

WHAT TO DO ABOUT VAGUE/FUZZY/UNDEFINED, YET SEEMINGLY MEANINGFUL, WORDS

An example of these kinds of words and the confusion that they can cause was introduced in the beginning of the chapter during the "job interview" for "investment rep." As a rule of thumb, whenever you are expected to perform some action to "satisfy" another person, you need to clarify exactly what they expect, that is, determine their criteria for "satisfaction." A customer saying, "I want you to give me good service," is an example of a statement that needs clarification (for reasons previously provided).

If you told each of your clients, "My job is to provide good service by helping you meet your needs and provide a timely response," the vast majority of them would nod their heads in total agreement, without having any specific understanding of what you mean by the words "service," "timely," and, possibly, "needs." Language has certain conventions that are theoretically understood. Yet one person may think that "service" means providing what is asked for, while another person may understand it to mean going the extra step and anticipating their "needs." "Timely" can mean anything from five minutes to five weeks. What is the response time that you require, in what context, and with what exceptions? Any misunderstanding or different interpretation could cause a problem for someone. Finally, try to define "needs." You may be able to help your clients meet their financial needs, *if* they are first defined in detail and *if* they are realistic. Otherwise, you will fail. Words that are subject to individual interpretation will often be interpreted in as many ways as there are individuals doing the interpretations. (We think this should be added to the collection of *Murphy's law* sayings, e.g., "If you need someone to understand you, they will misunderstand you.")

OVERCOMING MIND READING AND ASSUMPTIONS ABOUT OTHER PEOPLES' THOUGHTS, ACTIONS, BELIEFS, AND FEELINGS

"Mind reading" consists of making assumptions about what someone else is thinking. Earlier, we discussed the word "assumption" and its attendant dangers. Here are three more examples of assumptions people sometimes make:

1. "People don't want to work with me."
2. "My client is mad at me."
3. "I thought that is what you would have wanted."

Any of these statements requires some verification before it is accepted as fact. The most common questions to accomplish this are either "How do/did you know?" or "Have you asked that person?" You need the hard, objective evidence that will support their assertion.

A very common problem associated with mind reading is the hurt feelings that regularly occur when someone says the equivalent of, "She hurt my feelings" or "He should have known...." Unfortunately, due to a variety of reasons, some people are very easily insulted and easily get their egos bruised. At the same time, most of the hurts that people experience in life are the result of something that occurs in their own minds. What they've chosen to feel hurt about didn't happen with the intention that was taken. Think how this might affect your relationship with your clients. Sometimes, clients may assume that you made a recommendation just for the commission or that you are trying to sell them something they don't need. One way to avoid this is by constantly checking with your client to make sure that you understand each other.

One of the most common situations involving mind reading occurs when we feel insulted. If you ever think you have been insulted, try the following:

- Ignore it.
- Pretend that you heard a compliment.
- Ask them what they meant.

If you ignore it, chances are it will go away. If he actually meant it as an insult, he will try again. At the second occurrence, question him as to his intention. If you pretend that you heard it as a compliment, it will drive him crazy. If it were meant to be a neutral statement, then he will not correct you. *If he meant it as an insult, he will try again.* In both cases, assume that the statement was neutral in intent.

If you must question the individual, allow for the possibility that a miscommunication has occurred by try paraphrasing what you think they said and repeat it back to them (see "CLAPing," in Chapter 4) and ask for verification. For example, it sounds as though you are concerned that I might not really know what I'm doing. Is that right?" Or "I heard that last statement as potentially insulting. Was it your intention to insult me?" Or "Is there something that I don't know? Your statement sounded like an insult." Again, the chances are that nothing was meant by it and now the individual will probably apologize and clarify what was actually meant. If, however, he indicates that his statement was intended as an insult, you can find out why and work to resolve any conflict. Of course, you should remember that he too may have misheard or misinterpreted something he thought you said.

Often, it is not *what* was said, but *how* it was said. The inadvertent use of a poor tonality or inflection can turn an ordinary statement into an insulting one. As a professional communicator, you have it within your ability to control potentially explosive situations. The other person probably doesn't have the knowledge or the ability to do it. We have found that as much as 99 percent of all such issues are immediately and easily resolved by clarifying and resolving potential misunderstandings before they escalate beyond repair.

All too often, people spend days or weeks fretting about some real or imagined put-down. In a business where you have to call a hundred strangers each day just to open a new account, you will receive many rude responses. That's why a thick skin is very important for success as a broker. Besides, how personally should you take it when a stranger is rude. However, you may feel differently when a client is rude or unkind. Remember, as a professional, you are doing your best to serve their needs. There may be miscommunications, but you should never have to feel defensive. In our opinion life is too short to waste that much time, effort, and energy on such trivia. Its easier said than done, but the effort you spend in educating your people about this approach can pay substantial dividends in improved employee relations.

OVERGENERALIZATIONS

"*Every* time I call, they give me a hard time." "*Nobody* in the branch *ever* lifts a hand to help me." These exaggerations may all seem true at the time they are spoken. When people are frustrated, it *does* seem like absolutely nothing is going right or will ever go right. All they can do is focus on the problem at hand. In addition, because of the very narrow focus and the feelings associated with the problem, they don't, and perhaps cannot, remember what normally happens.

If clients or coworkers make such a complaint to you, the easiest way to break their thought pattern is by searching for the exception to their mental rule. For example, "Do you mean that *every* single time, without exception, they give you a difficult time?" Or "Not one single person in the entire branch ever helped you out or gave you a hand?" If the person can come up with *even one* exception, the discussion will take on an entirely different tone. Yet, until you bring it to their attention with your question, they actually cannot see that they are involved in the exception rather than the rule. Of course, it could be that, for whatever reason, their coworkers do not help this individual. If this is the situation, then you face a different problem. Normally, though, because of your question, their hard-line statement no longer has its previous power over their feelings. More importantly, one or more of these questions will also usually lead the complainants into a mental state more conducive to logical discussion.

UNRAVELING BELIEFS THAT PEOPLE USE TO RULE THEIR LIVES

Throughout our lives, we hear short statements that provide some truth or rule of thumb to live by. These adages serve the valid purpose of teaching children and provide a clear, concise statement that makes a particular point. "A penny saved is a penny earned," addresses thrift. But "Never talk to strangers" (when providing individual coaching and counseling to brokers, we often find this hidden, heretofore unconscious belief to be the cause of reluctance to cold call) and "Don't speak unless spoken to" are sayings that would be decidedly disadvantageous to salespeople. Once we accept one of these "statements of authority" as a child, it can take on the power of a major belief that controls our behavior and feelings into adulthood.

These are the unspoken rules of the office that govern procedures and, often, office behavior—sort of the "This is the way that it's done attitude." New ways are not sought because the old ways are so entrenched. You can know when this is the situation when you hear definitive statements like "This *is* how it is done!" or "They say that. . . ." Who is "they"? you might ask. Needless to say, you may not be encouraged to explore new ways of doing things. When you first begin in a new office, this makes a certain amount of sense. First, you need to follow the established rules to make sure you can do your job. In addition, if you spend too much time trying to improve the efficiency of your office (your manager's job), you may end up unemployed because you haven't spent enough time cold calling or helping customers.

However, blindly following rules without exception can also lead to problems. We know of one situation in which a huge account would have been lost because a clerk refused to entertain the possibility that there might be an exception to the rule and basically set his heels in and refused to budge. Sometimes this is good, but in this situation it was in direct conflict with the manager's wishes. The clerk's bureaucratic attitude was not appreciated. In trying to determine why the clerk had been so rigid, the manager later found out that another clerk had lost his job for granting a similar request. The only thing that our clerk did not understand was that the clerk who lost his job did something on his own authority and in substantially different circumstances than was currently the case. However, the impact of someone getting fired instilled the equivalent of a phobic response in this one employee. Thus, when in doubt, ask your manager.

Whenever you hear someone say, "*They* say . . .," find out who "they" are. Whenever you hear a statement about how something *should* be done, find out who issued the "order." Usually, no one really knows. Another way that these *imperatives* show up is through the use of statements that contain any of the following words or their equivalents:

- "Should"
- "Ought to"
- "Must"
- "Need to"

You will often hear these words from clients or peers who are anxious about their security, that is, clients who are concerned about the safety of their investments and their future and peers who are worried about the security of their jobs (e.g., when they are "burning out" or when they are not performing according to expectations).

When "burning out," most people have too many of these "shoulds" in their lives. They "should" cold call, and they "should" be calling their clients, and they "should" be getting more product knowledge and another dozen "shoulds" that are competing for equal attention. Such people literally pull themselves apart with all the shoulds they think they "ought to" be able to accomplish simultaneously. Unrealistic expectations? Absolutely! We call this, "Shoulding on themselves," and it becomes particularly important to address when setting your personal or professional goals because these things are often outside our conscious awareness.

Employees who are not performing to expectations may be "burning out," but they may also be involved in some internal "conflict." For example, we know of many people in the financial services industry who want to do a good job and put in the necessary hours to bring in the production. But they also want to spend time with their families, enjoy themselves, and exercise. Both parts of their lives are demanding attention, causing the "conflict" we discussed.

Throughout our lives we have been taught that we "should" be able to balance all the aspects of our lives. We've also been taught that we have an obligation to our job/career, our family, our religion, our country, and all the other things that we "ought to" be doing to demonstrate that we are successful and otherwise nice people.

Similarly, older customers, who have lived through difficult economic times, are often very concerned about their security. This is particularly true if they live on a fixed income from Social Security and their investments. If they lose money, they often have little or nothing to fall back on. Obviously, this can make anyone anxious and somewhat rigid when making investment decisions. One way of helping them might include educating them about the different kinds of risks they face, from loss of purchasing power to loss of principle (see financial profiling in Chapter 10).

If you find yourself falling into this pattern, begin by listing all of your "shoulds"; then prioritize them (sometimes with your manager's help). Then negotiate with yourself to sort out which ones really need attention and which ones can be temporarily or permanently postponed or eliminated. After all, you can only do so much.

One of the questions you need to ask yourself is, "Who or what gave you the rule that you 'should' do such-and-such?" More often than not, they won't be able to give you a viable answer. Yet, for years they may have been running their lives by these unconscious rules.

A final commentary regarding the "shoulds." These beliefs create a whole series of expectations that often determine how you react to the world in general and other people in particular. Virtually every personal conflict is based upon some "should" that the other person has violated. One key question to always ask yourself is, "What did you/I expect?" We only get angry, upset, distressed, or anything else when our expectations are *not* met. Ironically, most of us have several expectations that themselves are totally unreasonable. However, once brought to light, they become easier to handle.

BREAKING DOWN "ASSOCIATIONS"

Associations are very important when working on motivational issues and job satisfaction. In many ways, they determine the meaning we assign to many actions. An often used example in therapy would be "If he loved me, he would give me flowers." Somehow, for that individual, flowers = love. Her partner or spouse could do all of the other things that *other people* would equate with love, but she would need flowers. Unless she tells him, or he magically figures it out, he's caught in a situation in which he can't win. Ironically, she *expects* him to know that, to her, flowers = love. Your clients may also expect you to magically know/understand what they need or what motivates them (don't assume it will always be money). Unfortunately, if you don't know what motivates your client, it can be very difficult to help them, because they often won't commit to a decision.

The question is, "What motivates people?" The answer often depends largely on what form of reward an individual associates with personal success or security. If you know what to search for, it is easy to pick and choose a reward system that matches the needs of your client and motivates them toward making a commitment. Despite your best intentions, however, if you always assume that making money (or greed) is the only real motivation for all of your clients, you will not have motivated many of them and could be thought of as not caring.

While the techniques we've presented are just a more sophisticated way of saying "Huh?" it is important to start saying "Huh?" more often than you may be used to. If you do, you'll find that problems become more easily resolved and that you know your people more completely. You'll become more effective in your job and help more clients by motivating them to action.

6

Generating Trust and Confidence

Psychologists tell us that up to 93 percent of the meaning of any communication is transmitted nonverbally in our tone of voice, the emphasis we place on the words we use, our speed of speech, and our posture. That means less than one-tenth of what we communicate is the result of the denotations (definitions) of the words themselves. In Chapter 5, we discussed the importance of the private meanings people assign to such words as "service," "success," and so on and their impact on a customer's expectations of you as their financial professional. In total, everything we say, or fail to say, and how we say it, as well as everything we do or fail to do (including our appearance, posture, tone of voice, speed of speech, breathing and others), combines to communicate important information about us and our message. We may build rapport and trust or destroy a relationship before it begins.

What is *rapport*? Rapport might be defined as feeling that someone else is just like you. It is very much like empathy and helps us to communicate our understanding and acceptance of the other person. Yet the ability to develop rapport with others goes far beyond the words we use when we speak. That is why it is possible to develop deep levels of rapport with someone with whom you disagree. For example, do you know anyone with whom you seem to have a great deal in common (e.g., same employer, same school, same age, same hobby) but with whom you do not enjoy spending time? How about someone with whom you appear to have very little in common who you really enjoy? That is the difference between having rapport and not having it. You do not have rapport with the first individual, but you do with the second.

Have you noticed that some of us seem to just establish rapport naturally, while others have great difficulty? Frustrating, isn't it? Why is one broker is very popular, successful, and listened to very carefully, while another, who may be much more intelligent, is ignored and has difficulty developing client relationships? One reason may be their level of interest in people. Their warmth and desire to be with and please others (see psychological profiling in Chapter 9).

If the second most fascinating person in the world is someone who is like us, surely tied for second is someone who communicates a genuine interest in us. Whenever we really focus our attention on someone and try to understand what they are saying, we almost automatically begin to build rapport. How to develop, enhance, and maintain rapport on the unconscious level is the subject of the next sections.

PACING

Key to the development of unconscious rapport is a process called *pacing*. We pace another person to the extent that we are in physical, mental, and emotional alignment with him. Essentially, it is a way of becoming similar to another person.

Since we respond to people on three primary levels—physical, mental, and emotional—people to whom we can relate on multiple levels often become our friends. Those with whom we don't relate never get close to us. One way to increase the chances of making someone a client, or a friend is to become as much as possible like them.

We have already pointed out that you unconsciously use many techniques in building rapport whenever you genuinely attend to someone in whom you are interested. Conscious appreciation of what you already know how to do will enable you to become consistent in your ability to accomplish the same thing whenever you wish. It will also help you to deepen any rapport that you have already established.

You should recognize that pacing is made up of a number of different aspects, no one of which is sufficient to accomplish your task by itself. *It is the combined effect of all the methods of pacing that will virtually guarantee your ability to establish rapport with anyone that you wish.* Rapport has a number of aspects, and while each is important, it is the cumulative effect that makes each powerful. What we are saying is that no single pacing method will automatically enable you to establish rapport with another individual. However, *the cumulative effect of these basic techniques will assist you in creating a "chemistry" with virtually anyone you wish.*

RAPPORT THROUGH UNCONSCIOUS PHYSICAL AWARENESS

Have you ever been in a restaurant and, without even hearing what's being said, been able to tell who the friends and lovers were? Or those who were angry? How did you know? Unconsciously, we can tell who is in rapport and who is not.

As we said before, whenever we are very interested in someone (or even just what they have to say), we tend to psychologically open ourselves to their influence. In doing so, we also tend to follow their lead and unconsciously seek deeper levels of rapport. Matching their body posture is just one of the five ways we do this. Others include matching their breathing and rate of speech, speaking in positives, and dealing flexibly with their relationship style. All are used simultaneously, but will be presented separately in the discussions that follow. Note: In our classes, we involve participants in exercises and experiments that demonstrate the power and effectiveness of the techniques presented here.

MATCHING YOUR CLIENT'S BODY POSTURE—MIRRORING

We like those who are most like ourselves—literally and figuratively. Matching body posture is one of the easiest and most effective ways of unconsciously influencing your client. Match, almost as a mirror image, your prospect's or client's posture, breathing, and gestures. This doesn't mean that you have to be exact, and it certainly doesn't mean mimicking your client by moving as he moves (that would be noticeable and insulting). What it does mean is that if someone were watching you and your client, they would notice many similarities in both posture and gesture.

When you first meet someone, observe how he sits and then sit the same way. If you allow him to sit first, it becomes easy to sit the same way. If you are already seated, simply readjust your posture after he sits down. For example, have you ever gone to a party and looked at three people sitting together on a couch? Interesting isn't it? They almost always sit the same way. And, if one of them changes, they all change or readjust themselves to the others. That's matching on an unconscious level.

When your client adjusts, or changes, his posture, wait a few moments and then *casually* adjust your own posture to match his. As long as you wait a moment first, your shift will rarely be noticeable. Remember, we are social beings, and it is natural for us establish rapport. As you sit, or stand, or gesture like your client, you communicate a shared means of expression to him on an unconscious basis. This is true because the way we sit, stand and gesture are all means of communicating, and anyone who does them like we do is communicating like us in some way. Thus, they are already "speaking our language" at one level.

Matching may feel awkward, at first. Sometimes it may even feel as though there are too many things to attend to at once. That's natural. What is ironic is that you already do this very well at least part of the time, and without even thinking about it at all. With a little practice, you'll be able to do it whenever you wish without having to think about it.

Test it for yourself. During a conversation with a friend or family member, begin by matching him. Notice how the conversation progresses. Then, after a few minutes, change your posture and mismatch him as completely as possible and notice what happens to the conversation. Again, after just a few minutes, match him again and notice again what happens to the conversation. What differences did you notice? In yourself? In him?

Initially, some people feel awkward following this procedure. However, after doing it a few times, it becomes automatic. You will soon find that your interactions with people are even more comfortable and easygoing as you employ these techniques. Remember, any time you give someone your undivided attention (that means *not* thinking about what you want to say), you will almost automatically match them.

You may notice that the other person may shift his body posture so that you are no longer matched. Merely wait a few moments, and then *casually* change your position until you are again somewhat matched. The key is to do it casually and to be as subtle as possible.

Sometimes simple matching isn't enough. Occasionally, you will run into someone who is so restless, or fidgety, that it seems that he just can't sit still. Trying to continuously match him would not only be difficult, but would also make you uncomfortable. A technique for dealing with this is called *cross-matching*.

CROSS-MATCHING

When you are with clients who often shift their body position, matching them move for move would almost have to result in their becoming aware that you are mimicking them and would hurt the very rapport that you are trying to establish. To avoid this, while continuing to "match," you can utilize a technique known as "cross-matching" in which you match some part of your body to another part of your client's body. For example,

- If your client is sitting with his crossed legs, cross your arms but keep your feet flat on the floor.
- If your client's arms are crossed, cross your wrists, your legs, or your ankles.
- If a prospect leans back on his chair, lean to the side and slightly back.
- If he puts his hand on his chin, put your hand near your head. As long as your hand is in a *similar* position, you're fine.
- If a prospective customer is sitting with his legs spread apart, have your arms open. (This is especially useful for women to know.)

The real key to matching is to adjust your body so that your posture resembles your client's posture. Now, what about that restless, or fidgety client?

- If your client likes to slowly bounce or move his legs to some internal rhythm, tap your fingers at the same rate he moves his legs. There is very little chance that he will become conscious of what you are doing. Yet, unconsciously, you will maintain your rapport.

An alternative to tapping your fingers could be a slight, almost unnoticeable, movement of your head (like nodding your head slightly to their rhythm). Again, there is very little possibility that he will ever notice this minute movement. Yet, *his unconscious is aware* and this awareness will correlate the rhythm of the two individual movements and will maintain or deepen your rapport.

Something this subtle might be difficult for a third person to observe. However, as long as you do this, you will increase the rapport you need to develop really effective communication. Matching body posture to obtain rapport is nice. But how do you know that you've achieved your purpose? The next subsection provides a procedure to test for rapport.

LEADING TO TEST FOR RAPPORT

Just how do you test to determine if you really have established rapport? One way to do this is through a process called *leading*. To test via leading, follow these simple steps:

- Once you have matched a person's body posture for several minutes, change your posture slightly and wait a few moments (typically between 2 and 40 seconds) and notice if your client readjusts his body posture to match yours. That is, once you change, does he follow your lead by repositioning himself?
- If he does, then you have established rapport on the unconscious level. If not, go back to matching him for a while, and then test again.

Note: It is important to realize that often a half a minute will pass before he will follow your lead by changing his posture. Don't expect him to follow your lead immediately. You should also realize that it often takes several minutes of matching before you can successfully lead. While verifying rapport is very useful, leading has several other important applications:

- It can affect your own mental state.
- It can be used to help a client become more excited about your presentation.
- It can be used to reduce aggressiveness in an angry client.
- You can lead your client to move from one posture to another. When he does this, the physiological change will often bring about a corresponding psychological change. For example, be aware of your own internal, emotional changes as you conduct the following experiment.

Notice exactly how you are currently sitting or standing and the internal feelings that you associate with that body position.

Now change your posture to one that is either more relaxed, or less relaxed, and again notice any changes in your internal feelings.

Now sit absolutely straight, and then allow yourself to sink into the chair. Again, notice your internal feelings.

In which position could you most easily carry on a casual conversation? In which would it be the most difficult? Do you associate specific emotional states with certain body postures? If you associate certain emotional or psychological states with corresponding physical states, then consider the ramifications of this thought: *You can influence your mental and/or emotional state just by changing your posture!*

Try it out. Take a moment and stand in the way that you stand when you are really proud of something you've accomplished. Be sure that if someone were watching you, he would be able to tell that you were really proud of something. Stand tall, throw your shoulders back and your chest out and smile. Notice how easy it becomes to suddenly remember the many times when you have felt proud of something you've done. Notice how those feelings return and how proud you begin to feel. Take a moment and relive one of those moments, fully. Experience it now as if it were happening again. Fantastic, isn't it? How might this help you when making a presentation?

Now, change your posture and let your shoulders slump. Just slouch and let your chest sink. Lower your head and your gaze. What happened? Note how the intensity of the feeling changed. Now, return to your original "proud" position again. Psychologists call these positions, or postures, *anchors*. These anchors allow you to modify your internal state by changing your body posture and can be used to create a personal "state of excellence."

LEADING YOUR CLIENT

You have just demonstrated to yourself that you can change the way that you think and feel simply by changing the way you sit, stand, or even breath. Wouldn't it be useful to be able to motivate your client the same way? Now you can. When you are speaking to a client who is in a "negative" state (any state which would keep them from listening openly and positively to what you are saying), you can *lead* them into a more positive state of mind by following these simple steps:

1. Establish rapport by matching your body to theirs.
2. Gradually shift your body into a posture which will lead them into a different mental state as their own "anchors" take effect.

Remember that they may have different anchors from your own. So, if the first state you lead them to is not an improvement, continue to lead them through different postures until you obtain the response you desire. Here are some examples:

- You may wish to lead an anxious client into a relaxed posture/state from a stiff or rigid one.
- Try leading a customer who is very relaxed into a posture/state normally associated with paying close attention (e.g., sitting up straight, leaning slightly forward, maintaining good eye contact).
- Lead an irritable customer into a relaxed posture/state.

- Lead an indecisive client into a dynamic, decisive posture/state (e.g., such as the "proud" pose you experienced).

Pretty exciting, isn't it! As you combine leading their posture with leading their breathing and their rate of speech as well, you will be able to achieve even deeper levels of rapport and even greater influence.

MATCHING BREATHING

Matching your rate of breathing to that of your client is one of the most powerful techniques for enhancing rapport. This is a simple technique whose impact occurs below the level of conscious awareness and, if combined with the previous techniques, can significantly increase your level of rapport. To match breathing, simply breath at the same rate as your client.

- If you are conversing, time your breathing to match the inhalations and exhalations of your client's speech rate, and/or time your sentences to match their breathing. This can be especially effective when speaking on the telephone, since it is one of the few things you can match over the phone.
- Watch the rise and fall of your client's shoulders since this correlates with her breathing.
- Remember that there will be times that you do *not* wish to match a client's breathing (e.g., if they suffer from asthma or emphysema). When this occurs, use a cross-matching technique such as moving your head, finger, or foot at the same pace as their breathing.

As we mentioned before, matching your client's breathing along with their posture can significantly enhance the depth of your rapport. When you combine matching with the other rapport enhancing techniques you are about to learn, you will become even more effective.

TOO FAST? YOUR RATE OF SPEECH

The "fast-talking broker" and "slow-minded customer" have become clichés. Yet, have you ever spoken with a person who talked so quickly that *you* felt rushed? How about a person who spoke so slowly that *you* wanted to try to speed them up? How did you feel as you conversed with them— comfortable or uncomfortable? At some level, most of us feel at least some form of discomfort when this happens. Even when we can't put our finger on just what, it's obvious to us that something is wrong.

However, if you felt uncomfortable when your client was too fast, or too slow, for you, he probably felt the same way. If the client that was too slow for you, you were probably too fast for him. And vice versa. Now both of you are having that slightly uncomfortable feeling. Even though you may not be consciously aware of it, such differences contribute to what some call "bad vibes."

Think about the traditional fast-talking broker. He is always portrayed as speaking too quickly, and rushing his clients into a sale before they are ready. It could be that he's just so excited about what he's selling that he gets carried away. Or he may be afraid that if he doesn't get his message out fast, his customer will hang up before he gets to the close. Or maybe he's just nervous. In any case, his rapid speech pattern can be self-defeating unless his customer speaks as quickly.

Think about the last time you were a customer and the salesperson spoke so rapidly that you became uncomfortable. While he was giving you fast-paced information, you may have needed time to think. However, to give you that time to think, he had to slow down. Did he? After all, its not easy to listen to someone *and* process what they're saying at the same time. If he didn't slow down, one of three things probably happened:

- You processed the information you caught but probably didn't hear everything he said.
- You listened to him but didn't get a chance to think about it.
- You tried to do both and ended up confused.

When you think about it, frustration is the almost inevitable result of any of the possibilities. After all, asking someone to just absorb information and make a decision without thinking about it doesn't show much respect for the client and frequently makes him feel "pushed." At the same time, speaking too slowly can leave him bored, and just as frustrated.

Remember, whenever you think, you need time to do it. If you get the time you need, you can make a decision and act upon it. If you don't, you are likely to feel pressured and frustrated or confused. Show your client the same thoughtful respect you would like.

Of course, some people are very fast thinkers, even if they don't speak quickly. How can you tell when your client is following you? Note their expression, the relevance of their questions, and changes in their voice quality, speed, tone, or affect that might be indicators for them. Remember, if you speak slower than your customer, speed up. If you speak faster than he does, slow down.

LEADING YOUR CLIENT'S SPEECH

Earlier, we showed how you could test for rapport through leading; that is, once you have established rapport, simply modify your posture slightly and see if the client follows your lead. If she does, you have established rapport. You can also test for rapport through modifying your speech. Once you have matched the speed and intensity of your client's speech, you can *incrementally* change your speed and intensity, increasing or decreasing them, and see if she follows your lead. If she does, you have established rapport. In most cases, they will follow you without even consciously becoming aware they are doing so. Think of some of the ways this might help you:

- Increasing the effectiveness of any sales presentation. For example, suppose that in a previous conversation, your client had spoken enthusiastically, *and quickly*, when referring to a great business triumph (or even a hobby, or something else that interested her). You realize that, for her speaking quickly is correlated with positive enthusiasm. Having mentally noted this, you might incrementally increase the speed of your presentation until both *you* and your client were speaking at her "enthusiasm" rate. While this won't guarantee the sale, it will significantly increase your chances.
- Building additional rapport during a prospecting interview.
- Making a proposal to your manager.
- Trying to calm down a client. Initially, match the speed and intensity of her speech and then lead her into a calmer state by gradually lowering your own speed and intensity of speech (this can be particularly important for customer service people).

SPEAKING POSITIVELY

How many times has someone told you, "Don't worry?" What did you do? You worried! After all, "What am I supposed to not worry about?" The problem is that to not do something, we have to think about doing it first, and then add "don't." Doesn't help much, does it. Try this: "Don't think about the Statue of Liberty!" How did it work? If you're like most of us, you thought about the Statue of Liberty, even if only for a microsecond, before moving on to something else.

Interesting isn't it? When you are on a diet, what are you supposed to *not* think about? Food, right? But what is almost every waking thought filled with? Food! The harder you try to push the thought out of your head, the more attention you must focus on the thought (food) to do it. No wonder so many of people have difficulty "losing weight." The point is that in order to *not* think of something, you *have to* think about it first. That's because your language mediates the way that you think. Remember, you also communicate with yourself, and communication is the purpose of language.

Here's another thought: What do you do when you lose something? You look for it until you find it. For many of us, the same thing happens when we lose weight. We seem to search until we have not only found every pound we've lost, but a few more that we weren't even looking for.

Don't think or speak negatively! Or, in other words, *Think and speak positively!*

Considering the previous comments, have you thought about the effect of negative statements upon clients? For example, "Don't worry about the dividend." Your client has to think about potential dividend problems to *not worry* about them. You have just increased the probability that the client will become concerned about problems with the dividends. After all, why did you bring them up unless you thought that they might cause a potential problem. Makes sense, doesn't it? How about a few others:

- "Don't make a decision until you've heard what our research department has to say about the stock."
- "Don't buy certificates of deposit at a bank."
- "Don't forget."

This may explain a lot of misunderstandings and "surprises" that occur with clients who forget something important, or bring up concerns about future dividends. All they are doing is exactly what we unconsciously directed them to do. We literally set ourselves up to obtain the very results we wished to avoid. Think about what might happen differently if we speak in positive terms. We might say

- "You can depend upon the dividend."
- "Look at all your alternatives carefully. We're confident you'll purchase your CD from us."
- "Look over what our analysts have to say before you make a decision on the stock."
- "Remember."

Our words are very powerful because they can direct the thoughts and memories of our listener. These thoughts and memories then influence their attitudes, behaviors, and beliefs. If we accept the idea that our unconscious mind cannot deal in negatives (try to think of nothing) *or* that our minds have to focus briefly upon the unwanted concept to make sense of a negative statement, then we get the following communications formula:

The original statement (OS) minus the negation (N) equals the unconscious message received (UMR).

$$OS - N = UMR$$

What this means is that a negative statement becomes unconsciously transformed into literally the opposite of what we intended, whether we are talking to ourselves (thinking) or to someone else. For example,

- Do not feel bad.—Not = Do feel bad.
- Do not forget.—Not = Do forget.
- I do not want to be late.—Not = I do want to be late.
- Do not worry about your principal.—Not = Do worry about your principal.

It's obvious how easily we can program ourselves to fail in obtaining our objectives. Speaking in positives is much more effective.

RELATIONSHIP STYLES

The key to relating to others is flexibility. When we always relate to someone the same way, regardless of the context, we become locked into a rigid system that becomes self-defeating. As a broker, you will frequently run into clients or prospects who will relate to you in a rigid style, always acting the same way. For example, have you ever had a client who always wanted you to make the decisions, but always found some reason for not going along with your idea? Pretty frustrating isn't it? How about a client who always tried to demand that you do things his way even when you knew he was wrong? And then blamed you when it didn't work?

How did you respond to these individuals? When the first client left all the decisions to you, did you make the decisions or try to involve him? When the second client tried to dominate you, did you give in and let him, or fight back? When we get locked into a relationship where we are always dominant when the client is submissive (or just the opposite), we have developed a "relationship style" with that client that will ultimately be frustrating and self-defeating at best.

Relationship style is basically a way of describing the way two people commonly communicate within a given relationship, the pattern of their relating. Usually, the way an individual relates varies with the context and the person to whom he is relating. However, their pattern, or style, can become common to all contexts with a given person or even to all relationships. When this happens, problems almost always occur. We will describe three basic styles, or patterns, of relating: complementary, symmetrical, and parallel.

A Pattern of Opposites: The Complementary Style

This pattern is one of opposites, that is, dominant-submissive, introvert-extrovert, hostile-warm, "healthy-sick," and so forth.

The most common form seen is in the dominant-submissive mode. This is a rigid mode in which one person is *always* in control while the other is *never* in control. Conflicts are generally solved by either the submissive person withdrawing in defeat or by the dominant person handing down an edict. For example,

- The aggressive broker and the pliant, eager-to-please client
- The dominating broker and the resistant prospect who is finally won over, but who never sends back the necessary paperwork to open the account
- The hostile client and the overaccommodating broker (who can't seem to make a sale)
- The hostile prospect and the broker who caves in rather than attempt to overcome resistance

You should recognize that your submissive client receives a great deal of "payoff" for maintaining his submissive role and will therefore try to maintain that role in your relationship. Don't let him. Lead him to make his own decision, and then support his decision (even if it's not the one you wanted). As you do so, he will begin to see you as a source of support instead of a threat and will begin to take more responsibility for his decisions.

In addition, the submissive client carries an all-powerful veto—he needs only to appear to "surrender," seeming to go along with what you wish, and then fail to follow through with whatever has been "agreed upon." This could place you in the position of having "won" without obtaining your goals anyway. Deal with "buyer's remorse" before it occurs! Remember, dominating your clients can become very self-defeating.

Pattern of Sameness: The Symmetrical Style

This style may be found in situations and relationships in which both individuals respond identically, such as both dominant or both submissive. When power or control is sought, neither gives in and the struggle escalates until serious difficulties may arise. Neither feels sufficiently secure in himself, the other person, or the relationship to relinquish control voluntarily. As a result, "power" becomes the primary source of validation in the relationship: "If I were really okay, I'd win."

When you run into an aggressive prospect or client, do you find yourself confronting him and trying to overpower him? Or when you work with a passive client, do you have difficulty closing the sale because you can't make yourself close for a commitment? In both situations you and the client are responding identically to each other, and nothing is accomplished. Frustrating, isn't it? And, in both cases, the client holds the ultimate veto. All he needs to do to "win" is *nothing*. He can even just hang up. The best way to handle this situation is to adopt the more flexible style, discussed next.

The Flexible Pattern: The Parallel Style

The parallel style of relating is the healthiest and most effective of the three because it is the most flexible. It's a style in which neither you nor your client feels anxious about the other, and you both feel able to express yourselves without a struggle developing. In addition, you both decide the issues of power and control by the needs of the situation rather than by arbitrary or conflicting expectations.

In practice, as the leader in the relationship you are able to maintain the necessary flexibility by supporting your client's needs for self-esteem while providing the leadership to solve his problem. It is a relationship in which neither of you "wins" all the time, and it consists of honesty, openness, trust, and cooperation.

In the financial relationship, this more flexible, or parallel, style occurs when you and your client work together to solve his problems. In most cases, a parallel relationship will result in your taking the lead in seeking and proposing solutions to the client, but in every case, it allows the client to accept responsibility for the end decision: *Flexibility is an important key to communicating.*

There are four common elements that occur in all three relationship styles. These processes are control, communication patterns, change, and decision making. It is the variations among and within these four areas that determine the style of interaction or relationship.

- *Control* consists of the way each person in the relationship attempts to manipulate or coerce the other in an effort to maintain control of a situation and/or the relationship itself. This can be seen whenever either you or your prospect/client attempts to manipulate the other to obtain your own ends. Note: Attempts to "manipulate" are almost always construed as negative by the person being manipulated and almost always hurt your relationship.

- *Communication* consists of each person's willingness to participate in two-way communication between peers rather than attempting to control the flow of information between them. How open is the flow of communication between you? For example, are you perceived as someone who communicates freely with your client or who only calls when you have something to sell? Do you perceive your client as clearly sharing data about his needs, goals, and concerns, or as someone who only calls when he has a complaint?

- *Change* consists of each person's willingness to risk change in their own behavior as well as the relationship itself without being threatened. This can be seen when you feel the need to suggest a change in strategy from one product line to another. How well does your client handle the change?

- *Decision making* consists of each individual's ability and willingness to place the needs of the relationship above his own desires relative to the decision at hand. At times, you may feel that a particular product or service is exactly what your client needs to solve a given problem while he may not agree. Are you prepared to follow his inclination rather than risk damaging the relationship by insisting on your own point of view? Is the client willing to trust your judgment?

Remember that effective, long-term client relationships are based upon mutual respect and consideration for your clients needs. While the elements of control, communication, change, and decision making will vary from relationship to relationship, in a parallel relationship, each of you will take your turn at the appropriate time. Be flexible! "Winning" over a client may be satisfying in the short term, but can cost far more than its worth over the long haul. The dominance, that is, overuse, of any characteristic is usually less effective than an intermixing—more or less equally—of these four factors.

Effective communication takes place on many levels that extend far beyond the mere dictionary definitions of the words we use. Everything we say and do communicates something about our message and our relationship with our client. In the end, the most important message we can send is that we value (care about) that client and his needs, and, after everything has been said, only actions will really speak with authority. Combine this with a reasonable level of flexibility and you can relate to almost anyone.

Rapport, that sense that we are "just alike," that we share something important in common, is the basis of comfort and trust in any relationship. By being aware of, and flexibly matching, all that your client communicates through his posture, level of excitement, speed of speech, and more, you can build that comfort and trust in minutes instead of months.

PRODUCTIVE PROSPECTING

Most brokers wish to expand their business and compensation and are, therefore, constantly seeking new clients to help. Prospecting is the traditional method of accomplishing these goals.

The purpose of this section is to provide a summarized overview of the prospecting process. The three chapters here deal with the following topics:

- Finding prospects by the thousands
- The nine steps to prospecting
- Managing your business and maintaining your efforts

There are four keys to successful prospecting:

1. Always remember that the *purpose of prospecting is to find people that you will be able to help.*
2. *Prospecting is a numbers game.* Even the worst prospector in the world will find clients if he makes enough phone calls. The name of the game is to increase your calls to accounts ratio.
3. As long as you use a qualified list, it *doesn't matter which prospect becomes a client.* Prospects who "reject" you quickly are doing you a favor by helping you find your next client more quickly.
4. *Use a good script and practice it.*

7

Prospects by the Thousands!

WHY PROSPECT?

When you prospect you are developing a continual source of new clients to further develop your business. Unless you are in a firm in which prospecting is inappropriate or unnecessary, the need to bring in additional clients is essential. It gives you additional money, which is always nice to have. (People who have had or are having tax audits may debate the previous sentence.) Additional clients also allow you to maintain your current standard of living, which would otherwise be reduced, because of client turnover. In our industry the rule of thumb is that you will lose 20 to 30 percent of your clientele each year due to clients moving, switching to the competition, dying, being dissatisfied, taking a large loss and blaming it on you, or whatever. The income loss that you experience due to this turnover requires that these expected losses be replaced. Continued prospecting allows you to insert some control into your business growth. It also allows you to progress beyond those who are complacent. Remember: *If you're not going forward, you're going backward.*

There are numerous approaches to prospecting. *All* work some of the time. *All* involve effort and continued prospecting consciousness on your part. *All* have certain advantages and disadvantages. Listed next are the six most popular prospecting methods. Each will be briefly discussed within this chapter.

1. Firm-generated leads or reassigned accounts
2. Client referrals
3. Business networking
4. Letter writing campaigns
5. Seminars
6. Cold calling

Let us examine the least viable method first.

RELYING ON FIRM-GENERATED LEADS OR REASSIGNED ACCOUNTS

There are many brokers who pick up the phone only when they get a "lead" from their manager. To a large extent, these brokers are doing themselves a major disservice because they are placing their entire future in the hands of the manager, who may be transferred tomorrow or who may stop providing these clients with little or no notice. We believe that such a reliance is the harbinger of ultimate failure in the business. In reality, firm-generated leads normally go to those brokers who have already proven themselves successful using other methods. Newer brokers often have unrealistic expectations, bordering on fantasy, that the business will come to them without any real effort on their part and that most, if not all, of the best leads will be handed to them.

Other brokers apparently rely on accounts reassigned to them when another broker leaves the firm. Most new brokers pray for such reassigned accounts and quickly find that they are often more trouble than they are worth. The larger accounts tend to go to the larger, proven producers who have been in the office/firm for a number of years. In addition to rewarding those brokers for productivity, the firm is also trying to retain the client relationship (which may best be accomplished by having the large clients work with brokers who have been in the business for a few years). Note: The dilemma faced by firms is the actual or perceived reward to brokers doing highly transactional business. Rewarding such brokers may prove counterproductive to the firm as other brokers may become transactional so that they, too, may be rewarded. Upper management must be extraordinarily conscious about such perceptions.

REFERRALS

Referrals are an excellent source of new business. If you ask for referrals often enough, you will get them. The beautiful thing about referrals is that you have a much more receptive person at the other end of the line. Most satisfied clients will be happy to provide referrals if requested nicely. How to ask for referrals is described in detail in Chapter 21.

The vast majority of leading brokers leverage their time and efforts by consistently requesting referrals from their prospects and clients—they realize that they have everything to gain and nothing to lose. Once requested, people tend to be on the lookout for people who have needs similar to their own. Once you contact a referral, you usually get good receptivity because people usually take the advice of their friends, and they don't want to run the risk of offending them by rejecting you out of hand. Note: Make sure that you periodically thank the people who give you referrals. People will do virtually anything for you if you are appreciative.

Anyone can sell financial products and services. But people need a professional who is ready, willing, and able to help them achieve their financial goals. In essence, the idea behind prospecting is that there are usually many people out there who need your specific product or service. The trick is to ask questions and to keep your eyes and ears open to opportunities. Remember, if you want to increase your income or opportunities within the company, you must get more clients.

One of the funniest incidents concerning referrals during prospecting occurred to a stockbroker who was talking to the president of a large manufacturing company. After finally getting through, the president ranted and raved about how he had lost money in the stock market, about his view that all brokers were crooks, and a host of similar statements. The broker allowed the client to vent and, because he had nothing to lose, asked for a referral. The president, of course, would not give the broker the names of any friends or associates because he believed that the brokers would merely lose their money. "Give me the name of your biggest competitor," said the broker, "so I can lose him money." The president provided the name. Being a professional, the broker then called the competitor and related the entire story. The competitor, after a good laugh, opened an account. The broker then called the original person back to thank him for the referral. The president was so intrigued with the broker that he also opened an account.

GIVING REFERRALS AND BUSINESS NETWORKING

In your day-to-day conversations you will undoubtedly discover needs that you cannot fulfill. Someone may tell you that they're painting their home or he's looking for a car. Rather than merely continuing to talk about financial products, it is occasionally nice to refer them to someone who may be able to help them. You could say, "I know someone who may be able to help you. Would you like his or her name? (for him or her to give you a call?). If you have developed a list of contacts within your network, *you become a center of influence.* "One hand washes the other." It is another way of maximizing your effectiveness. Make sure your client uses your name when contacting this other person/business. Also, send this person a note indicating you gave his name; he may reciprocate by giving your name when appropriate or assist you in other ways such as sponsoring you to give a talk at a trade association meeting.

There are also business networking clubs available in which a series of professionals meet on a regular basis and exchange leads. A club may consist of a realtor, attorney, CPA, broker, and so on. Each person tries to refer potential prospects to the others. However, before you participate in such a club, check with your firm's compliance posture regarding clubs. Also, be careful of breaching client confidentiality.

BEFORE YOU BEGIN A SALES CAMPAIGN . . .

Before a letter writing, cold calling, or seminar campaign is launched there are three preliminary procedures that will be extremely beneficial to you. Understanding your market and contacting the right people are essential to any effective campaign. These approaches can be used in conjunction with each other or one at a time. They are

- Understanding how to market to the affluent
- Conducting your own demographic study, simultaneously creating centers of influence
- Discovering thousands of "ideal" clients

Marketing and Selling to the Affluent

As brokers, we wish to deal with wealthy people. If brokers had one wish it would possibly be that all of their clients were millionaires. Dr. Thomas Stanley spent years studying the millionaires of America and wrote two books that should be required reading for any financial professional. *Marketing to the Affluent*[1] shows how to find and market to America's wealthy. *Selling to the Affluent: The Professional's Guide to Closing the Sales That Count*[2] discusses, among other things, ways to work with millionaires. Here are some points from the books worth noting:[3]

- When prospecting for the affluent, beware: luxury goods are often the replacement for wealth, not the symbols of it. Most millionaires wear Timex or Seiko wristwatches.

- Sales and marketing executives frequently make the mistake of targeting the "pseudoaffluent"—those with the trappings of wealth. Stanley defines as affluent those with households earning $100,000 or more a year, or with a net worth of $1 million. Most are business owners. With 1 millionaire for every 100 households, the group is growing and has an average income of $120,000. About 20 percent are retired.

- Millionaires are a frugal bunch and tend not to live in the fanciest neighborhoods. They are generally not well known, and many of the business owners don't even incorporate. Korean Americans are three times more likely to have $100,000 households than the average American.

- Because they've accumulated their own wealth, they appreciate courage in others—something to keep in mind for the salesperson about to make a call.

- For every household worth $10 million in a so-called affluent neighborhood, there are many more with net worth of under $500,000. They have virtually no money to invest. But they may have a difficult time admitting that to you. You must discipline yourself to recognize that symbols of wealth and dollars to invest are not complementary to each other; they are substitutes for each other.

Conducting Your Own Demographic Study

Here is an approach which can be used with a variety of professions. CPAs and accountants will be used as the primary example. Most CPAs service

[1]Thomas J. Stanley, *Marketing to the Affluent* (Homewood, IL: Dow Jones-Irwin, 1988).

[2]Thomas J. Stanley, *Selling to the Affluent: The Professional's Guide to Closing the Sales That Count* (Homewood, IL: Business One, Irwin, 1991).

[3]Thomas J. Stanley, "Feeding on the Rich: Find the Investors with Real Money," *Success*, Date unknown.

the people living in the immediate area of their offices. Although there are exceptions, each CPA has a good understanding of the financial needs of his clients—especially regarding taxable and tax-free investment needs. Since these needs may vary from one geographic subsection to another, checking with some CPAs may give you insight into the needs of the specific area. Even if only one out of three provides you with the information, you are still doing very well because

- You may be able to fine-tune your mailing (i.e., target market) by high-lighting financial products that the CPA may have already recommended.
- You may learn of small geographic pockets that have specialized needs.
- Those CPAs may become centers of influence for you.

This strategy is similar to our *Adopt-a-Town* approach. Search for a town that has no brokerage firm or bank offering brokerage services. Meet with the town's centers of influence and poll them about the financial needs of the citizenry. Offer seminars on the recommended topics, becoming the town's broker. (Although the approach is more complicated than outlined here, this provides the basic idea.)

Discovering Thousands of "Ideal" Clients

Who would you most like as a client? Eliminating any billionaires or mere multimillionaires, what are the characteristics of an ideal client? You can pick virtually any economic level, background, or characteristic you can imagine. What prospects do the other brokers dream about having? As long as you stay within the bounds of reason, there are hundreds or even thousands of people who fit the majority of the characteristics that you want. Here are some areas to consider when determining your ideal client:

Age	Magazines read	Business owners
Own home	Hobbies	Occupation
Vacations	Marital status	Schooling
Income	Children (number and ages)	Etc.

Part of the problem for some brokers is that they try to go after any-body and everybody who has a dollar. While it may seem to be the most log-ical way of doing things, it is not really as efficient as focusing your efforts.

During your initial start-up efforts it *is* logical to explore all avenues. Shortly thereafter you should become more and more focused as you pursue certain types of clientele. For example, a broker may begin by selling any type of financial service possible to anyone wishing to buy, but may find that some of her best clients are parents of school children. They refer her to parents, which causes the broker to become even more expert in educational funding and related areas. At that point, she may wish to devote even more of her time and effort developing this particular market.

Begin your prospecting efforts as if you were a strobe light.[4] You want everyone to know that you exist and are willing to pursue a variety of markets. As you obtain success with any particular group, devote more of your time and energy to similar prospects. As you become even more knowledgeable about a particular market segment, you will become a recognized expert. At that point you will have shifted from being a strobe light to being a laser beam.

Ideal Prospects by the Thousands!

The sources of names of potential prospects are limited only by your imagination. You can use trade associations, church groups, owners of small pleasure craft, members of certain clubs, professional groups, and so on. Again, depending upon the industry you are focusing on, you can find a wealth of information in your local newspaper and the local court: marriages, estates, and new business formations are examples of the items commonly available from either source. It may take some time to find out what is available, but once you do, you can hire a high school or college student to do the legwork for you. The more names of potential prospects that you have, the better your probabilities. There are even companies that will, for a modest price, compile lists of thousands of people for you to either call or mail.

Using a Mailing List Company Effectively

Companies that specialize in providing mailing lists can be a great source of qualified leads. However, there are some important things to consider whenever you use a mail list company:

1. There are many list companies that have information about your area. Look in the Yellow Pages under "Mailing Lists." However,

2. The standard lists have probably already been used by others in your

---

[4]This idea was originally provided by Art Mortell of Systematic Achievement Corp. in a private interview with Steven Drozdeck.

profession. The next paragraph will show you how to quadruple the value of your list, because

3. You can create a personalized list that will find people who are very close to ideal prospects.

4. If you buy a list, make sure that the company has a "guaranteed delivery rate of 90 percent or better. This helps insure that the names and addresses are relatively current. (Some list companies get their "Change of Address" information directly from the U.S. Postal Service.

5. Phone numbers are available from most list companies for an additional charge. (It can be cheaper to let a student look up the numbers from a reverse directory such as a *Coles Directory*.)

6. Some companies will provide your list on a floppy disk or CD-ROM for your computer.

Think again of an ideal prospect, perhaps by thinking of the common characteristics of your best current clients. For example, you may want to search for people who are married, between 40 and 50 years old, own their own homes, take vacations by flying first class, have 2.3 children, and read a particular business magazine. The list company can probably provide you with thousands of names of people who meet all or most of the criteria you established. The idea is that you can be highly specific and selective. Create an ideal prospect and let the list companies find people who match most of the criteria.

Of course you have to pay for these supercharged lists. There is usually a slight, incremental charge for each additional criterion that you wish. For instance, the list company might search for all the married couples and then "cull out" anyone who does not own his or her own home. From this smaller listing, the company would eliminate anyone who is less than 40 and older than 50, leaving a smaller list. It might then search the readers of whatever magazine(s) you wanted. The process goes on and on until you have the names of a few hundred or thousand highly qualified individuals. You have just increased your efficiency because you can tailor-make your mailings to meet their probable needs.

If you are too narrow in your focus, the list company will let you know that it cannot supply the quantity of names you requested. It wants you to be successful because you will then use the services again and will therefore help you modify your selection criteria. (Be aware that there probably are a few list companies that have what you need. Check with two or three companies.) Often they will provide useful ideas that can be incorporated into your prospecting program—mail or phone. Because your success ratio usually becomes significantly higher and your time and energy are being used much more productively, you are often reimbursed for the increased cost of the list within the first few new accounts. Although these super-charged lists may be about twice as expensive as ordinary lists, they pay for themselves with the significantly increased value of each name.

LETTER WRITING CAMPAIGNS

This is one of the most popular and costly methods of reaching prospective clients. Even with the best lists, a response rate of only 1 or 2 percent is all that can be expected. You may wish to mail a letter to the people on your "ideal client list (created or purchased) to inform them of your product and offer them the opportunity to call or write for additional information. You would probably be wise to ask someone in your company's advertising department to help you compose a letter specifically designed to meet the needs of that select listing. Most firms have a list of preapproved letters. Remember that industry rules require that most sales oriented letters be pre-approved by a duly licensed principal of the firm.

Those who respond to your mailing are the people you contact first. The people who do not respond to the mailing can still be easily called using the "Did you get my letter?" approach. For example, "Mr./Ms. Prospect, last week you received a letter from me which. . . ." At this point it is no longer an absolute cold call. You realize that the person probably didn't read the letter. That doesn't matter. Tell him about what the letter contained. At that point, you will be simultaneously qualifying the person with respect to your products and services.

Remember that you already know quite a bit about them. Each of the people on the list is all highly qualified by definition of the list you had the list tailor-made. The only purpose for the letter is to determine which individual members on the list were hot prospects—the ones with an immediate interest that you should call first. Try two or three variations on the same letter. Send out 200 or 300 of each letter and find out which one provides the best response. Then go with the best. After calling the few people who respond to your initial mailing, seriously consider calling everyone else at a later date.

SEMINARS

Seminars are another popular and effective prospecting method. Here are some thoughts that represent things to watch out for when conducting a seminar:

- If possible, avoid poor speakers by making sure that the presenter has a good speaking reputation. Even though he or she may be a whole-saler or an analyst, check with other offices to make sure he or she presents well. If not, get someone else.

- If you are going to present, be certain that you use slides or overhead transparencies. Insure that people at the back of the room can easily see both you and your visual materials. Provide participants with a small handout of key points made during the presentation, allowing them to focus on the presenter rather than on taking notes.

- Use a wireless mike or a microphone with a long chord. Avoid stand-ing behind the podium and conducting an entire speech from there.

- When someone asks a question, repeat the question and then make sure that you explain its relevance to the entire audience. Often, other people will not have heard the question, and an answer without the context of the question make not might sense. Look at the person ask-ing the question, but direct your answer to the rest of the audience to make sure they understand the relevance of the answer to themselves. Otherwise, you'll lose the majority of people.

- If other brokers will attend, insure that they will sit and listen. Too often, brokers stand in the back and talk. The latter is unprofessional and distracting.

- Collect the names of all who attend and offer an inexpensive door prize. Make sure you can follow up with the participants.

- Include humor. It keeps the presentation alive.

- Tell stories and anecdotes. They make it real.

- Rehearse your speech. (In our courses we suggest that each subtopic should have a condensed *and* expanded version, allowing you to shorten or lengthen the speech at will.)

- Avoid jargon. Keep it simple.

- Keep it relevant and to the point.

- Read your firm's compliance requirements for speech giving.

Other Seminar Ideas

- Address a topic that has been appearing in the newspapers, and ad-vertise the seminar extensively.

- Call people and invite them to attend. Confirm their attendance by calling again the day before or the day of the seminar. It is amazing how many people fail to attend unless constantly reminded. Offer non-alcoholic refreshments, plus something light to eat.

- Consider sponsoring your seminar with a local center of influence such as an attorney or CPA. Let them invite their clients and do the majority of the legwork. After they present their specialty, for example, estate planning, you present all the ways that the estate can be funded.

The same idea can be used with local charities. We know of a broker who became expert in gift giving and charitable remainder trusts. A local charity sponsored a black tie affair and allowed her to be a key speaker. A large amount of business (both charity and noncharity oriented) came her way as some wealthy sponsors contacted her for investment advice and services. Her rehearsed, polished presentation made her a popular speaker (and highly successful broker) as other charitable organizations also asked her to speak. (Of course, when a patron/sponsor asked technical questions, the charity referred the question to their financial expert—the broker).

QUALIFY FOR YOU

Regardless of how you get your list of names, you will still have to initiate the first phone call. When initially speaking to prospects, you are in a fact-finding process in which you are qualifying the client in two ways: *Do they need you?* and *Do you want them?* Additionally, you are positioning yourself and them for a future contact.

Prospecting Purpose #1: Do They Need You?

Can you and your firm supply what they want or need? If not now, how about in the future? If the answer is "No," then remove that person from your list of names. Before you do that, however, you have the opportunity for a referral and potentially for some networking. The "Do they need you?" question is important. Equally important is Prospecting Purpose #2.

Prospecting Purpose #2: Do You Want Them?

When making prospecting calls, one of your main purposes is to determine whether it is worth giving this person a follow-up phone call. While closely correlated with "Do they need you?" it goes further because you must also evaluate the time and effort needed to make this person/company a client.

At this point you must be very "bottom-line oriented." The prospect may only have a limited amount of money available, yet demand a great deal of attention. The person may have an abusive personality, which makes dealing with him psychologically expensive.

Because "time is money," you should devote your attention to those who are worth your while. Remember: There are thousands people who need your assistance. However, while you may accept a limited number of small accounts as a personal favor, too many of these small accounts make it impossible to support yourself—and you won't be able to help anyone. Similarly, evaluation of a prospect's potential is an ongoing process. From week to week, circumstances can change for you or for them. You must always make a determination regarding the most effective use of your time and energy. Remember that while you are talking to a low-probability candidate, you are *not* contacting someone with greater potential. The next chapter will explore four qualifying questions that will help you determine whether the prospect is a viable candidate for your prospect list, as well as the other things to accomplish during the initial call. The four areas that may be explored during the first conversation are

- Brokerage affiliation
- Investment objectives
- Investment history
- Available funds

Knowing when to "let go" is something that comes with practice and effective questioning. Newer financial salespeople tend to hold on too long. Experienced salespeople often let go too quickly. Many studies have shown that most new accounts are opened after the sixth phone call, while most financial salespeople give up after the third. This may be part of the reason that a relatively small group of leading brokers take home the vast majority of commission revenue. In the next chapter we will also discuss "the numbers game" and ways to keep yourself motivated.

Prospecting Purpose #3: Commit Them to a Profiling Meeting

The final purpose of prospecting is to commit prospects for future profiling meeting and to establish yourself as the person who can meet their needs. Through effective profiling, you will discover not only each prospect's financial goals, but their key "buying criteria" and motivations. Your subsequent sales presentations will be more powerful, effective, and persuasive as a result of this knowledge. While determining their needs, desires, and motivations, you will also develop a very deep level of rapport so that the person both likes you and wants to do business with you.

CHAPTER
8

The Nine Steps to Prospecting Success

During your career, you will be exposed to a variety of ways to prospect by phone, as well as several prospecting philosophies. The following approach, and the psychology behind it, have proved successful for thousands of brokers. It is a simple, yet effective, prospecting track (sequence) that we introduced in our first book, *Consultative Selling Techniques for Financial Professionals* (Simon & Schuster, 1990).

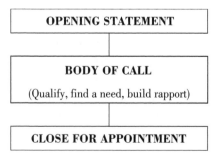

| OPENING STATEMENT |
| BODY OF CALL |
| (Qualify, find a need, build rapport) |
| CLOSE FOR APPOINTMENT |

There are four things that you must accomplish during the initial call to prospects or to referrals.

1. Introduce yourself and briefly explain how you can assist them.

2. Identify their key needs and begin to financially profile them. (Financial profiling is an ongoing process and will be discussed in greater detail in the next section.)

3. Establish yourself as a "valuable resource person" who will assist them.

4. Form the beginnings of a relationship that will allow you to fulfill their financial needs.

At the end of your conversation with a prospect, that person should have a positive feeling toward you and your firm and should be willing to have follow-up discussions sometime in the near future. Using the appropriate telephone and financial profiling skills will help ensure that a positive relationship is established.

All this can be accomplished if you use sound, selling principles during the process. You will be successful if you apply a consistent, systematic approach which has stood the test of time. Eventually it will become second nature—allowing you to spend your time *really listening* to the customer and making the minor adaptations necessary to make it more individualized and effective.

The information gained in the prospecting sequence will allow you to efficiently motivate the customer to meet with you to profile his or her financial needs.

OVERVIEW OF THE NINE PROSPECTING STEPS TO SUCCESS

In essence, the prospecting sequence employs the following steps:

1. Review any information about the person that you are aware of (address, occupation, referral source, etc.) and identify actual and/or probable needs for your products and services.

2. Select an appropriate opening statement that you will use at the first phone call. This statement introduces you and your services while creating an environment in which the customer will answer your questions.

3. Deal with any initial barriers that might stop the conversation.

4. Ask profiling questions and generate customer interest in your products and services.

5. Respond to any concerns while enhancing the relationship.
6. Go to the next step, which may be
   a. Additional follow-up phone calls
   b. Referring the customer to the appropriate department
   c. Arranging a meeting
   d. Mailing literature
7. Complete the appropriate paperwork.
8. Schedule the next phone call or profiling meeting.
9. Dial the next customer/prospect/referral. *Ultimately, this is the most important step. Persistence is the key to success.*

THE NINE STEPS TO PROSPECTING SUCCESS

Step 1: Review the Customer Information Form and Identify Actual and/or Probable Needs for Products and Services

Your prospecting list was created with certain key criteria in mind. Briefly examine any information you know about the prospect and be prepared to use the information in either the opening statement or within the discussion. For example, if you know that the prospect has previously purchased annuities, you would want to discuss annuity oriented concepts such as tax deferral, rates of return, future uses of money, and so on. It would increase your probability of generating interest. Similarly, if you are calling accountants, you might wish to discuss your firm's tax-planning strategies. Therefore, if you know something about the prospect, use that information in the opening statement (or early in the conversation) rather than using a totally generic opening statement.

Step 2: Select an Appropriate Opening Statement to Use During the First Phone Call

This statement introduces you and your services while creating an environment in which the customer will answer your questions. When you are prospecting by the phone, you usually have only 10 to 20 seconds to say something that is interesting and exciting and causes the prospect to want to hear more. Depending upon the background information that you already have, this can become rather simple. Businesspeople like to know what their competitors are doing. People generally like to hear what other people are doing. Your initial statement should include solutions that would probably appeal to the individual with whom you are speaking. For example, if you know that the person has a child in high school (you could have created a list that includes this as a criteria), you would have a higher level of receptivity if your initial statement included something that would appeal to people in this situation. For example, "The costs of higher education are becoming enormous. If I could show you a way in which some of those costs could be offset, would you be interested?" (You already know that this is a probable concern.) The prospect can answer either "Yes" or "No." In either case your next question is "Why?" This question has a good probability of getting them to talk. The response will further qualify the person regarding your product. Even if there is no need, in which case you have limited the amount of time and effort you have spent, you can ask for a referral.

Essentially, the opening statement should also be personal and specific, assertive but not threatening, a disarming agent, and tailor made for each group. The primary purpose is that the prospect should understand that he will receive a benefit from dealing with you. However, he has to be willing to listen.

You may as well think of your job as interrupting people for a living. In reality there are very few people out there who are sitting by the telephone saying to themselves, "I sure hope a salesman calls me today." They were, almost by definition, doing something else when you called. Your call may or may not be a welcome diversion. Having an effective initial opening increases your initial response rate. However, regardless of the effectiveness of your initial opener, you will still regularly experience initial stalls and objections.

There are two basic types of opening statements: (1) product or service specific and (2) generic. Each works, each appeals to specific personality types, and each has advantages and disadvantages. Because different openers contain different levels of threat to a prospect, each will result in different levels of resistance on his part. We will provide examples of several types of openers, who they appeal to, and how much of a threat they might represent to a prospect.

Product/Service-Specific Openers   This opener is exactly what it appears to be: calling a prospect to determine whether she would be interested in buying a specific product or service. For example, if your firm were participating in a new stock offering for the local utility company, the broker might inform the prospect about the new stock offering and ask if the prospect would like to participate. Whether it be a stock offering, a municipal bond, unit investment trust fund, and so on, this type of product-specific opener remains popular.

Being so direct is advantageous if you know that the prospect will be interested and it obtains an immediate commitment (or, at least, an indication of interest) in the offering. However, these product-specific openers can be disadvantageous because, unless you know something specific about the individual, the chances of the prospect wanting this particular product at this moment in time rather remote. The product specific opener elicits a "Yes/No" response. Unfortunately, the probability of a "No" is substantially higher. The product-specific opener tends not to be viewed as "consultative" and may therefore set the wrong tone.

These openers appeal to aggressive financial consultants. Their chief advantage is that they will elicit an immediate response from prospects and will end a call quickly if they are not interested.

Additional Disadvantages of the Product-Specific Opener

- Product-specific openers immediately identify you as a "salesman" in the mind of the prospect. Once this mind-set has been established, it is almost impossible to change.

- Because of the sales bias of the approach, this opener can be very threatening to many prospects, resulting on increased "sales resistance" on their part.

- This kind of opener appeals primarily to "sophisticated" (experienced) investors who already understand your product/service, and who know exactly what they want. Prospects with less financial sophistication will feel more threatened.

Note: To some brokers, "sophisticated" prospects may at first appear to be ideal clients because they can often result in a quick sale and commission. However, they rarely give any one broker more than a small percentage of their total assets, frequently know more than the new investment rep, and tend to quickly transfer their accounts when the market turns or someone else calls with a "better" new idea. Many new brokers appear to prospect almost exclusively for this kind of client and, after doing well initially, frequently lose many of their clients when the market turns because they have never established a solid relationship.

- Despite what many brokers appear to believe, it can be very difficult to move from a product-specific opener to determining a prospect's overall needs. You may end up appearing to say, "Since you don't want to buy this product, is there something else I can call back with to sell you later?" (Reading a laundry list of products and services is a very poor sales strategy.)

Examples

"Hello. This is _____, with Prudential Securities. I'm calling with some information on our latest municipal investment trust, which is currently yielding _____% tax free, paid monthly. Do you have a need for tax-free income?"

"Hello. This is _____, with the investment firm of Merrill Lynch. I'm calling investors to determine their interest in receiving our investment newsletter. It's published weekly, and it provides up-to-the-minute advice on the market, interest rates, and investment recommendations. Do you currently invest in the market?"

"Hello, this is _____, with Legg Mason. I'm calling the owners of sporting goods stores with information on our newest offering of stock in Reebok Athletic Shoes. If you sell Reeboks, I'm sure that you already know how well they are made and how quickly they are selling. Would you like to hear more?"

Service-Specific Openers   This opener is essentially the same as the product-specific form, but offering a free service. However, if the service with which you are calling is "free," it is considerably less threatening to a prospect, for example, your firm's services, such as your version of a central asset account, or an IRA, free portfolio or tax analysis, or free retirement planning.

This type of opener appeals to financial consultants who are warmer and who wish to establish rapport with the client for a longer term relationship. It is appealing to prospects because

- Depending upon the service specified, he may be able to more quickly see the benefit to himself than with a specific product opener.
- There is far less pressure to buy something. As a result, it is easier to keep the prospect on the phone to qualify them and build rapport.

Disadvantages of the Service-Specific Opener

- This opener may not carry as much sizzle as a product specific.
- Given encouragement, some financial consultants can become tempted to spend more time socializing than is effective.

Examples

"Hello. This is _____, at Citibank. I'm calling to introduce our new central asset account. It provides more than twice the services as most banks, and at lower cost to you. Do you currently have a central asset account?"

"Hello. This is _____, at Donaldson Leften and Jenrette. As April 15 approaches, I'm calling investors to determine if you currently have an IRA. Despite the recent changes in the tax laws, a great many people are still eligible to open and contribute to an IRA account before taxes. That can result in substantial tax savings while providing a nest egg for retirement. Do you currently have an IRA?"

Generic Openers   The generic is the broadest of the openers. If the product-specific approach is like hunting with a rifle, the generic is like hunting with a shotgun. Its broader appeal makes it easier to hit more targets. It may refer to a wide range of products or services, or to a generic concept. This kind of opener is particularly useful if you are calling from a list that has not been prequalified for a specific product or service, for example, financial planning (the generic concept); your firm's broad range of banking, information, or insurance services; information on the latest tax law changes; and so on.

Because they tend to be nonthreatening, generic openers appeal to prospects in the same way as the service specific openers do. As long as you are able to come to the point and quickly demonstrate a benefit to your prospect, most will listen. They are particularly useful in their ability to provide greater flexibility in establishing a smooth transition from the original purpose of the call to identifying a more pertinent need of the prospect.

The generic, like the product-specific, opener can be a two-edged sword. We mentioned that the product-specific opener is not only the most exciting, but also the most threatening. Similarly, while generic openers are less threatening, they can also be the least exciting.

Advantages of the Generic Opener

- They enable you to present yourself as a professional who is calling to determine how you can help your prospect rather than as a salesperson who is calling to determine how you can use him.

- They are generally nonthreatening. Hence, they do not generate additional barriers to overcome in establishing rapport with your prospect.

- They provide an easy vehicle for qualifying the prospect and setting up future contacts to profile him and open the account.
- They focus the interaction on you and your firm. This enables you to project more of your personality to your prospect as you establish the relationship.

Disadvantages of the Generic Opener

- You must move quickly to elicit a need, and to show that you can meet that need. If you don't, you may irritate or even alienate many prospects.
- It can encourage unassertive financial consultants to talk too much.
- It may not be as exciting as a product-specific opener. You should note that, while all these disadvantages are possible, none need occur if you can get the prospect talking.

Examples

"Hello. This is _____, at Dean Witter. I'm calling to introduce our financial planning services. Essentially, this is a group of services that we have developed to help you plan for your retirement, your children's education, your taxes and even, Heaven forbid, death or disability. Do you currently have a financial plan?"

"Hello. This is _____, at Scott & Stringfellow. I'm calling with some information on the latest changes in the tax code and how they could effect your investments. Are taxes currently a concern for you?"

"Hello. This is _____ at First Source Securities. I'm calling to introduce our investment products and services. Essentially, we have developed these products and services to help you with your retirement, your children's education, your taxes, and insurance needs. Which of these are important to you?"

"Hello, This is _____ with _____ branch of National Westminster. I'm calling to introduce some of the services that we think you would useful to you (and your business). If you have a couple of minutes now, I'd like to explore how we may be of even greater service to you in the future."

The "No-Frills Approach" to Opening Statements for Inactive Customers:

"Hello, Mr(s) Customer, This is _____ from _____ (optional). May I have a few minutes of your time?"

"I'm calling to find out how we can improve our level of service to you." (Listen and make note of their answer. Then CLAP to verify. When they finish, thank them and say:)

"In response to requests from other customers we are now offering the following services (Give list.):

"I would like to sit down with you to help develop a financial profile of your needs and how we might be able to help you."

Note: We've taught this particular technique at many banks and have gotten fantastic results from this approach. Another opening statement for inactive accounts that has proved successful is:

"The reason for my call is that I've been asked me to contact you regarding some of the additional services that (name of firm) may be able to offer you. For example, we've been very successful in helping customers (state a need while using one of the verbs below). Would something like this be of interest to you?"

Verbs to use:

- benefit from
- prepare for
- evaluate
- plan
- cope with
- etc.
- consolidate
- organize

If YES

"That's great! What are you currently doing to accomplish this?" Or ask some other qualifying question. Continue qualifying.

If NO

"Oh, why is that? Are you currently working with someone else?" Continue qualifying.

If NOT INTERESTED

"Oh, why is that? Try to explore another need."

"What would you like your money to do for you and your family? or What is something that the bank might be able to do for you even better?" Continue profiling.

Step 3: Dealing with Any Initial Barriers
That Might Stop the Conversation

Regardless of the effectiveness of the initial opening statement, there will be some people who initially respond negatively. It is typical to hear statements such as

"I don't have the time."

"Just send me your card."

"Just send me some information."

"I'm perfectly satisfied right now."

"I already have another broker/banker/representative."

"No money."

Etc.

Most initial prospecting calls result in the prospects' automatic defensive mechanism coming into play. People are conditioned to react defensively to salespeople. The easiest example we know is what happens when a clothing store clerk asks if we need assistance. The almost universal, automatic response is "No, I'm just looking" or something similar. Likewise, because of the vast amount of unprofessional solicitation that is constantly bombarding our senses, most people will automatically respond in the negative to any prospecting approach that identifies you as a sales person.

Remember that this automatic response is merely a put-off, an initial stall. It does not necessarily indicate a permanent "no," nor is it a rejection of you as a person. You have two choices at this point. Hang up the phone and try someone else, or try to respond to that initial stall. The first alternative is promoted by some approaches who suggest that success is assured to those who persistently call and constantly dial the phone. While this is true, it is not as efficient as attempting to respond to or bypass the initial barriers.

Assume that only 1 out of every 10 people who hear from you has an immediate interest, and that 9 out of 10 will respond with one of the automatic responses. If you try to overcome the initial objection you will probably qualify an additional 2 people out of the 9. Now you are qualifying 30 percent of the people you contact instead of only 10 percent. Over thousands of phone calls it becomes significant. For example, over the course of 10,000 prospecting calls, which is what many salespeople make annually, qualifying 3,000 people versus 1,000 people gives much better probabilities. Some of those additional 2,000 are going to become good clients. Of course, the other alternative is to make an additional 20,000 phone calls and only qualify 10 percent of these people. (Brokers taking the latter course are encouraged to have their finger calluses removed regularly.)

Standard Stalls and Your Potential Response   Traditional sales
courses identify a prospects' natural hesitation or suspicion as "stalls" or
"objections" that must be overcome. In consultative selling we recognize
that prospects are naturally hesitant to accept any sales call at face value.
Rather than increase potential "resistance" by trying to overwhelm or get
around it with slick answers, being by CLAPing (see Chapter 4) to make sure
you understand the prospect's real concern. Then respond to that concern.

By doing so you will demonstrate that you are a helping professional
rather than just one more sales person. You should note that there are about
six to ten common responses that prospects give when called to show their
hesitation, lack of interest, or distrust. Here are some typical "stalls" with
some useful responses. They work partly because you demonstrate your desire to understand and have an immediate comeback which takes the prospects comment into consideration. They should be previewed, modified to
meet your individual style or situation, and then practiced so that you have
an automatic response to their automatic stall.

Stall: "No money" or "Not interested"

Response 1: "It sounds as though this isn't a good time for you to consider investing. Is that right? " YES. "I can understand that the chances of me calling you at a time in which you had money available for an immediate investment in _____ product are rather remote. The reason for my call
is to find out if we can establish a relationship for the future."

Response 2: (*Not* designed to win friends and influence people, but we thought
you'd get a chuckle from it.) "Is this a permanent or temporary condition?"

Stall: "Been burned/hurt by your product/service/company before."

Response: "It sounds like you had a bad experience and don't want to risk another loss. Is that right?" YES. "I'm sorry to hear that. What happened?"

People sometimes need to vent their anger or frustration. While they review the situation, you are gathering valuable information about what they
consider to be important. They usually feel good that someone listened to them
and often appreciate you in the process. Remember that you are part of the solution, not the problem. You are only part of the problem if you don't listen.

Stall: "Already have another agent/broker/representative."

Response 1: "So you basically feel that all your needs are already taken care of. Is that correct?" YES. "Many of our current clients *had* another broker before they began working with us. I'd like the opportunity to earn your investment business."

Response 2: "Many people in your situation have more than one broker. If I can provide as much added value to you as I have to my other clients, are you willing to work with me?"

The key to dealing with a prospects' hesitation or suspicion is to never defend. By CLAPing you are readdressing or redefining their question. Realizing that many responses are purely automatic, it becomes worthwhile to try to go to the next step. Thus, you are trying to ask the question: "Are you potentially interested in how I can help you?"

There are undoubtedly other typical "stalls" that are standard for the financial services industry. Make a list of the ones you hear in the next 100 phone calls you make. After 100 calls you will have heard it all and have developed a response to virtually everything. When someone does offer something new, you can honestly say, *"That's interesting. I've never heard that comment before. Can you tell me why you said that?"* Once they start talking, you achieve your objective of qualifying them.

While you will qualify many additional people because you are willing to go the next step, you will still get a significant number of "No. Not interested" responses. The ability to continue searching for those who *do* need your product/service while disregarding the numerous negatives that you will receive is what brokers are paid to do. If all you had to do was take orders, you would have substantially less earning potential.

Remember, while we are suggesting that you respond to their automatic responses, we are not suggesting that you become a punching bag. You will significantly increase your success ratio if you accept that reactive responses will occur and plan for them. You can almost make a game out of it. Since nine out of ten people will have an automatic defensive response, try to figure which one they will use. Search for a new, more effective response. Try different ways. Have fun with it. (Additional ways of dealing with rejection and keeping track of your effectiveness are dealt with in Chapter 9.)

Step 4: Asking Profiling Questions and Generating Customer Interest in Other Products and Services

At this point in a conversation you can start to explore the two key questions: "Do they need you?" and "Do you want them?" A "No" to either question should result in you politely discontinuing the relationship. You may refer the prospect to someone else, but you have made a determination that your time will be better spent pursuing other possible clients.

During your first conversation with a prospect, you should try to get answers to as many of the following questions as possible. *These questions represent areas to explore* and will help determine the "economic and time value" of your prospect. While it is not important, or reasonable, to get this information from each prospect you call, the more information you obtain on the first call the more efficient you will become.

- *Determine their current brokerage/bank/investment advisor affiliation.* If it is already with someone at your firm, it is usually wise to politely discontinue the conversation. However, if the prospect has a relationship with a competing firm, then they have met the first criteria. Remember: *Your best prospects are already someone else's best clients.*

- *Discover their investment objectives* (retirement, kids' college, etc.). While there are many ways to ask this question, during the first phone call you want to know if there is something you can do for them. Sometimes, rather than provide concrete investment goals, people will test you by indicating that they want unusually high yields with little or no risk or something else that may be equally unrealistic. Your professional response to these requests will let such investors know that you are too professional to "jump through the hoop" and try to achieve the impossible. Of course, an unsophisticated prospect may honestly have unrealistic expectations which may require that you educate them.

- *Learn about their investment history.* What have they done to achieve their objectives? What stocks/bonds/financial vehicles do they currently own? What types of products might they have purchased in the past? This area also includes their current portfolio, other financial assets, and so on. Note: You will rarely obtain a totally honest answer to this question during a prospecting call. A response to this question may simultaneously answer the next question.

- *Determine if they will be able to pursue their goals now or in the near future.* If they are destined to remain a small account, you may wish to reconsider dealing with them yourself and suggest either that they deal with some form of managed money (with a minimal involvement on your part) or that their needs may be more fully met by dealing with a different broker or firm. You may wish to refer them to one of the newer brokers in your office.

Of course, everything can change. This "small" client may come into substantial money from a variety of sources—but what is the probability of that happening? How many small accounts must you open and how much time and effort must you devote to such accounts before one of them becomes truly worth your while?

Having explored one or more of these areas, you now have a better idea about the potential value of adding this person's name to your inventory of prospects. Because of the number of prospects and clients you are dealing with, the fact that records must be kept, and it is virtually impossible to service hundreds of people, you must be very selective in who you work with. The next chapter deals with ways to maintain your prospecting efforts, as well as prospecting organizational systems.

Note: Many prospects will hesitate to answer personal financial questions from a stranger over the telephone. This is another good reason to use prequalified lists and to recommend a face-to-face meeting.

Step 5: Responding to Any Concerns While Enhancing the Relationship

During the conversation you may discover concerns that the prospect has concerns regarding the attainment of investment objectives, the economy, the current administration, where interest rates are heading, and so on. This will give you an opportunity to send information to the client, or verbally respond to their concern. Meanwhile, you will be demonstrating your professionalism and enhancing the budding relationship.

Step 6: Going to the Next Step

Send a short note (which you can have preprinted) indicating that you enjoyed the conversation and will call again on a particular date. Also, if appropriate, include promotional and/or informational literature that the prospect will find interesting or useful. Such notes are a normal and expected business response. Failure to acknowledge the conversation may be considered impolite.

Beware of sending too much sales literature. Some newer brokers have been known to send packets of "everything" their firm offers, their quotrons, sales assistants, and the last six years of *Money Magazine* in an effort to impress the prospect.

Step 7: Completing the Appropriate Paperwork

In the next chapter we've provided samples of prospecting cards/forms that we've found helpful. Whether you use a preprinted form or blank paper, keep track of the conversations and key data that you've obtained. It is embarrassing to have a prospect say, "I told you that last time."

Step 8: Scheduling the Next Phone Call

Calling the prospect to follow up on a timely basis is important to the new relationship. As a rule of thumb, give them four to seven days after they've received your literature before you call again. The time suggestions are neither so close as to be intrusive, nor so long that they forget who you are. Calling them again allows you to follow up on any literature you've sent, reinforce the relationship, and begin the in-depth profiling process (the subject of Section IV).

Step 9: Dialing the next Customer/Prospect/Referral

As discussed in the next chapter, it is vital that you make a number of calls each day. Many brokers fail in this business because they do not continue "Dialing for Dollars" and do not allow the "numbers" to work in their favor. Without doubt, staying on the phone can be difficult to do, especially after you've gotten an extended series of "Not interested" responses. Yet maintaining an ongoing prospecting effort is essential to success. (These calls to prospects can be to seminar participants, people who responded to your letters, referrals, and so on. Most "rejection" comes from pure cold calling. Interestingly, many top producers attribute their primary success to pure cold calling. To a large degree, your reaction to rejection is based upon your personal attitude. See the next chapter for additional commentary.)

Remember that one of the primary purposes of prospecting is to determine if you ever wish to speak to this person again in your lifetime. If they disqualify themselves for your product or service, you have merely come one step closer to working with someone else. One way of thinking about sales is that you are paid to get through all the initial rejection so that you connect with those people who need your assistance.

You want to get them talking. There is an old adage that "no one ever hung up on themselves." Once you get them talking you are obtaining the information that you need. Through the use of short-answer questions, you can direct the conversation to gain the additional information that you need to help them. These questions will be covered more fully in subsequent chapters.

The Nine-Step Prospecting Track represents a logical sequence of events. It works because it takes many factors into consideration and doesn't try to go too far with the first phone call. Rather than trying to make a sale, the consultative selling approach concentrates on establishing a stronger relationship through the subsequent profiling interview. Then, having discovered the client's objectives, you have set up the next five or six sales. That is efficiency!

9

Maintaining Your Prospecting Momentum

Prospecting can be easy or difficult. A task to look forward to or a task to dread. Something to actively pursue or procrastinate doing. It's all a matter of how you look at it—your attitude. The wonderful thing about life is that *you can choose your attitude.* Your prospecting attitude is partly dependent upon your organizational system, your understanding of the "rules of the game," and your internal drive and motivation. This final chapter on prospecting will deal with these important issues. In addition, this chapter will provide some tools which will allow you to more effectively implement the nine prospecting steps to success presented in the last chapter.

THE VALUE OF EACH PROSPECTING CALL

How much is each phone call worth? The answer is easy to calculate, but it is computed differently depending upon whether you're on salary/draw or commission and how long you've been a broker. For new brokers who are on a draw and bank investments representatives who are on salary, a computation that takes into account your draw/salary on a daily basis and the number of prospecting calls you make can be used. More experienced brokers should take the average value of a new account and divide it by the number of calls it takes to generate a new account. Illustrations of both computations are provided here:

> For those on draw or salary,
> Annual salary
> Divided by 244 (average number of workdays/year)
> Equals approximate salary per workday

Divide by number of prospecting calls you are expected to make each day to get the value of each phone call. For example, a new broker at a $30,000 per year draw/salary is paid $122.95 per day. If he is expected to make 100 phone attempts per day, the value of each phone call is $1.23 (rounded). (Important note: Some brokers try to double the value of each phone call by only making half the phone calls. This is not a good long-term career strategy.)

> For more experienced brokers,
> The average commission value of a new account
> Divided by number of prospecting calls to get a new account
> Equals the average value of each telephone call

For example, assume that it takes 10 calls to get a prospect and 10 prospects to get a client. This means that 100 phone calls be made to get 1 new client. Assume, further, that each new client generates $200 in commissions. Therefore, each prospecting phone call was worth $2 in eventual commission business. *You had to get 99 "no's" before you got the one "yes" worth $200.*

Leading brokers have a prospecting call value substantially higher than $2 per call. Many of these brokers obtain new accounts primarily from referrals. While every referral does not open an account, even if only one out of every five did open account (still assuming a $200 commission value), then every call would be worth $40. In reality, the initial commission value is usually substantially higher. We have seen prospecting call values (from referrals and firm generated leads) in the $200 to $500 range for some leading producers.

Whether you are a new or experienced broker, here's the key question: "If someone gave you $2 (or whatever your computed value is) each time you dialed the phone, how many times a day would you be willing and able to pick up that receiver? It wouldn't matter if you spoke to a person, got a busy signal, the wrong number, no answer or a "no" response. Each time you picked up the phone and dialed a number you would receive $2. In our seminars, most people indicate they would be able to make a lot of phone calls *and feel good about each one!*

Since it is doubtful that your manager would be willing stand over you and physically hand you a dollar for each phone call, *you can give yourself a dollar—physically or mentally—every time you pick up the phone.* If you think about it this way, prospecting becomes much more enjoyable. Some people actually start to look forward to the turndowns because they realize that it merely brings them one step closer to their goal of obtaining an account.

Keeping Track of the Numbers

To determine your personal efficiency, you must keep track of your daily productivity. It is only through measurement and self-assessment that you will know how you are performing. This fact is true whether or not you use the information to maintain your ongoing personal motivation.

Your long-term results will be based on what you do every day. Studies of the most successful brokers indicate that a primary reason for their success is their consistency. They realize that they cannot control the market, the economy, whether someone is interested or not, or even if a sale will be made today. They do know that "its a numbers game" and "the harder I work, the luckier I get."

They also know that they can control their personal effort. Hence, they realize that even if they don't make a sale today, they can still be successful if they gave it a good effort. They can feel good about themselves because they did their best, today and every day. In essence, they are "successing." The following tracking system was designed to achieve two purposes:

1. To insure that you can measure your effort
2. To insure that you can both measure and increase your effectiveness

Use a daily activities form similar to the one in Figure 9-1. (A complete form will be provided later.) These numbers represent phone calls you have made and will be marked in the manner indicated here:

Figure 9-1 Part of Daily Productivity Analysis Form

1	2	3	4	5	6	7	8	9	10
11	12	13	14	15	16	17	18	19	20
21	22	23	24	25	26	27	28	29	30
31	32	33	34	35	36	37	38	39	40
41	42	43	44	45	46	47	48	49	50

Each number represents a phone call, and whenever you dial a prospect you will check off one of the numbers using the following system.

／ = Dialed but no answer, busy, wrong number, and so on. Basically you tried to call someone but were unable to contact them.

⊘ = A circle is drawn around the slash if you connect with the person that you wanted. If you go to the next step. If you only talk without qualifying him or her, leave the mark alone.

⦸ = A second slash is added to the circle if you qualified them.

⑧ = An "S" is added if you open an account. (Essentially, you have put $ in your pocket.)

After a couple of weeks, you will get a good idea about your actual productivity levels. You will also be able to analyze the results to determine your level of efficiency and effectiveness.

Analysis of Performance Patterns

Look at a few examples of daily forms (see Figure 9-2) and draw your own conclusions based upon the various marks. Consider the comments below to each of the six patterns. Assume that each example is a representative sample for six different brokers.

You can see how your performance can be analyzed and, therefore, improved upon. Lists can be changed. More attention to qualifying prospects can be given. Fewer nonproductive phone calls can be made. It is impossible to make improvements in your personal performance unless you know what you are doing now. Too often, brokers work very hard doing nonproduc-

Figure 9-2 Analysis of Performance Patterns

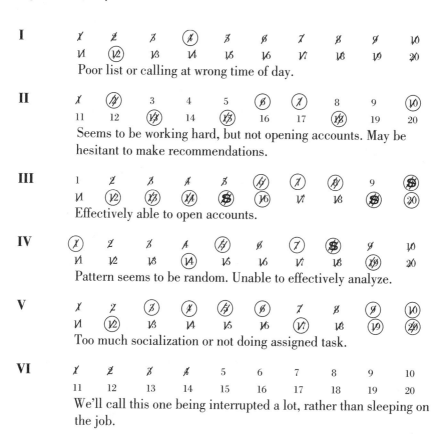

I
Poor list or calling at wrong time of day.

II
Seems to be working hard, but not opening accounts. May be hesitant to make recommendations.

III
Effectively able to open accounts.

IV
Pattern seems to be random. Unable to effectively analyze.

V
Too much socialization or not doing assigned task.

VI
We'll call this one being interrupted a lot, rather than sleeping on the job.

tive activities and feel both exhausted and frustrated at the end of the day. When we've provided individual performance coaching sessions for brokers, we've found that they quickly discontinue unproductive activities once they see their performance illustrated so graphically.

A shortened version of a daily productivity page is provided in Figure 9-3 for your consideration, followed by an alternative method (without using a form) to keep track of the information.

A Daily Tally Sheet

If you keep a daily tally sheet of the number of dials you make, the number of people reached, the number of people that you qualified, the num-

Figure 9-3 Daily Productivity Analysis

Date:_____

1	2	3	4	5	6	7	8	9	10
11	12	13	14	15	16	17	18	19	20
21	22	23	24	25	26	27	28	29	30
31	32	33	34	35	36	37	38	39	40
41	42	43	44	45	46	47	48	49	50

...

Prospect Name	Action Needed / Comments	New Acc't No. or Follow-up
1 _____		
2 _____		
3 _____		
4 _____		
5 _____		

...

ber of accounts or sales that you make, and the average commissions generated on each sale, you would be able to make the computations. Keeping a daily tally is a good idea because you can measure your levels of efficiency in a number of ways. The tally sheet could look something like that in Figure 9-4:

This tally sheet can be analyzed in a number of ways to measure the relative efficiency of your efforts:

- It took 50 dials to reach 25 people. This 2-to-1 ratio is excellent for most prospecting efforts. The list that is being used is a very good one.

Figure 9-4 Daily Tally Sheet

Number of dials: JHT JHT JHT JHT JHT JHT JHT JHT JHT JHT = 50
People reached: JHT JHT JHT JHT JHT = 25 (unusually high)
Qualified prospects: JHT JHT = 10
New Accounts: 1   Commissions: $200.00

A ratio of 5 to 1 would also be considered acceptable, while a ratio of 20 to 1 would indicate that you probably need to change your prospecting list or the time at which you are trying to contact the people on the list.

- Being able to qualify 10 of the 25 people is also excellent. Usually the figures are significantly lower. You would immediately realize that the list you were using was bad if your qualifying ratio dropped significantly.

- Opening one new account generated $200 in commissions. Assuming that this was an average day, this salesperson was earning $4 for each and every call made. *Not bad for dialing the phone.*

If you think of your prospecting efforts as a machine, the constant monitoring would let you know when you had high performance and when you needed a tune-up. *Prospecting is a "numbers game." The more people you dial, the more you succeed. You are literally Dialing for Dollars.*

THE SYSTEM

This system has been successfully employed by thousands of professionals who must systematically keep in contact with their clients. It is designed to require an absolute minimum effort for daily upkeep while providing reminders for periodic follow-up. It is also designed to keep unnecessary paperwork to a minimum. It is composed of three key components, which will be examined separately.

- An account book
- 3 × 5 index cards (one for each prospect and customer)
- A file box with tabs for the days of the month and the months of the year

Account Book

Your book of accounts is an alphabetical listing of all of your prospects (using profiling forms (such as the one we've developed) or blank pages. Note: Because of changing economics and personal situations, it can be easily argued that a profiling or account form is never completed and represents a "living document." Each prospect is listed in alphabetical order with investment objectives listed, and a record of your conversations. Eventually, these prospecting pages can be transferred to your client book once they become a client.

Prospect/Customer Index Cards

Put the name, address, and phone number of each prospect and client on an index card. (You can also place prospect labels on 3 × 5 index cards so that you have one card for each prospect and can easily integrate the call back system for prospects and clients.) These cards will be used in the tickler file system that will be introduced shortly.

Place (or have preprinted) numbers across the top of each card to represent different investment objectives, such as retirement, education, taxable income, and so on, which your firm can fulfill (see Figure 9-5). Circle the number of each investment objective that the prospect or client currently has or in which he has indicated an interest. Over time, your goal is to determine whether or not the prospect is appropriate for each of the areas/numbers available. In the long run, using circles and Xs, you will insure that you have covered all of the bases with each customer. Remember that due to changes in economic and/or personal circumstances, financial needs, and goals also change.

The prospect's or client's specific financial goals are actually listed on your account page where a complete record of your conversations and referrals is contained. The numbers on the cards merely represent product needs/interests that you can easily see at a glance, allowing you to quickly identify appropriate clients for a particular mutual fund, municipal bond,

Figure 9-5

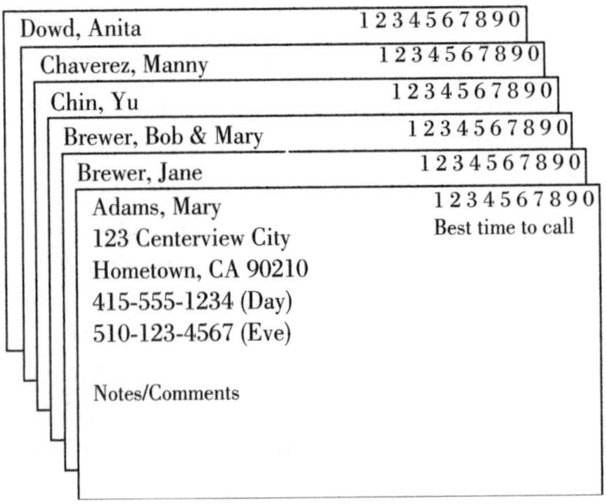

and so on, as well as immediately identify areas in which you must still qualify the investor.

The Card File

The index cards are placed in the card file based upon when you want to call the prospect back. You'll have a set of monthly calendar cards as well as a set of date cards numbered from 1 to 31 (available in virtually any office supply store).

It Works Like This

If you've spoken to a prospect and want to call her back next month, you would place her index card behind November 19, for instance. When November 19 arrives, you would call this woman as well as everyone else whose card was placed behind this date. If someone isn't home when you dial, merely move the card to the bottom of the day's pile. If you haven't contacted them by the end of the day, merely move their card to the next day or next week. This insures that (1) prospects don't get lost in the shuf-

Figure 9-6

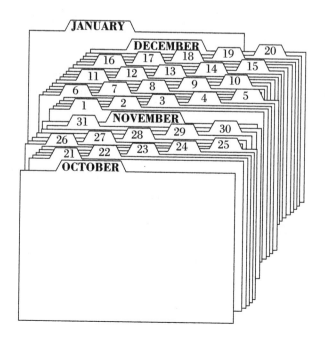

fle (every pun intended), (2) a minimum of paperwork is done—you only make a notation when you actually speak to them, and (3) you can easily organize each day.

Whenever you call someone, you *always* place her card to call again sometime in the future. Depending upon the situation, you may wish to contact this person one day, three weeks, one month, or five months from now (see Figure 9-6). Then, at the appropriate time, you'll be reminded to give her a call. Some suggested follow-up times will be provided shortly.

Alternatives to using a card file include a daily calendar or computer program specializing in "prospect contact." A daily calendar that requires constantly making notes and jotting down callback dates requires a lot of time and energy to maintain. You may wish to include a daily calendar with this system, but keep the writing to a minimum. Computer "prospect contact" programs are ideal. They do virtually everything just described while allowing you additional options.

WHEN TO FOLLOW UP

Since the key to your success is maintaining prospect contact and regularly introducing your prospects to various products and services, it is imperative that you schedule your calls at the most opportune times.

Although you will normally be in contact more often, the maximum time between phone calls to a particular prospect or client should be six months. This would only occur in unusual circumstances. Normally, the maximum time between phone calls should be three months for those who have actually expressed no immediate interest or need for assistance.

You'll probably be speaking with most of your prospects once a month, with some prospects—at least initially—once a week.

Events/Circumstances	Time
Between initial introductory letter and first phone call	5–7 days
Between sending literature and verifying receipt	5–7 days
Thanking customer for a referral which opened an account	1–2 days
When you're working on a problem	Every 2 weeks
Updating a financial profile	4–6 months
After the prospect receives a promotional letter	5–7 days

DEVELOPING AN EFFECTIVE TELEPHONE "PRESENCE"

Even though your prospecting efforts are organized, you must develop an effective telephone presence to maximize your effectiveness. Although presented earlier in the book, a synopsis is provided here for your convenience. Among the elements necessary for telephone effectiveness are

- *Make effective opening statements.*
- *Respond to prospects automatic responses of hesitation or suspicion.* ("No money," "Too high," etc.)
- *Use appropriate voice tones.* Your emotions are reflected in your voice. The simplest way to ensure good voice tones is to smile while you are talking.
- *Strive for congruence.* Your voice should reflect confidence, enthusiasm and concern. Shakiness, boredom, and anger are easily heard and would cause immediate distrust or rejection of your ideas. If you feel "off," take a break and put yourself into a better mental state. Effective methods include read or listen to a joke, take a 60-second relaxation break, and visualize yourself succeeding, sitting or standing "proudly" and "confidently," doing a different task, reading promotional literature, and so on.
- *Adjust your rate of speech.* Try to speak at the same rate of speech as your prospect to help maintain rapport. Avoid speaking much faster or slower than they do since these differences create unconscious and unnecessary barriers.
- *Speak in positives.* Remember the effect of "Don't think of a pink elephant." Create mental imagery that supports your purpose of assisting the prospect to more effectively manage his or her money with you.
- *Use effective verbal techniques,* such as

    Open and closed probes. In general, try to listen more than you talk. Use open probes ("Tell me more about…") to gather information and closed probes to verify information.
    Bridging. This ensures that prospects know what you are talking about.
    Building. Building adds additional emphasis or support to prospects' positive statements.

Acknowledging. Make sure prospects know you are really listening.
Use of analogies. Allow prospects to more easily understand new
or complex ideas.

- *Respond to customers' concerns by CLAPing.* Allow prospects to know
  that you value their input and want to ensure that their concerns are met.

YOUR PROSPECTING ATTITUDE AND EFFORTS

Even with an effective organizational system and a good telephone presence,
many brokers don't prospect with enough effort or consistency. There are a
number of reasons, including

- Not having enough time to prospect because they're dealing with their
  current prospects or with day-to-day business problems.
- Not giving appropriate mental value to prospecting efforts. (Review the
  "Value of Each Prospecting Call" presented earlier in this chapter.)
- Believing that prospecting is a waste of time and effort. (Review the
  "Value of Each Prospecting Call" presented earlier in this chapter, as
  well as in Chapter 7.)
- Too tired or burned out. (Consider employing stress management tech-
  niques.)
- Inability to deal with rejection (in industry parlance, the "R" word).
  (See next section within this chapter.)
- Having the dreaded malady, *"telephone-a-phobia"* (discussed later in
  this chapter).

Dealing with Rejection

Inability to deal with rejection is probably the single greatest reason for brokers failing and dropping out of the business. Intellectually, we know that
nine out of ten (+/−) prospects will have a "no" automatic, defensive response. The best prospects are being solicited, seemingly, by everyone. Of
course they're going to have an automatic defensive response. Intellectually,
we know that it has nothing to do with us personally. Yet the majority of brokers *do* take it personally and are negatively affected by something that
should be totally immaterial to them.

Part of the reason is preconditioning. If many people tell you something is bad, horrible, or difficult, the chances are that your mind is condi-

tioned to view the event/task with a negative mental reference. Then, at the least sign of difficulty, the preconditioned response alters our perception and colors our thinking. This has generally been true with prospecting. As Kathryn Napier said, "Everyone kept telling me how bad it [prospecting] was, and I believed them. I eventually realized that it wasn't so terrible after all. In fact, it was relatively easy when compared to most other things. At that point, prospecting became a simple, not quite enjoyable, thing to do. Most of my best prospects came as a result of my realization that my manager, and all of the people giving me advice, were wrong [about the difficulties in prospecting]." Kathryn was very astute, and lucky, to come to that important realization early in her career. While prospecting may not always be easy, it certainly is not the terrible task that some have made it out to be.

Fortunately, the consultative selling attitude significantly reduces the fear of rejection because you're calling to do the prospect a favor. The traditional methods of prospecting imply a confrontational, win-lose situation, with the prospect holding the key. With the correct attitude, if you're able to qualify a person, great; if they disqualify themselves by declining your services, great. It becomes a win-win situation with your attitude being the key.

Dealing with "rejection" may also require additional attitudinal adjustments. Art Mortell is rated among the most popular public speakers in the United States. His unique presentations actually change how people perceive and react to rejection. In his speech "How to Enjoy Failure, Be Amused by Rejection, and Thrive on Anxiety," he makes the following points.

- "You know, from childhood we are conditioned to feel successful only if we succeed most of the time. If we get 19 out of 20 on a test, then we get positive feedback. In selling, however, the ratios are the other way around. People are often rude to us. We confront resistance. We get 19 wrong out of 20, or 95 negatives out of 100. We call 100 people and only 5 may be receptive and only 1 person may buy and it's very discouraging. And yet, people realize, as they grow up, that they need to change their attitudes towards negative experiences. It's a matter of percentages. The meaning of the ratio has changed."

- "The idea of feeling successful in an environment in which failure and rejection are normal indicates that failure and rejection may have tradeoffs and benefits after all. In fact, that's one of my major theses— that failure is only an experience that was less than what we expected. If we can somehow change our expectations, our perceptions and our reactions, our feelings will start changing."

- "All the sales training in the world won't help if you allow rejection to overwhelm you. Becoming defensive, depressed or discouraged by rejection will make it impossible to use your sales training successfully. By raising your level of awareness, you can have more control over your feelings, thoughts and behavior, and that will translate into sales success."

As Art says, "Be amused by rejection and thrive on anxiety allowing them to motivate you to higher levels of achievement.

"TELEPHONE-A-PHOBIA"[1]

You see it everywhere. People staring at the phone as if it were going to bite. Brokers unable to lift the receiver and turning gray at the thought of calling another prospect. Anticipation anxiety can be cloaked under many guises: "I'm too busy doing something more important," "My ear didn't get enough rest last night," or "I will as soon as I get organized."

Telephone-a-phobia (the unreasonable fear of using the phone) has reduced many brokers to total ineffectiveness. There are many reasons for not picking up the phone, including stress, rejection, disorganization, being overwhelmed with other things to do, being burned out from making too many phone calls that day (or within the last half hour), having a "bad hair" day or month, a telephone receiver that weighs too much, and absolute boredom. Picking up the phone to make another call virtually becomes an intolerable thought. For this to occur occasionally is to be expected; for it to occur regularly is a warning signal.

Telephone avoidance patterns can be resolved in a number of ways, for example, by

- Identifying that a problem exists and examining the probable causes behind it.
- Laughing at it.
- Examining your personal beliefs about what a professional should and should not have to do. (We have coached brokers who believed that talking to strangers was beneath them or that they should not have to make outgoing calls.)
- Not having appropriate goals or having conflicting goals, and resolving any goal conflicts may take care of the problem.
- Not knowing *how to* make effective calls or not knowing what to say.

[1]Originally introduced in our book, *The Effective Manager: Being the Best in Financial Sales Management* (New York: Simon & Schuster, 1991).

(If a person doesn't know how to do something, unconsciously he often creates rationales as to why he can't or shouldn't do it.)

- Not *wanting to* because there is no intrinsic payoff.

- Not having the *chance to* because of some environmental reason like having no sales associate and having to do all the paperwork yourself, being disorganized, or constantly being interrupted.

- Having a mental image of a terrible person about to answer the phone. If every time a broker were to pick up the phone a mental picture of a horrible person giving them a hard time were to pop in front of his mind, that broker will hesitate or avoid picking up the phone. Normally, understanding this is happening is enough to resolve the problem. If not, then change the picture in your mind to more pleasant person by mentally practicing replacing the bad picture/feeling with a pleasant picture/feeling. (This technique is explained in greater detail during our workshops, or can be reviewed in our book, *The Effective Manager: Being the Best in Financial Sales Management.*)

- Having a negative/unpleasant feeling that is automatically "triggered" when picking up the phone. This is often based on one or more bad experiences that have become overgeneralized in our minds. The approach similar to the one taken in the previous paragraph often resolves the problem.

- Talking to other brokers about it and realizing that you're not alone and that "this, too, shall pass." Having a support system of other brokers that you can talk to is an important aspect of long-term motivation and can often be used when difficulties arise. (The use of a support system of brokers with similar production levels to your own, and from different offices was strongly emphasized by Prudential's West Coast training manager, Gene Ingargiola.)

If you have or get "telephone-a-phobia" (or any of the other dreaded maladies), consider trying one of more of the preceding suggestions. The chances are that it will be resolved and your personal productivity will be substantially increased.

EVALUATING YOUR PERFORMANCE

Because of prospecting's importance, it is also useful to periodically monitor your performance by conducting a self-evaluation. The form in Figure 9-7 will assist you in these efforts. Merely tape record some of your tele-

Figure 9-7 Follow-up Evaluation Sheet

Getting Attention

Introduced yourself and your firm   ___Yes   ___No
Stated the reason for the call   ___Yes   ___No
Offered a benefit   ___Yes   ___No
One way this skill could be improved:

Handling Indifference

CLAP for understanding   ___Yes   ___No
Asked closed probes to uncover specific needs
    or dissatisfactions   ___Yes   ___No
Asked open probes to get the suspect to begin talking   ___Yes   ___No
One way this skill could be improved:

Qualifying the Prospect

Qualified in terms of budget   ___Yes   ___No
Qualified in terms of objectives   ___Yes   ___No
Qualified in terms of attitude   ___Yes   ___No
One way this skill could be improved:

Gaining Commitment for a Profiling Interview/Appointment

Appealed to a need   ___Yes   ___No
Offered benefits   ___Yes   ___No
Asked for a specific commitment   ___Yes   ___No
One way this skill could be improved:

Comments:

_____

phone conversations with prospects. Then use this sheet to make notes concerning your own skills when playing back the tape. When thinking about your skills, give yourself specific, supportive feedback. (Important note: Check regarding your firm's policy on tape recording as well as your state laws. You may be required to inform the other party that the conversation is being recorded.) An alternative is to allow an associate to listen to and evaluate you while you are on the phone.

IV

REALLY KNOW YOUR CUSTOMERS

Regulatory agencies say you must know your customer. Their concern is that you can't be sure that your investment recommendation is suitable if you don't know your customer financial needs, resources, and risk tolerance. However, really knowing your customer means understanding not only his financial needs, but also the way he thinks and makes decisions about investments (i.e., both the criteria and the strategy he uses to select something), as well as any hidden emotional agendas that might affect how he reacts to the helping relationship so you can match his needs.

Understanding motivation is key to selling from your customer's point of view. Each of us is motivated by a wide variety of factors that affect everything from the way we make decisions to the products and services we select. Ironically, *most brokers tend to emphasize factors that appeal to them during the selling process instead of those which appeal to their clients.* In addition, they also tend to assume that their clients make purchasing decisions in the same way that they do.

Sounds pretty silly when you think about it, but most of us still do it. It is natural to assume that everyone else is just like us (after all, they look like us—no one is running around with two heads, and must therefore share our tastes, interests, and thinking processes. This may explain a great deal of the frustration felt by many brokers when they present a product or service that is really just what the customer needs, and the customer isn't inter-ested. Remember, most brokers waste up to 80 percent of their presentation time trying to overcome unnecessary resistance, which they, themselves, caused the moment they opened the call.

Earlier, we emphasized the need to communicate from the customer's point of view. Combine that with the concept of rapport, in which it is im-portant to convey how much you have in common with your customer and it makes sense it find out how she thinks and what criteria she needs before she will be attracted to a given product or service.

As an investment advisor, your job regularly requires you to under-stand how your clients make their decisions and the forces that motivate them. The purpose of this section is to provide you with the skills necessary to meet the mental and emotional needs, as well as to match the internal model of your clients so you can keep them motivated and "sell" them on your solutions to their financial goals. By doing so you will not only increase your overall productivity, you will also meet enough of your clients internal needs to increase the strength of you relationship with him in good markets and bad. In addition, these same skills can be used when "selling" your sales manager on meeting your needs.

Profiling is the key to consultative selling and the engine that ulti-mately drives all sales. In the past, many brokers have simply assumed that greed was what motivated all investors and spent their time selling "get-rich-quick" stocks. However, we now know that most investors are far more motivated by concrete goals for which they are willing to take a managed risk. In fact, surveys by individuals like Tom Stanley, author of *Selling to the Affluent* and *Marketing to the Affluent*, indicate that even "millionaires are more concerned with things like protecting their business and their children's education than they are in making a quick "killing" in the stock market.

We've already discussed the importance of knowing your customer's buying criteria, motivational and decision-making strategies, and hidden emotional agendas, because they can strongly influence the outcome of any sales presentation. However, none of that information can make up for try-ing to sell a product that doesn't meet your client's real financial need(s). In this section we'll present a profiling technique that will not only give you all the information you ever wanted from a client, it will also help to increase the amount of assets under management, increase client loyalty, and presell several solutions before you ever make your first sales call.

10

Financial Profiling Strategies

WHY PROFILE?

There are several reasons for profiling a prospect or client, not the least of which is the information it provides. In addition, the New York Stock Exchange (Rule 405), and various insurance and banking authorities, require you to "Know Your Customer" before making recommendations for appropriate action. Failure to profile a client adequately not only makes it very difficult to determine the type and quantity of product or service most appropriate for him, it may also leave you vulnerable to suit if your recommendation does not perform as your client had hoped. Ideally, an effective profiling session you should achieve the following objectives:

- Elicit the prospect's/client's financial goals and the parameters of each goal.

- Establish rapport and a professional image in the mind of the prospect/client.

- Discover the prospect's/client's private language (the private meaning some words have for them, as well as the sensory orientation of their speech—visual, auditory, or kinesthetic), psychological profile, buying criteria, and motivational strategies.

- Build a commitment to achieve the prospect's/client's financial goals with you.
- Increase the percentage of the prospect's/client's assets under your management for investment.

Consider one very successful broker who was promoted to management in his firm. Just before he entered management training, he distributed his accounts to the other financial consultants in the office. To one new man, he gave Mrs. X, an elderly lady who was "fully invested" for whom he had bought a $100,000 certificate of deposit.

"She's fully invested," he said. "But at least the account will increase your assets." The young broker thanked him and he left for management training. When he returned, the young broker ran up to him and dropped on his knees to thank him, practically kissing his feet. At first, he assumed that this was merely respect for his new position as sales manager. However, he asked. The new broker told him he wanted to thank him for the account that he had given him. "What account," he asked.

"Mrs. X. Last month we did $60,000 of production in her account, and this month we should do even more."

"Are you crazy," said the new sales manager. "You'll go to jail."

"Not at all," replied the broker. "Didn't you know that when she told you that she was fully invested that she thought that $12.5 million in a money market fund was an investment. When I *profiled* her, we determined what her goals were, and we've made several investments to help her radically reduce her taxes." The new sales manager had to be sedated.

- Increase the number of products held by your client. This is particularly important in light of a survey conducted by the Chicago Board Options Exchange in which they found that if you place a client in only one kind of investment (e.g., stocks), you have only a 33 percent chance of *not* losing him within the next year. If you placed him in two kinds of investments (e.g., stocks and mutual funds or bonds), you have a 67 percent chance of keeping him for the next year. But, if you have placed your client in three, or more types of investments (e.g., stocks, bonds, and an annuity), you have an 83 percent chance of keeping him. The reasons for this are

- The broader the product mix, the greater the professionalism you demonstrate.
- It increases your client's dependence upon you for advice and support.
- The broader the product mix, the less likely you are to be effected by negative economic events (such as a major market or interest rate move).

During your sales career you have probably been exposed to several techniques for profiling. All are excellent, and the authors would suggest that you determine which you are most comfortable with and use it or modify it to your needs. *But profile!* It is one of the keys to long-term success.

Profile—The career you save will be your own.

WHEN TO PROFILE

Some financial consultants wait until they have had clients on the books for months and have made several sales before they profile them. We would suggest that this just doesn't make sense. In addition to the reasons just provided, profiling can be an excellent way to build the rapport and the trust necessary to convince the prospect to open an account and/or encourage an existing client to transfer a larger portion of their assets to your care.

Throughout the book we have stressed the importance of stepping into your client's world so that you can sell to him from his point of view. This is the essence of consultative selling and begins the moment you first make contact with a new prospect. Formal profiling is just one way of gaining information regarding your prospect's or client's needs. Similarly, there is nothing wrong with an in-depth profile after a client has been on your books for a while. This can show the need for further planning or specific planning needs, such as a different product or service.

Profiling actually begins during the "cold call" with the questions you ask to qualify the prospect. It continues through follow-up calls and your first face-to-face meeting. When properly done, profiling will become a habit that will continue throughout your relationship with the client, updating the information you have on file with almost every contact.

Profiling During Follow-up Calls

Sometimes, there will be several follow-up calls between your initial contact with a prospect and your first face-to-face meeting. These contacts provide an excellent opportunity to increase the amount of information you have about your client's overall financial needs/goals as well as his or her personality type, buying criteria, and decision-making strategies. Thus, profiling during follow-up calls should accomplish three things:

1. It should elicit additional information regarding the prospect's interests, needs, and sophistication as well as how he thinks and makes decisions. (See Chapters 12 and 13)

2. It should further qualify the prospect.

3. It should help lead the prospect to the conclusion that he needs to meet with you personally to discuss his situation more fully.

Begin each follow-up call by bridging to the preceding conversation and previously elicited needs. You should then deal with questions that may have been generated by any literature you may have sent. Next, move to questions that will provide additional detail on the prospect's investment history. Remember that detailed, potentially threatening, questions are not necessary at this point. You can ask them more effectively in person.

Once you've obtained sufficient new information to justify the call and the need for a face-to-face meeting, set up the meeting. If you can give a sufficient benefit for meeting with you, most prospects will meet. Some brokers have told us that it makes no sense to waste time in face-to-face meetings, just to profile a prospect when they already receive 80 percent of their business from 20 percent of their clients. However, it should be noted that most brokers never receive more than 10 to 20 percent of their customers' financial assets to manage. It is interesting that, in most cases, the 20 percent that provides most of their business consists largely of those clients whom they have actually met. Thus, one reason for not obtaining significantly larger percentage of assets to manage is that they never develop the deep levels of rapport and trust needed for an individual to commit larger portions of their assets to a single individual or firm. In fact, Dick Green, one of the most successful brokers in the entire industry, says that he will not accept clients who will not meet with him.

We realize that, eventually, you will probably develop clients whom you will never see, either because of distance or other problems. In those cases, your entire relationship will be mediated by the phone, and you will need to profile them completely over the phone rather than in person. However, if at all possible, meet.

PROFILING FACE TO FACE

As a tool for building rapport, meeting a prospect face to face cannot be overestimated. When meeting someone over the phone, you have to project your entire image through a single medium, your voice. This forces your prospect to imagine what you look like. It also makes it much harder for you to overcome any biases he may have regarding brokers.

Its much easier to communicate your interest and professionalism face to face. In the same way, it is much harder for clients to establish trust with a faceless voice than with someone they have met. Think about it: Would you make a large purchase over the phone from a stranger? The first few minutes of the meeting should be directed toward building rapport and setting the client at ease. Once this is accomplished, move on to the primary purpose of the meeting: obtaining information.

THE PROFILING TRACK

Like prospecting and selling, effective profiling follows a specific series of steps designed to bring you and your prospect or client to a desired conclusion (in this case, commitment to further action). These steps are

Step 1: Establish rapport with your prospect/customer and place her at ease.

Step 2: Discover her needs/goals/problems (e.g., children's/grandchildren's college, retirement). Be concrete. If discussing colleges, get the names of the schools; if discussing retirement, determine where specifically do they wish to retire.

Step 3: Prioritize customer needs/goals.

Step 4: Determine the parameters of each need/goal. That is,
How much time to reach the goal (e.g., how many years before he retires or before each child reaches college age)?
How much money will he need to achieve his goal (what will the tuition be at Harvard or your intended college when the children arrive, or how much money—in today's dollars—will he need to live on when he retires, etc.)?

What steps have they already taken; that is, what investments has he already made with this specific need/goal in mind?

How much do they want to commit to solving this problem/achieving this goal *at this time*? Does he expect to make additional investments for this goal? When? How much?

Determine their risk tolerance by educating him about the types of financial risks he faces regardless of what choice he makes (i.e., theft, interest rate risk, loss of buying power—inflation, market risk, economic risk, etc.)? With which risk are they most comfortable? How comfortable? Are there any investments they specifically wish to avoid? Why?

Step 5: Once you have established the parameters of each goal/need with the customer, ask if they have any other investments, assets, income or liabilities—or expect to receive any in the future—which might affect their ability to obtain their goals.

Step 6: Ask for permission to review each of the goals and the parameters of each goal before suggesting any solutions so you can make certain that whatever you suggest will be appropriate. Then review them.

Step 7: Establish an appointment to call or meet again to present/discuss possible solutions to his needs/goals. Then find a solution. Sometimes a client may want an immediate solution to a need. If this occurs, suggest an appropriate one before he leaves. At the very least, fill out the paperwork to open an account if they do not already have one. Otherwise, thank him for his time and give him a copy of the goals and parameters you have established together. Include your card.

There is an art to asking questions. Remember that, given the proper motivation, anyone will answer any question. When profiling, remember (and remind the client) that the purpose of your questions is to help him achieve his goals. Before you can do anything for him, you need to know his current state and where he wants to go. Thus, you must begin by asking the nature of his destination (i.e., the financial need or goal) and follow that by determining the parameters of that goal.

Remember that each question the prospect answers makes it easier for him to answer your next question. This is true because each time he answers a question, he makes himself just a little more open to you. Thus, once you have determined the client's goals, it is important to ask questions that obviously relate to each goal. Keep your questions focused on one goal at a time. If you jump back and forth from one to another, you will not only appear disorganized and unprofessional, the questions may not make sense and you may find yourself developing resistance and losing their trust. For example,

> *Broker:* "Mr. Jones, you indicated that your primary goal is to prepare for your retirement. You also said you were forty years old. At what age do you plan to retire?"
>
> *Client:* "Sixty."
>
> *Broker:* "What college were you thinking of sending your children to?"
>
> *Client:* "Michigan State."
>
> *Broker:* "That's great! In today's dollars, how much money do you think you'll need each year to maintain your desired life-style, after you're retired?"
>
> *Client:* "About $50,000 per year."
>
> *Broker:* "What other investment services are you using?"

The example we have provided is not as extreme as it may first appear. Unfortunately, many brokers often find themselves asking profiling questions in such a disorganized manner.

Always take notes during a profiling interview. Few people have photographic memories, and unless you're one of them, you are bound to forget something important. However, before taking notes, explain why you are doing so and ask their permission. Then take notes of his answers, and represent them graphically. Some firms require their brokers to use specific profiling forms to make certain that they obtain any information required for compliance purposes, while some financial professionals like to use special profiling forms they have developed, themselves. This is fine, but can be threatening to some prospects. How did you like filling out your last medical history? We like to write "free hand" using a pad of legal paper.

If you do use a form, avoid letting it dominate the profiling interview. While forms can add a useful sense of completeness to the interview, and ensure that multiple needs are addressed, they can also become a crutch and a distraction for the broker when she should be attending fully to her prospect. Remember, you can always fill it out, or consolidate it, later. We'll now explore each step of the profiling process.

Step 1: Establish Rapport

When you first meet your prospect, take a moment to put her at ease and establish rapport. Begin matching her posture, speech, and private language. Start listening for clues about her buying criteria and motivational strategies. If you listen carefully, your prospect will provide you with all the information you will need to help her during this interview.

Bridge back to your first contact and remind her of why she came, and find out if she has other needs that might require your assistance. Then take a moment and explain how you work. This is a great time to demonstrate how you differ from other financial professionals by emphasizing that you are there to help her attain her financial goals and *not* just to sell her financial products and services. Once you have accomplished this, move on to steps 2 and 3.

Steps 2 and 3: Elicit and Prioritize the Client's Goals

If she hasn't already done so, ask your prospect to tell you her goals. As we've already mentioned, it is important to elicit specific, concrete goals. "Growth," "income," and "tax reduction" are all *abstract* goals. While common, they are not as meaningful or effective as they may initially appear. The key question is: "What do you want the growth or income *for?*"

Psychologists have found that concrete goals (such as a home, car, college, or retirement) are generally far more motivating than abstract goals (like getting more money). Thus, the more concrete you can help your clients make their goals, the stronger their commitment will be to those goals during bad economic times as well as good. When a client mentions that his financial goal is to make more money, ask him what he wants the money for; then give him a few examples, such as college, retirement, and so on. In most cases, he will then provide you with a concrete goal. Next, ask questions that will help him be more specific in their description of his goal. For example,

"Mrs. Brown, you mentioned that you want to invest for your daughter's education. Have you thought about the kind of school you'd like her to attend?" Wait for an answer. If no answer, then, "Perhaps your alma mater?"

Another good question might be

"What would you like your daughter to be able to do when she grows up?" To be a professional anything requires a great deal of money and education. This may cause your client to rethink their asset allocation for their educational fund because this may be the goal of their goal. "I want her to follow in my footsteps and be a lawyer."

If they mention a specific school, encourage them to talk about it for a few minutes. The more they discuss it, the more real and *motivating* it will become to them. Show your interest. Remember, over the long term, every investment has bad times as well as good. When those "bad" times occur, your clients may need the mental image of their goal to keep their commitment to invest and stay the course. Experience has shown that abstract goals just don't have the motivating power necessary to accomplish that.

Once your prospect has told you his goals, ask him to prioritize them so that when you discuss them (and later, when you present solutions) you will be dealing with the most important goal first. For example,

> "Mrs. Brown, you mentioned that you have three investment goals: your retirement, your children's education, and a larger home. Is retirement the most critical of the three goals, or is one of the others more important at this time?" Or "Which of these is the highest priority?"

Step 4: Establish the Parameters of Each Goal

Each goal has a series of parameters that you must first establish before you can begin to seek an investment solution. Once you know the values of each parameter, actually selecting a specific course of action to recommend becomes easy.

- *Time.* Once you know how much money you'll need to complete each goal, you need to know how long you have to obtain the necessary funds. For example,

> "Mr. White, you indicated that your primary investment goal is your child's education. How old is your child? We'll need that to determine how much time we have for your investments to grow to achieve your goal."

- *Amount of money ($) required.* The first thing you have to know about any goal is the amount of money you will need to attain it. For example, in the case of college, once you know the name of the college and the year the child will be attending, it becomes relatively easy to determine the expected cost using the Rule of 72. For retirement, ask them how much money they will need to live *in today's dollars.* Once you know the expected year of their retirement and an assumed rate of return for that year, you will have a working dollar amount as an investment goal. For example,

> "Mr. Johnson, you mentioned that you want your child to attend your alma mater, Brown University. By the time your daughter is old enough to attend, they expect their costs to be about $50,000 per year. That means we'll need approximately $200,000 by then to achieve your goal."

- *Steps already taken.* What steps have they already taken to achieve this goal? Most brokers just ask what other investments a prospect has made or what's in their portfolio. Such questions can result in the prospect's becoming defensive because they are very invasive questions and most people either won't answer them or will lie which can be very frustrating for you. For example, some prospects will exaggerate their net worth, level of sophistication, and so on, when asked. It is important to note that in response to traditional questions about portfolio size, their history of investments, and so on, these prospects may wish to impress you ore bolster their ego. Our method, because of its focus on specific goal attainment will reduce any "departures from the truth" because (1) you are doing financial diagnostics, (2) the method asks for specific information and has checks and balances, and (3) you will be writing it down. Thus, if you ask what steps they have taken to achieve *this specific goal* (your justification is that you need the information to determine your starting point for achieving the goal), they will almost always tell you the investments they have made which they consider to be related to this goal. For example,

You: "Mr. Larson, what steps have you already taken to prepare for your children's educational needs?"

Client: "Why do you ask?"

You: "If we are going to develop a plan to help you pay for their education, we have to know our starting point. Your current investments may already be enough to achieve your goal, or it may be necessary to start fresh. Until I know what you've already done, I won't be able to tell."

Client: "When the baby was born, we invested $10,000 in the XYZ mutual fund."

You now know not only the starting point for achieving this goal, you also know part of their portfolio. By the time you have completed this step for all their goals, you will know a significant portion of their entire investment portfolio.

Buying Criteria and Motivating Strategies   This is an excellent time to elicit your prospect's buying criteria (see Chapter 12) and motivational/decision-making strategies (Chapter 13). After he has told you the investments he has already made toward achieving his goal, ask what he likes about each. Then ask if there is anything he dislikes about each. The answers will provide the information you need when presenting your solution to his need. For example,

> *You:* "You mentioned that you had previously purchased $10,000 of the XYZ mutual fund. To help me understand your needs better, may I ask what is was about the XYZ fund that made you select it over other funds?"
>
> *Client:* "I *recognized the name,* and the prospectus said that it invested only in blue-chip stocks and bonds, so it seemed pretty *safe.*"

- *How much does the client want to invest in a solution?* A big mistake made by most brokers is to ask their prospect or client how much he has to invest. This is an intrusive question that sounds as though you are reaching for his wallet. Instead, ask him how much he *wants* to invest in a solution to this problem, at this time. This leaves him in control of the investment process and is far less threatening. This will also tell you, by definition, the proper order size to recommend when you make your sales presentation. For example,

> *You:* "How much do *you want* to invest in a solution to your goal *at this time*?"
>
> *Client:* "About $15,000."
>
> *You:* "That's fine. Are you planning to make additional investments for this goal?"
>
> *Client:* "Yes, we are. We'll probably add another $5,000 to $10,000 each year in February when I get my bonus."

Now, unless you believe that the amount he is about to invest will be sufficient, by itself, to achieve his goal, you must also ask if he expects to make additional investments directed toward this goal and when he expects to make them. Again, you need this information if you are to help establish a plan for achieving his goal.

- *Risk tolerance.* This is a key question to avoid compliance problems. (See the next few paragraphs for a discussion on risk and reward.) Unfortunately, most brokers have solved this in the past by simply asking a customer how much risk he or she can handle. The problem with this technique is that it assumes the customer really understands the nature of investment risks, when most don't. Every investment decision involves some form of risk. Even hiding money in a mattress or a safe deposit box entails the potential for loss of buying power through inflation or even theft. Given the proper motivation, anyone will take almost any risk. However, without enough motivation, some people won't take any risk at all. Thus, it is important to find out what your prospect means by the word "safe."

First, educate the customer by explaining that *any* decision he makes about his investments contains some risk, inflation (loss of purchasing power), economic, market, interest rate, and selection risk (i.e., loss of principal). Explain loss of purchasing power in concrete terms, perhaps by comparing the difference between college tuition when he attended to tuition now or the expected tuition when his child is ready to attend. Another simple comparison can be made using the price of a loaf of bread when he was a child versus the price now (you can also use the Rule of 72 here). Once you have explained the different types of risk, ask him with which he is the most comfortable and how comfortable he is with that risk. This is important because many people still think that risk of principal is all they have to worry about, yet many short-term fixed-income investments virtually guarantee an after-tax loss of purchasing power. Finally, remind the client that they are investing for a long-term goal and that all investments go down briefly some of the time, but that, in the long run, a good investment will grow toward achieving their goal. For example,

> *You:* "Mr. Samuels, I'm sure you realize that every investment decision you make involves some form of risk, even deciding to do nothing."
>
> *Client:* "What do you mean."
>
> *You:* "One form of risk is inflation, or loss of buying power. This occurs when you leave your money in a safe deposit box or a low-paying savings account. Your principal is safe, but the amount you can buy with it gets a little less each year. For example, when I was a child, a loaf of bread cost 25 cents. Today, it costs over $1.50. Do you see what I mean."
>
> *Client:* "I see what you mean. What other kinds of risk are there? I just want to preserve my principal."
>
> *You:* "In addition to inflation, there is market risk. What type of risk are you most comfortable with?"

Client: "I can handle some risk, but how can I be sure you will make the right selection? What if you put all my money in a stock and it goes down?"

You: "That is handled by diversifying your investments, that is, not putting everything in one basket. One way people do that is to divide their investments into several different stocks or purchase something like a mutual fund where that is done for you. Do you understand?"

Client: "Yes. That's fine. Then I'd have to say that inflation is my biggest concern."

You: "Good. How much risk are you prepared to take to avoid inflation and achieve your goal?"

Client: "I realize I'll have to take some risk, but I'd like to minimize it. I want to stay with the highest quality of investment, whether it's a mutual fund or bonds or something else."

You: "All right. Do you realize that even the price of the best blue-chip stock can drop as much as 10 percent in an hour and can take weeks or even months to recover?"

Client: "Yes. I can handle that, as long as its a good investment and will perform over the long term."

It may also be helpful to further clarify their ability to handle risk by asking additional questions about their need for "safety." It is critical that you understand exactly what "safety" means to them before you make any investment recommendations. In addition, industry regulations require that you warn your client of any potential "risks" involved in an investment (e.g., banking regulations require that bank investment reps specifically warn customers that annuities and mutual funds are not FDIC insured).

Allied to risk tolerance is the question of specific investments that the prospect would rather avoid; for instance, some people are willing to buy equity mutual funds but will not buy individual stocks regardless of their rating. Others refuse to purchase investments involving certain specific companies (the tobacco industry, or mining companies, etc.). There are many other potential questions that can be asked about individual investments that the prospect has either already made or wishes to make (these will be explored in more detail in the next chapter). The important thing to remember is that whatever questions you ask should relate logically to their goal. For example, if their goal is lowering their taxes, you can ask their tax bracket and income almost immediately because these questions are immediately relevant to their goal. However, asking these questions up front when discussing college or retirement would probably be considered intrusive and cause resistance. The next chapter contains a list of relevant questions to help you explore various goals in greater detail.

Step 5: Other Assets and Liabilities

Once you have established the parameters of each and every goal/need with the customer, ask if they have any other investments, assets, income, or liabilities (or expect to receive any in the future) *that might affect their ability to obtain their goals.* Just asking for other investments or assets, much less liabilities, is likely to provoke resistance. However, if you connect these questions to their goals, they are more likely to be answered. For example,

> *You:* "Do you have any other assets, income, or liabilities that might affect our ability to achieve your goals? For example, are you expecting any windfall in the future that may help with retirement or the children's college?"
>
> *You:* "Do you mind if I ask what tax bracket you are currently in? It will affect the growth of some investments which we might consider for achieving your goals."

It is at this point that you will also need to ask about their tax bracket (if you haven't already obtained it) and their level of insurance coverage for their goals. For example, do they have enough life insurance coverage to pay for their children's education should one or both die before the children reach college. This question is especially important if you don't sell life insurance yourself, because it demonstrates professionalism and concern for their needs rather than just interest in commission.

Note: You should have been taking notes on their goals and parameters, and so on, throughout the meeting. At this point we recommend that you draw an investment pyramid (such as in Figure 10-1), or use one of the examples provided in the next chapter, on your notes and place their current investments within the pyramid, demonstrating not only the level of safety of each, but also each investment's relationship to the overall asset mix. Then take a minute to discuss the appropriateness of each current holding relative to their stated goals and risk tolerance. If they match, congratulate him. If they don't, check to determine if you have misunderstood his goals or risk tolerance. If there has been no misunderstanding, you have just demonstrated your professionalism to your prospect. You may also have just earned your first trade. However, if their goal is unrealistic, it may be necessary to "educate" them about it.

Figure 10-1 Investment Pyramid

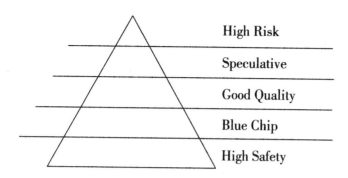

This educational process, of explaining to a prospect that their goal is unrealistic (e.g., given the time allowed and their risk tolerance, they will not be able to achieve their goal with the level and type of investments they have specified), is extremely important. It one of the things that will set you apart from the competition. When you have completed the profiling interview, give them a copy of your notes (so write neatly). For most people, this goal sheet will represent the first time they have ever seen their entire financial picture and goals on a single sheet of paper. In addition, it tends to represent an informal, almost unconscious, contract between you to work *together* to help him achieve his goals.

Step 6: Review the Parameters

Ask for permission to review each of the goals and the parameters of each goal before suggesting any solutions so you can make certain that whatever you suggest will be appropriate. Then review them. This accomplishes two things:

- This review not only shows your professionalism, it helps ensure that the information you have is substantially correct, avoiding mistakes or potential compliance problems when you make your recommendations, later.

- As you review the parameters of each goal, your prospect actually commits himself, unconsciously, to work with you and act upon any solution you present that meets or exceeds those parameters. This helps to presell each investment recommendation you make before you even present it, making future sales calls considerably easier. Once you have finished this, it is up to you to complete the necessary new account forms before he leaves.

Step 7: Establish an Appointment

Once you have completed steps 1–6, the last thing you must accomplish before the interview ends is to establish an appointment to call or meet again to present/discuss possible solutions to their needs/goals. Then find a solution. If you set a specific time to call or meet, be certain that you are ready at that time. Being late can destroy everything you have built to this point. After all, promptness is often psychologically associated with precision—a very good trait for a financial advisor.

Occasionally, you will meet a client who needs immediate action. If he needs an immediate solution, suggest an appropriate one before he leaves. Thank him for his time and give him a copy of the goals and parameters you have established together. Include your card.

Normally, you will *never try to sell them something during the profiling meeting*. If you do, you destroy the impression that you are a helping professional and confirm in their mind that you are just one more salesman out for a commission. Even if you know the perfect solution, it is better to wait several hours or days before presenting it because, in the client's mind, this will give you time to do the necessary research to develop an appropriate recommendation and will give the client the feeling that you gave it some thought.

Profiling is the heart of consultative selling. By the time you have completed the profiling session, you should know everything you need to properly develop and present an appropriate and effective solution to their problem. Effective profiling can easily increase not only the amount of assets under your management, but also develop a level of client loyalty that will remain steadfast in good times and bad.

11

In-depth Financial Profiling

This chapter reviews the investment and resource pyramid as a profiling tool and suggests ways to more fully determine suitability. It is our contention that an investment representative must know what questions to ask to truly determine the appropriateness of a particular product or service. Unfortunately, many newer or untrained representatives ask too few pertinent questions, which can result in less than appropriate recommendations, customer dissatisfaction, and legal issues. In most cases, these reps were not trained to know what questions to ask and how to go beyond the surface issues.

Consider the following analogy. If you went to a doctor and said, "Doctor, doctor, my stomach hurts." And the doctor, without further examination says, "It's probably your appendix. Go inside, lay down, and in 5 minutes I'll cut it out." You would probably run, not walk, to the nearest exit. You would expect the doctor to ask you a host of questions, such as "Where does it hurt?" "When does it hurt?" "Describe the pain," and so on. Furthermore, you would expect the doctor to do a series of diagnostic tests to determine what was wrong before prescribing a solution to your problem.

In a very real sense of the word, investment advisors are "financial physicians." They need to ask appropriate diagnostic questions to determine the nature of the problem/goal and the solution(s). Clients often place substantial portions of their life savings in the hands of their brokers. To some degree, many clients achieve financial wellness or destitution based upon the advice of their brokers. Without asking enough of the right questions, the broker relies on pure luck.

For example, a client saying that he wants "growth" does not constitute enough information to recommend a particular growth stock or mutual fund. Before any recommendation can be made, the representative must know such things as the following:

- What specific investment objective (e.g., retirement, children's college) will this growth vehicle help attain?
- What is the client's specific definition of growth?
- What percentage growth rate (e.g., 5 percent or 25 percent) does the client need? Does the client expect?
- Is this percentage before or after inflation?
- What will be the basis of comparison? to the S&P 500? the Dow?
- For large clients, how much money will be allocated to the growth portion of the portfolio and what percentage of the client's assets does this represent?
- Is short-term, intermediate-term, or long-term growth desired? What are the specific time frames?
- Is their desired growth rate reasonable when time considerations are taken into account?
- What is the client's risk tolerance? Does he truly understand the risk-reward parameters?

The following are some of the areas/topics that any investment representative should be able to competently explore:

- Retirement planning
- Income enhancement
- Savings plan(s)
- Taxable income
- Stocks
- Risk
- Educational funding
- Tax relief
- Loans/financing
- Mutual funds
- Bonds
- Asset allocation
- Insurance
- Tax bracket
- Growth
- Annuities
- CDs

Identifying the parameters of the problem during the profiling interview will usually determine what product line(s) will be appropriate for the investor. However, it is usually necessary to fine-tune your understanding before a particular product or service is decided upon. Another difficulty faced by brokers is the number of products available. Depending upon their firm's product line, a representative might have to qualify a client for anywhere from 2 to 200 product lines. Even if it is unreasonable to expect any person to be able to fully qualify a prospect with respect to every product their firm offers, the representative should be able to at least ask enough question to know when to turn that client to a product specialist or someone else in the firm such as a commodity specialist, a lending officer, or retirement expert.

Lost Opportunities for All

Failure to be aware of a firm's product line and the basic profiling questions needed to determine suitability for each product means that numerous lost opportunities to assist the client. The broker is not maximizing his potential. The firm is not achieving cross-selling and account penetration. The client is not being adequately serviced and advised.

To explore a client's needs more fully, we suggest that each broker use an investment and resource pyramid when profiling a prospect/client because this tool allows you to

- Profile the person more fully.
- Do an initial resource allocation/strategy review.
- Discover hidden/unmentioned assets.
- Develop numerous account penetration and cross-selling opportunities.

However, to make full use of the investment/resource pyramid, you have to be able to ask numerous astute questions as you explore each aspect of the pyramid. (These questions are provided in the second half of this chapter.) Finally, the pyramid also becomes a tool for ongoing portfolio review (which is reviewed in Section VI.)

THE INVESTMENT/RESOURCE PYRAMID

The simplified Investment/Resource Pyramid (Figure 11-1) is a useful tool to help profile any client. Although a more comprehensive explanation is provided in Section VI, suffice it to say that a person would allocate resources (assets) to achieve both vertical (through different risk categories) and hori-

Figure 11-1 The Investment/Resource Pyramid

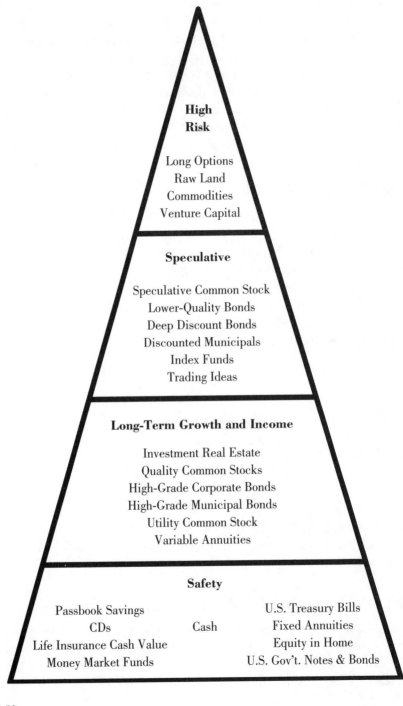

zontal (different assets within the same risk category) diversification. The shape of the pyramid and the percentage assigned within each risk category will vary depending upon such things as their personal net worth, age, current portfolio, discretionary dollars, yearly additional income available for investment, retirement plan, and so on, as demonstrated in Chapter 23.

The Investment and Resource Pyramid as a Prospecting Tool

Once you have elicited the parameters of your prospect's or client's financial goals and determined the general types of products that might solve those goals, you may need to further refine your understanding to determine the suitability of any specific product you may wish to recommend. For example,

> A prospect sits down with you. After developing rapport and beginning the conversation, you pull out a blank investment and resource pyramid and begin circling the products that the prospect currently has or is interested in. For example, you might ask, "What investments do you currently own?" The prospect might answer that he has some speculative common stocks, some discounted bonds, some index mutual funds, and commodities futures. (You circle each of the items and add the mutual fund to the speculative portion of the pyramid, as in Figure 11-2.)
>
> "What are you interested in doing at this time?" you would ask. The prospect responds with, "I'm interested in buying a junk bond, a bond fund, and some trading ideas." (Meanwhile you circle lower-quality bonds and add "trading ideas" to the speculative section.)

When you then ask what else he has or needs, the prospect basically responds with, "That's all for now." *Here is where the Investment and Resource Pyramid becomes so effective.* You begin by reviewing the purpose of the investment and resource pyramid and how the majority of the assets belong in the base or foundation; a lesser amount in long-term growth and income; still a lesser amount in the speculative area; and the least amount in the high-risk category.

"It seems to me that you are overweighted in the speculative and high-risk area," you might point out to this prospect. At this point, the prospect will give you one of two responses: (1) "I never considered that"—which does occur on rare occasions, or (2) "I'm already fully taken care of, thank you" (the more common response). "Oh? How?" you ask. *You have created a psychological hole that the prospect must now fill in.* "I have some muni bonds, some money market funds, CDs, and variable annuities." (Meanwhile you are circling or adding in the appropriate items.)

Figure 11-2 shows how the Investment and Resource Pyramid might look after you have circled and added the appropriate items. Two things become evident when you look at this information:

1. The prospect is possibly underinvested in the long-term growth and income area. You may have determined an investment need and will more easily work with the prospect to appropriately fill-in the missing area.

2. You have discovered very valuable information about this prospect. Even if the prospect doesn't allow you to manage everything they own right now, you can use the time to periodically send him information on municipal bonds and annuities. Some day, he may see something he likes or may become dissatisfied with his current broker and transfer the account to you. You would never have gotten this future business if you had not known about these other assets. Only by asking questions can you get this type of valuable information. The investment and resource pyramid allows you to more easily obtain this information.

Using the investment and resource pyramid effectively presupposes that you can ask the appropriate questions about each item within the pyramid, as well as knowing where additional items (not appearing on this pyramid) should be placed. It further presumes that you can ask the questions in a conversational manner so that the prospect does not feel interrogated.

Figure 11-3 lists some of the areas/topics that you may wish to fully explore. The illustration represents a series of 4 × 6 or 5 × 8 index cards that are arranged in a flip file (in any order you wish) where each card overlaps another. Each card represents a different topic and can be raised to reveal a series of questions that allow you to qualify a person with respect to that investment objective, product or service. The order presented is random. Topics that have been expanded in subsequent pages are highlighted in **bold lettering.**

Figure 11-2 Completed Investment and Resource Pyramid

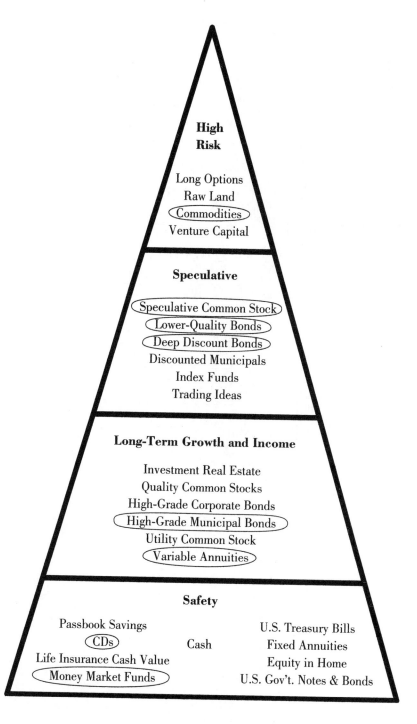

Figure 11-3 Areas/Topics to Explore for Investment Potential

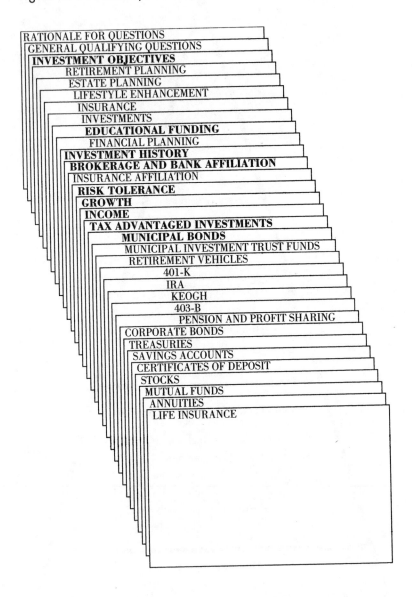

RATIONALE FOR QUESTIONS
GENERAL QUALIFYING QUESTIONS
INVESTMENT OBJECTIVES
    RETIREMENT PLANNING
    ESTATE PLANNING
    LIFESTYLE ENHANCEMENT
    INSURANCE
    INVESTMENTS
EDUCATIONAL FUNDING
    FINANCIAL PLANNING
INVESTMENT HISTORY
BROKERAGE AND BANK AFFILIATION
INSURANCE AFFILIATION
RISK TOLERANCE
GROWTH
INCOME
TAX ADVANTAGED INVESTMENTS
    MUNICIPAL BONDS
    MUNICIPAL INVESTMENT TRUST FUNDS
    RETIREMENT VEHICLES
    401-K
    IRA
    KEOGH
    403-B
    PENSION AND PROFIT SHARING
CORPORATE BONDS
TREASURIES
SAVINGS ACCOUNTS
CERTIFICATES OF DEPOSIT
STOCKS
MUTUAL FUNDS
ANNUITIES
LIFE INSURANCE

GROWTH

INCOME

TAX-ADVANTAGED INVESTMENTS

What is your tax bracket? now? and anticipated?

Do you own any tax advantaged investments? Which ones and why?

There are generally three ways to approach taxes:

Reduce	See cards for: *LIMITED PARTNERSHIPS, *GIFTING, *TRUSTS, *TAX SWAPS.
Defer	See cards for: *ANNUITIES, *RETIREMENT ACCOUNTS.
Avoid	See cards for: *LIMITED PARTNERSHIPS, *MUNICIPAL BONDS, *MITFs.

Each topic represented with *CAPITAL LETTERS represents another card within the question series. Each card is also cross-referenced to other cards so a more complete profile can be accomplished.

INVESTMENT OBJECTIVES

- What are your investment objectives?
  (What would you like your money to do for you and your family?)
- What is the time frame we are working with? That is, when should the various goals be accomplished?
- Most people are interested in *RETIREMENT PLANNING, *CHILDREN'S EDUCATION, *INCREASING THEIR INCOME, and so on. What types of things are you interested in? (Go to appropriate topic for additional questions.)
- Others are interested in *GROWTH, *INCOME, or *TAX ADVANTAGES. Which are you interested in and why? (Relate back to *RETIREMENT PLANNING, *CHILDREN'S EDUCATION, *ESTATE PLANNING, etc.)
- Describe an "ideal investment."
  (Rationale: My firm has so many products and services that we can probably create an idealized investment package for your and your family—one that is specifically tailored to meet your investment goals and objectives. If you could fantasize about what you want, the chances are that we can create the right product/service mix for you.
- How are you addressing the problem of *INFLATION?
- Have you taken care of your future needs? How?

INVESTMENT HISTORY AND APPROACHES

- What have you done in the financial markets thus far?
- How have you done?
- Why did you take that approach? What purpose does it serve?
  (*Cross checking with investment objectives.*)
- What has been your best investment? How did you make that choice?
  (*Gives selection criteria and strategy*)
- What was an investment you wish you didn't get into? How did you get into it?

BROKERAGE AFFILIATION

- Which brokerage firm(s) do you currently have an account with? Why?
- Do you obtain financial advice from anyone? Or do you make your own decisions?
- Which banks do you deal with? (*If a person names a few banks, then the possibility is that he has gone to the maximum amount with each of them and has multiple banks to obtain additional FDIC coverage.*)
- Who is your current broker? How long have you been working with him or her? Are you satisfied with your current broker? brokerage firm?
- What do you like and dislike about your brokers?
- Describe an "ideal" investment representative for you?
- Who makes the recommendations? decisions? selections?
- Is your current broker fulfilling *all* your investment needs?
- What can I do to earn your investment business?

RISK TOLERANCE

- What do you mean by risk?
  - Give parameters, percentages, figures.
  - How much can you afford to lose? How would you feel if you lost it?
  - How much time before retirement do you have to recoup? (Becomes very important when making asset allocation decisions.)
  - What is the riskiest investment you have now? safest? (You are trying to really understand the customer's definitions.)
  - Have you taken into account *INFLATION/loss of buying power.
  - Have you assigned different levels of risk to different investment objectives? (The financial profiling form may assist here.)

GROWTH

- Define "growth" What do *you* mean by growth?
- What do you have or what do you consider a growth investment?
- What time horizon are you working with?
- What percentage of your portfolio/investments is allocated to growth?
- Parameters? ideal? least acceptable?
- Purpose of growth? How is it necessary for your short- and long-term goals?
- Correlate to *RISK.
- Purpose of growth with respect to goals/needs—*INVESTMENT OBJECTIVES.
- Willing to sacrifice income for growth? Do you want/need both?
- How are your growth investments correlated to your other investments?
- What are characteristics that a growth investment would have?
    - Time frame
    - Acceptable percentages: above inflation? above S&P or Dow? basis of comparison?
    - Give an example of a growth stock, bond, mutual fund, investment.
- What is more important? income or appreciation?
- Have you had investments that provided you what you wanted?

INCOME

- What type of income do you want?
- What is your tax bracket: now and anticipated?
- How much income do you need?
    - For what purpose? (*RETIREMENT, *EDUCATION etc.)
- How do you currently get your income?
    - Percentage from salary, percentage from investments.
- What do you mean by income?
    - Percentages?
    - Time frame: annual? semiannual? monthly? weekly?
- What income-producing investments do you currently have?
- Willing to sacrifice *GROWTH for income? Want both?
- Are you interested in
    - *TAXABLE INCOME: stocks and/or bonds (see *CORPORATE BONDS, *STOCKS, *PREFERRED STOCKS, *UITs)
    - *TAX-FREE INCOME (also see *MUNICIPAL BONDS, *MITFs)
    - *TAX-DEFERRED INCOME (also see *ANNUITIES, *RETIREMENT ACCOUNTS)

EDUCATIONAL FUNDING

- Number, names, ages of children.
- Anticipated needs?
- What are you currently doing to fund their education?
- Current program? (also see *UGMA, *TRUSTS)
- Number of years till college.
- Approximate costs, including *INFLATION.
- Will you fund all or part of it?
- Willing to make an irrevocable gift? No? See *REVERSIONARY TRUST.
- What if the kids don't want to go?
- Can you set up a program of regular contributions? (See *MIP, *MUTUAL FUNDS.)
- Does your current life insurance policy/program cover the educational costs in case of your death?

MUNICIPAL BONDS

What is your tax bracket? now and anticipated?
- If low, see *TAXABLE BONDS, *CORPORATE BONDS, *UITs, and so on.
- Do you own any municipal bonds? which ones and why?
- Do you own any other tax-advantaged investments?
- Criteria for municipal bond selection
    - Yield and yield to maturity
    - Rating
    - Discount or premium
    - State(s) of preference
    - Maturity
    - Amount of money (also see *MITF, *MUNI BOND FUNDS).
    - Diversification needs (also see *MITF, *MUNI BOND FUNDS).
    - Strategies employed: *TAX SWAPS, *MARGIN.

Selling During Prospecting

Because many of your larger clients will have already achieved their more concrete goals, such as college and retirement, it is worth your while to create or obtain a series of questions that allow you to fully qualify an individual for virtually any product. The product cards can be directly correlated with the features, benefits, and advantages of that product. Therefore, *as you ask them qualifying questions, you can simultaneously sell them the product!* The product cards could also be written in the form of a decision tree. As long as the investor answers "Yes," you continue on the same line. After 7 to 12 "yesses," you know the client is qualified. At any "No," the card would refer you to a different product. This method allows you to fully qualify virtually anyone and constantly remind yourself of alternative investment vehicles.

The following is a list of a series of broad topics and their subtopics that you can use to model our Financial Qualifying System™. (You can, of course, also place the information on a computer. We find, however, that the flip file works more efficiently for most users.) This system is especially helpful for new brokers. After you've asked the GROWTH questions, for example, a number of times, you can throw away the card and only retain the cards relating to products that you rarely deal with. These may include questions on COMMODITIES, 401-Ks, OPTIONS, ESTATE PLANNING, and so on. You can also adapt the system to suit a number of your other purposes.

General Investment Questions

Core qualifying questions
Rationale for questions
Investment objectives
Investment history
Brokerage affiliation
Amount of money
Risk
Reward
Inflation
Etc.

General Investment Goals

Retirement planning
Educational funding
Life-style spending
Insurance
Investments
Estate planning
Financial planning
Preservation of capital
Hedge against inflation
Wealth accumulation
Etc.

Growth

Stocks
Bonds
Mutual funds
Variable annuities
Options
Etc.

Income

Taxable

    Corporate bonds

    Treasury bills, bonds, notes

    Preferred stocks

    Utility stocks

    Savings accounts

    Certificates of deposits

    UITs

    Etc.

Nontaxable

    Municipal bonds

    MITFs

    Municipal bond funds

    Etc.

Tax Advantages

Reduce

    Limited partnerships

    Tax shifting

    Trusts

    Etc.

Defer

    Annuities

    Retirement accounts

    Etc.

Avoid

    Municipal bonds

    Etc.

Popular Investment Products

Stocks

Corporate bonds

Municipal bonds

Mutual funds

Commodities

Annuities

Certificates of deposits

Money market instruments

Zero coupon

Treasury bills, bonds, notes

Etc.

Corporate Needs

Retirement planning

Cash flow

Lending

Equipment leasing

Etc.

To be truly consultative, you must be able to ask a series of pertinent questions relating to a particular investment need, objective, or product. Once this information is obtained, you can organize it in a variety of ways, including the Investment/Resource Pyramid.

The net effect of asking questions and organizing the information in the manner described is that you are able to assist the client, yourself, and your firm more fully by providing a wider variety of products to meet the client's needs. This allows the client to achieve both vertical and horizontal diversification.

12

What Makes Us Buy?

Psychologists have found that each of us has various criteria that we use when making selections (e.g., a favorite restaurant, a job, investments). These criteria may deal with such things as price, appearance, service, quality, or a host of others. It is interesting that, depending upon the kind of selections we are making, we may use certain of these criteria consistently. How important any criterion is for us during a decision-making situation will usually depend upon the nature of the decision (e.g., ideally, "price" would rarely be an important criterion when selecting a friend). In addition, our basic criteria or, motivational themes, are quite consistent for each of us. That is, each of us has several consistent criteria that we use when making selections, or purchasing decisions, as varied as clothing to securities, and these criteria are important when making any purchase.

This is one of the concepts behind "benefit selling." Now, instead of hoping your clients correctly translate the features of your financial products or services into benefits that are personally meaningful to them, you can facilitate the process. By using their criteria to describe your products, you speak their language and, once again, demonstrate that you think in the same way that they do. Do you think this will assist in closing a sale? You can bet it does!

While not everyone has the same criteria, we have polled thousands of individuals and the results verify that we all have criteria that effect multiple decisions. However, while each of us may have as many as five or six key criteria that have to be met before we will make a purchase decision, there are so many available criteria (e.g., cost, quality, service, popularity) and so many possible combinations that only about 5 percent of the population will match our own criteria exactly. This becomes extremely important because we also found that *when trying to sell something, we naturally emphasize those criteria which are important to us.* Think about how that might affect your ability to convince a client to commit to a course of action. You have found the perfect solution to their need, but instead of emphasizing their criteria of *price, convenience,* and *popularity,* you stress the product's *quality, service,* and *name recognition.* You may not "turn them off," but you also won't really motivate them. You have missed the psychological themes that motivate them. In essence, these are some of the *psychological parameters* of their investment, and can be as or even more important than their financial parameters because they enable the client to feel comfortable, or satisfied, with your recommendation. Thus, true benefit selling occurs on more than one level. While a benefit may be defined as what the product will "do" for the client (e.g., help him pay for his retirement or children's education), the emotional impact of a purchase can also be a benefit. Learn someone's basic themes and you can always present your solutions to his or her psychological as well as financial needs. Take a moment, now, and explore your own buying, or selection, criteria by taking the "test" that follows.

YOUR BUYING CRITERIA

For each of the following six questions, please circle the words that are applicable to you for the situation described. You may circle as many words in each situation as you desire.

1. What do you want in a car that you might purchase?
   a. Reputation
   b. Style/looks
   c. Service from dealer
   d. Dealer integrity
   e. Warranty
   f. Available options
   g. Location of dealer
   h. Bargain
   i. Dependability
   j. Performance

2. What would you like about a company that you either work for or would consider working for?
   a. Reputation
   b. Appearances
   c. Service orientation
   d. Company integrity

e. Contract offered
f. Career alternatives
g. Location of office

h. Money
i. Reliability
j. Company track record

3. Why do you go to a particular clothing store?
   a. Excellent reputation
   b. Good looking store
   c. Helpful staff
   d. Good reputation
   e. Good return policy

   f. Good selection
   g. Easy to get to
   h. Good value for money paid
   i. Quality merchandise
   j. Keeps up-to-date styles

4. What do you pride yourself on? Or what would you choose as the attributes of a person you admire?
   a. Good reputation
   b. Provides good image
   c. Offers assistance
   d. Trustworthy
   e. Fulfills verbal word

   f. Seeks new challenges
   g. Ease of accessibility
   h. Paid for work rendered
   i. Reliable
   j. Constantly improving self

5. Why do you frequent certain restaurants?
   a. Reputation
   b. Atmosphere/ambiance
   c. Good service
   d. Integrity
   e. Satisfaction assured

   f. Good selection
   g. Location
   h. Reasonable prices
   i. Consistent quality
   j. Gets better and better

6. What are some of the qualities you would want in a friend or spouse?
   a. Confidence in person
   b. Attractive
   c. Helpful
   d. Trustworthy
   e. Keeps promises

   f. Wide range of interests
   g. Is there when needed
   h. They're worth the effort
   i. Dependable
   j. Self-improvement conscious

The letters listed below will allow you to indicate how often you chose a particular response. For example, if you chose the answers associated with the letter "g" on five of the six questions, you would write the number 5 at the appropriate place (i.e., g. 5). Please do this for each of the ten letters.

a. _____   f. _____

b. _____   g. _____

c. _____   h. _____

d. _____   i. _____

e. _____   j. _____

Most people have a few letters that received rather high usage. The words associated with each letter were synonyms of each other—all the letter "gs," for instance, mean basically the same thing. Any words or equivalents used on three or more occasions can be considered a personal "key criteria" or "motivation" for you or for whoever took the test.

We've presented variations of this exercise to over 6,000 people and found that almost everyone has at least two or three major criteria that affect multiple decisions. If you learn someone's basic themes you can make your presentation much more powerfully. What is interesting is that while each of us has two or three dominant criteria, we all have different combinations. In fact, when we polled the 6,000 participants in our study, we found that only 1 in 20 precisely matched someone else's criteria. This becomes particularly important when you realize that each of us tends to emphasize *our own* criteria when making a presentation, which means that, we will inadvertently mismatch 19 out of 20 clients. This may explain a great deal of the "sales resistance," or hesitation, you may face.

The following is a list of common buying motivations that we have elicited that appear to be common to most of us.

Buying Criteria and Their Equivalents

Advertising	Reputation	Familiarity	Awareness
Alternatives	Variety	Selection	Product line
Appearance	Looks	Atmosphere	Ambiance
Courtesy	Consideration	Service	Respect
Credit	Cash flow	Bargain	Discount
Dependability	Reliability	Reputation	Confidence
Habit	Tradition	Familiar	Sentimental
Image	Style	Status	Prestige
Integrity	Honesty	Trustworthy	Honor/trust
Professional	Competent	Expert	Authority
Quality	Value	Craftsmanship	Reliable
Relationship	Loyalty	Friendliness	Affiliation
Safety	Security	Guarantee	Warranty

Think of how many ways knowing your customers' criteria can make your sales presentations more effective. Instead of presenting a variety of features, benefits, and advantages and hoping your client can take them and "correctly translate" them into items that are personally meaningful, now you can elicit their buying motivations. This will allow you to tailor-make presentations that are both directed and highly meaningful to your clients. Now, you can create presentations that are formed entirely from their point of view, and in their language by combining an understanding of your clients':

- Psychological needs (see Chapter 13)
- Emotional needs (see psychological profiling in Chapter 14)
- Sensory style of thinking and speaking (visual, auditory, or kinesthetic; found in Chapter 4)

In fact, your presentation will appear to your clients as though they have written them themselves. Such presentations become almost impossible to resist. For example, here is an example of a presentation to a customer whose buying criteria are "popularity," "safety," "selection/variety," and "service," and who is primarily "visual" in orientation.

> *Broker*: "Mr. Jones, I'm sure that when you *look at* the annuity I am going to *show* you, that you will *see* why I think that it is so *attractive.* To begin with, it has *many features* which were *designed* to fit *beautifully* with your needs to improve your retirement coverage. That's why it is so *popular.* You can choose from a *selection* of several plans in which to invest, for example, a single-premium annuity, or we can even have payments automatically deducted from your checking account each month. And you will receive a quarterly statement of your account and its growth to review. This is just one of the *many services* offered by our firm. I think that you'll also like the convenience of our location, which will enable us to easily meet personally to *review and service* your needs. I'm sure you'll find our service both warm and *friendly. Many* of your *neighbors* will probably want to purchase a similar annuity when you tell them you are preparing for retirement this way. Finally, we've been in business for nearly 100 years, which should give you a real sense of *security.*

Discovering a few of your client's primary buying motivations can be as simple as asking a few questions and listening carefully to the answers. This can easily be done over one or more casual conversations or during the "get-acquainted" portion of any face-to-face meeting. It's really pretty easy.

Simply ask your client questions which might normally come up in a social or business situation/meeting such as what he likes about a given product, or restaurant, and so on and notice criteria that appear consistently. For example, read the conversation that follows and look for potential decision-making criteria from the client. We'll highlight the important probes of the broker.

> *Broker:* "Bill, I notice that you own a Jaguar. I'm thinking of buying one myself, but I haven't quite made up my mind. *What do you like about yours?*"
>
> *Client:* "Well, I think that it's a well-made car, and it's lots of fun to drive."
>
> *Broker:* "*Anything else?*"
>
> *Client:* "Yes. It's a sharp-looking car. Not like some of these 'boxes' they're selling today. And my family likes it."
>
> *Broker:* "Sounds great, Bill. But where do you get it serviced? I mean, I'd guess you must want a factory trained mechanic for it."
>
> *Client:* "That's for sure. I don't want to take any risks where a sixty thousand dollar car is concerned. I take it to the dealer where I bought it, in Smithtown."
>
> *Broker:* "That's a little out of your way, isn't it? *What made you choose that dealer?*"
>
> *Client:* "Frankly, Dick, I didn't like the quality of the service that I was getting at the dealer here in this town. The dealer in Smithtown always has the car when he says he will and does a quality job. For that, I don't mind the inconvenience of paying a little more and having the extra drive. Besides, he always gives me a loaner while the car's in the shop."

Did you notice all the information that the client provided? We'll provide it again, this time underlining possible criteria.

> *Broker:* "Bill, I notice that you own a Jaguar. I'm thinking of buying one myself, but I hasn't quite made up my mind. What do you like about yours?"
>
> *Client:* "Well, I think that it's a <u>well-made</u> car, and it's lots of <u>fun</u> to drive."
>
> *Broker:* "Anything else?"
>
> *Client:* "Yes. It's a <u>sharp-looking</u> car. Not like some of these 'boxes' they're selling today. And, my <u>family likes it</u>."
>
> *Broker:* "Sounds great, Bill. But where do you get it serviced? I mean, I'd guess you must want a factory trained mechanic for it."
>
> *Client:* "That's for sure. I <u>don't want to take any risks</u> where a sixty thousand dollar car is concerned. I take it to a dealer in Smithtown."
>
> *Broker:* "That's a little out of your way, isn't it? What made you choose that dealer?"

Client: "Frankly, Dick, I didn't like the <u>quality</u> of the service that I was getting at the dealer here in this town. The dealer in Smithtown <u>always</u> has the car ready when he says he will and does a <u>quality</u> job. For that, I don't mind the ***inconvenience of paying a little more and having the extra drive.*** Besides, he always <u>gives me a loaner</u> while the car's in the shop."

Now, lets list the criteria that the client provided:

- Well made = quality
- Fun
- Sharp looking = appearance
- Family likes it = opinions of others
- Don't want to take any risks = security
- Gives me a loaner = services
- Always has the car ready = reliability/dependability
- Inconvenience of paying a little more and having the extra drive = reinforcement of quality issues and price is not the primary criteria.

Two or three other questions (about favorite restaurants, etc.) can easily provide additional criteria while emphasizing those criteria that might be restated in different contexts. In addition, during the financial profiling interview, you should also ask questions about other products (yours or a competitors) that the client has purchased previously. These can be particularly useful because they are more closely related to what you are trying to accomplish. In addition, while the client is answering these questions, you are also finding out about their psychological profile and their preference in sensory systems/predicate. For example,

You: "Mrs. Jones, you mentioned earlier that you own $200,000 of Pennsylvania General Obligation (GO) municipal bonds and 5,000 share of McDonald's stock. May I ask what you liked about each that made you select them in particular?"

Client: "I bought the Pennsylvania bonds because I like the *security* of general obligation bonds and because I got them at a *good price*. And of course, they *save me money* on taxes. I got the McDonald's stock on the *recommendation of my broker* because she pointed out that they were of the *highest investment grade* and that they had done *nothing but grow steadily* since they opened when I was a little girl. We also picked them up at a *great price* during the crash in 1987. Finally, my *granddaughter* won't let me take her anywhere else to eat. With that kind of *popularity,* I'm sure *they'll be around for awhile.*"

Did you notice the repeated themes of *safety* and *price?* Also the emphasis on *steady growth* plus *around for awhile*, which are another way of saying *consistency*. It's possible that another criterion is the opinion of others (e.g., broker and granddaughter). However, there is insufficient data to be certain of that, and you would want to explore it in more detail with questions about other investments or interests.

Thus, if a person's primary motivations can be identified and listed in the order of importance to him, future sales presentations can be structured to address those preidentified needs/desires/motivations. Just take the features/benefits/advantages of your product or service and predetermine how each would address a prime motivation of your client. Continuing the example,

> *You:* "Mrs. Jones, there are two things I really like about this PFL Life fixed annuity is its *high level of security* and *its great yield.* For example, in *Best's Review*, PFL Life is rated as the best annuity on the market as measured by the fifth year surrender value. That's high praise from the number one rating service for annuities. I also just like the *overall safety* of annuities generally. They're issued by the same people who insure your home or car. In fact PFL Life's parent company, AEGON, is one of the largest both here and in Europe. Finally, this annuity has a *great yield,* which will remain substantially above the one-year CD rate regardless of how interest rates may change. That's true because the yield of the annuity is adjusted once each year to track interest rates. Which means you *won't lose principal* if interest rates go up. What do you think?"

One way that you can practice eliciting someone's criteria is to occasionally ask your friends or associates about what they like about something (just what, doesn't matter). After asking this a few times about different things, you will probably notice that you are beginning to receive similar responses from people. *Two key questions you can ask are*

- What do you like in a _____? (Provides criteria.)
- What would having _____ (use their answer to the first question) do for you? (Generally provides motivation behind the criteria.)

There are, of course, numerous variations on these questions. The answers provide you with significant data about the client.

Each of us is unique in so many ways. One of the things that makes us so unique, and such a challenge to effectively sell to, is the unique combination of private language, private motivations, and decision making criteria that determine how we will act and what we will purchase. In this chapter we have explored a simple technique for eliciting the criteria your clients use to make investment decisions so you can target each sales presentation to the specific client rather than the "generic" client. After all, how many generic clients do you expect to have? Remember, on average, one out of twenty people you meet/call will have the same set of criteria that you do. Nineteen out of twenty have a different set and will need you to emphasize slightly different aspects of your product or service than you might say.

13

How We View the World

Authors' Note: This chapter may be of greatest benefit to experienced brokers who already have a detailed knowledge of their clients' financial needs. Newer brokers, without that detailed knowledge, will still benefit, but possibly to a lesser extent.

Within the financial services industry, investment reps constantly seek to understand what makes their clients tick. How do they make decisions? What criteria do they use to make a purchasing decision? What makes them do what they do? In the chapters on rapport and communication, we discussed the importance of looking at things from your client's point of view, of speaking their language and developing a real understanding of their needs. While part of understanding their needs consists of establishing rapport and speaking their language, another part is made up of recognizing unconscious emotional needs and thinking patterns that account for the vast majority of any decision. The final part consists of eliciting the actual financial need itself (see Chapters 10 and 11 on financial profiling). Ironically, it is solely upon this financial need that most investment advisors focus, without considering the entire picture.

Clients are motivated by many factors, some by the need for power, others affiliation, and still others by achievement (see Chapter 14). Many people seek "security," others "income," and for years, brokers focused on selling "greed" in various forms. While these are all important, they represent only one portion of the complex configuration of needs, beliefs and attitudes that makes up the motivational system of any individual. In this chapter, we will investigate the other needs, beliefs, and attitudes that make up the rest of an individual's motivational system.

HIERARCHY OF NEEDS

To really understand a customer's behavior, it is important to understand that we all have many needs that affect what we buy and why we buy it. Some of those needs are physical (e.g., buying a bank certificate of deposit to provide income for daily needs of food and shelter), and others are emotional (e.g., buying particular stock because we identify with that company). Years ago, the psychologist Abraham Maslow arranged people's emotional and physical needs into categories and then listed them in a hierarchy of importance based upon their power to affect us. He arranged these needs in the form of a pyramid, with the most basic needs at the bottom (see Figure 13-1).

Physical Needs

Maslow considered these our most basic *primary needs* and put them first. They consist of survival-oriented drives such as the desire for food, water, shelter, and sleep (and, to an extent, sex) and must be fulfilled before our higher needs can be met. At this most basic level, Maslow viewed our drive

Figure 13-1 Maslow's Hierarchy of Needs

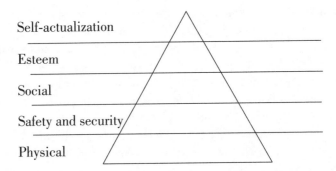

to survive as being the most powerful. After food and clothing, the first thing most couples save/invest for is a home.

Safety and Security Needs

After our need for food and water have been met, our next priority is safety and security. Hungry people will risk their lives for food. After we've been fed we want to be free from danger. Once they have a home, people next look for safety (e.g., insurance, retirement planning and emergency funds). People who lived through the Great Depression and World War II often tend to seek investments that are "totally safe" (examples of such totally safe investments might include savings accounts or bonds guaranteed by the federal government) even when they could make more money with something else. Part of the sales process may be to help such individuals to redefine their definitions of safety to include items that would help them solve their financial needs more effectively.

Social Needs

As social beings, we need association with other people and often seek their approval. Once our physical and safety needs have been met, these social needs become increasingly important to us. Investors with strong social needs will tend to be more interested in "popular" investments with names they recognize.

Esteem Needs

All of us need to feel that we are valuable and are valued by others. We also need to feel adequate/competent in what we do. Our sense of self-esteem is a powerful motivator that can often mean the difference not only between buying or not buying a given item, but also the career we choose, how we do business, or even how we treat our customers. Customers with strong esteem needs will be attracted to investments that build their esteem (by demonstrating their success, intelligence or general superiority, etc.).

Self-actualization Needs

Maslow perceived these as our highest needs and defined them as the need to feel that we are meeting our potential, using all our talents and resources to be all that we can. Your desire to be the best sales professional possible is an example of this need. Investors motivated by self-actualization are more likely to invest with the goal of being able to increase their quality of life, perhaps through trips and vacations or during retirement.

It is important to recognize that people will often try to fulfill several layers of needs at once. A customer may want to meet safety, social, and esteem needs while investing for a child's college education at her own alma mater. You must be alert for each of the customers needs. As a professional, the more needs you can meet, the stronger will be your sales presentation. Your mailings can be made more effective by taking these needs into account, as well as by incorporating other value systems.

BELIEFS AND EXPECTATIONS

When we go to make a purchase, we take a series of expectations and core beliefs with us. These *beliefs* consist of the core principles that rule our lives and largely determine what we expect in a given situation (our expectations). The impact of someone's beliefs may range from their expectations of a given product or service and what it will do for them to social customs and how they expect to be treated by the broker they invest with. When those expectations and beliefs are met, they generally feel happy with the investment and reward the broker with loyalty, perhaps even telling their friends about it. When their expectations are not met, they may become dissatisfied and judgmental, telling their friends how bad it was, perhaps even trying to move their account. Sometimes their expectations are very reasonable and their beliefs consistent with their investments; sometimes they aren't. But they are *always* important to them. As a financial professional, your ability to discover, understand, and meet your customer's expectations and beliefs will have a tremendous affect upon your success.

A client's beliefs include what he hopes a product or service will do for him, in fulfilling a particular need. For example, he may hope that buying a particular mutual fund will enable him to pay for a child's education or give him the income to entertain more lavishly.

Beliefs also have a powerful effect upon our behavior and largely determine what we *expect* from ourselves and others in any situation. Beliefs are generally formed as a result of experience and our interpretation of that experience and, once formed, act like filters that affect the way we interpret new experiences. For example, consider the feelings that most people had immediately after the stock market crash of 1987. People who had invested heavily in the stock market were frightened that day. Their very foundations were shaken, and long-held beliefs about the financial security of their future were undermined. The results were expressed in major changes in the way they invested their money, as people became very cautious and began to invest in financial instruments that were considered "safe" (such as bank certificates of deposit, blue-chip bonds and stocks, etc.).

Because the savings of many individual's were "destroyed" overnight, their confidence in the future was similarly affected. Many people, who had been purchasing all the toys of the "Yuppie" generation had suffered a substantial "erosion of capital" and went into a survival mode with a change to "safe" investments being the theme of the day. Without belaboring the point, the investment game changed on that day. In one form or another, everyone reading this book was at least mentally affected. Your subsequent response, as well as the responses of your prospects and clients, was partially determined by what each of you saw, heard, and felt over the days that followed the crash. It was also determined by your background and the way you usually approach the world in your experience. Thus, those investors who lost money in the crash of 1987, or those who grew up during the Great Depression, may have formed the belief that preservation of principal is the only safe investment goal, and they will not consider any investment that does not virtually guarantee their principal, regardless of its poor performance, against inflation. In addition, if an individual lost money while investing before, he may hesitate to trust brokers in the future for fear of doing so again.

People also tend to look for evidence that supports their beliefs, proving they were right to believe something. Thus, our beliefs and expectations affect our *perceptions* (what and how we see things). Ironically, this may cause us to see only things that support our belief and to ignore evidence that would contradict it. Thus, during times of high inflation, many investors will ignore evidence of the dangers of loss of buying power and stick with short-term, "guaranteed" investments with negative real rates of return.

EXTREMES IN THINKING

Individuals who think in terms of black/white, good/bad, right/wrong, and so on literally tend to think and respond in extremes. They appear to be very definitive and opinionated. They see the world through their own "rose-colored glasses," and as far as they are concerned, everyone should think and believe exactly as they do. These individuals have made up the ranks of the world's zealots since history began.

It is very difficult to argue with people like this concerning one of their beliefs. They are right and they know it and are willing to tell anyone and everyone who will listen. Confronting them in front of a group is usually a disaster because they just dig in their heels and stay put. This can easily lead to an escalation of the argument where either you back down or are forced to take corrective measures. Obviously, neither solution is desirable.

You must deal with them one-on-one. When you need to convince them that there is something beyond the level of their own experience, merely *search for the exception that negates the extreme statement.* Usually, if you find even one exception, they have to admit that, just possibly, they do not have all the answers. For example, during one sales presentation a customer informed his broker that he had no intention of buying a particular mutual fund because the fund was worthless. The broker made a statement something like the following: "You sound very certain. What specifically did you read in the prospectus that lead you to that conclusion?" The customer got flustered and had to admit that he associated this particular mutual fund with another fund that had performed poorly in the past. The broker then spent a moment reestablishing rapport and brought up several points about the fund that matched the customer's buying criteria and successfully closed the sale.

PAST—PRESENT—FUTURE

One's orientation to time is an important key to how some people think, respond, and are motivated. We all know people who constantly refer to the "good old days," while others regularly refer to "how things will be." Whether the individual is oriented to the past, to the future (as illustrated earlier), or to the present (one of those popularly called the "now generation"), knowledge about people's orientations can be very important to the process of committing them to a course of investing.

Past Orientation

Past orientation is exemplified by the individual who constantly reminisces about "the good old days." Many people seem to live their lives in the past and use it as their primary basis of reference. "They don't build cars like they used to," and a series of other past-oriented phrases would let the astute broker know that the key to dealing with such a client would be to emphasize "the continuance of quality the way we always have" and the "enhancements to the basic products and services that have served us so well over the years." The phrases used by the broker indicate a past reference, which would then match the client's past time orientation. The way to demotivate such a client is by emphasizing the modern, state-of-the-art, breaking-tradition aspects of the product or service. These emphases, of course, would appeal to people with the "present" or "future" time orientation.

Present Orientation

Individuals with a strong orientation to the present are involved in what is happening at the moment. They occasionally review past memories and plan for the future, but they live in the present. "*Now* is the time to get things done." As clients, these individuals can make a decision, if they can see an immediate benefit, for example, an increase in *current* income.

Future Orientation

People with a strong future orientation are more concerned with the way things will eventually be rather than working right now. They often tend to live in a fantasy world in which things will always work themselves out. They are always talking about the things they are about to do. "Things will be better/different, tomorrow" is typical of the way they deal with problems. Unfortunately, many of them never get anything done. However, a healthy future orientation enables many to focus on planning for future needs, such as retirement and children's education. These individuals tend to look for long-term investments rather than short-term gains.

PEOPLE—PLACES—THINGS—ACTIVITIES

"*People-oriented*" *individuals* are usually talking about others. *Relationships are very important* to them. This person can be motivated by making references to the popularity of a product or service and is often best prospected and "sold" in a seminar setting. Discuss how their entire family might benefit from a particular investment decision. For example, "You'll be able to proudly tell all of your friends," would be another approach to persuading this person.

"*Place-oriented*" *people* generally talk about all the places they have been. "Last year we went to Europe and spent some time in Paris. Oh, what a wonderful city. Have you ever been there?" This person may be motivated by investing for a trip or the fact that a global mutual fund invests throughout the world.

"*Thing-oriented*" *people* are exemplified by the "Yuppies" who accumulate things for the sake of ownership. "He who dies with the most toys wins" was a popular saying. While making fun of the extreme, it is interesting to note how many people get motivated by being able to purchase things with money they've invested.

An excellent time to gain insight into a client's orientation is during the profiling interview when you ask them what they want their money/investments to do for them, or what their goals are. Some people may respond by saying that it will let them travel, or spend time with their children and friends, and so on. Each of these ties into one of the orientations discussed.

GLOBAL VERSUS LINEAR

Global thinkers often see the big picture and are generally not interested in the details of a situation. Present a concept and they grasp the meaning and are often mentally exploring other potentials and ramifications while their contemporaries are still trying to understand the basic ideas. While global thinking is great for some things it can be disadvantageous for certain types investments which require a more detailed understanding before making an informed investment decision, for example, certain forms of retirement accounts.

    Linear thinkers take things one step at a time. They tend to be great at procedures and relatively poor at "what if" scenarios. When presenting a solution to such individuals, avoid giving them a variety of investments to choose from. Provide one solution and show how it directly related to their need. Avoid extraneous information that might confuse them.

CHUNKING

Chunking refers to the detail required in presenting information or ideas. Information chunk size can often be correlated to global or linear thinking. However, the correlation is not precise. If a client needs a tremendous amount of detail to understand an investment and make a decision, provide it. Make note of it on his account holding page, and the next time you make a presentation, you'll be able to provide it in the most advantageous way for the individual. When in doubt, use the K.I.S.S. principle when making presentations. You can always add more detail. (See Chapter 16).

    Of course, you must take into account the person's relative familiarity with the product in which they are about to invest. Even a global thinker, who prefers the big picture, may need additional details if he is unfamiliar with the product type. The trick is to be able to explain something using both extremes—details vs. global. If you can do that you can then explain to anyone.

EMOTIONAL VERSUS LOGICAL

"I *feel* that this is the right way" or something similar. "I just know that...." These people often have an intuitive method of coming to a conclusion. They often "react" very quickly and with a great deal of emotionalism. Thus, they may be extremely happy when you help them solve an investment need, and quickly angry and upset if its value goes down briefly. They have little emotional detachment. These individuals will often tend to use kinesthetic, or feelings-oriented, words when they speak (see Chapter 4). They rarely get very excited, nor do they easily get depressed.

The emotional client may expect you to "share your feelings" with him. Similarly, he responds more readily to the rah-rah of some sales presentations. Of course, he could have the opposite response and be turned off by such a presentation. Either way, he will have an emotional response.

The *logical person* responds to appeals to the intellect. She tends to be more detached from things than her more emotional counterpart. Try to sell her with an emotional appeal and you'll find she has a decided lack of interest and even the possibility of mild disgust that someone would do something so illogical. Give her the numbers and show her how a given investment will help her achieve her desired results, and she will usually respond.

I VERSUS WE ORIENTATION

"*I* think that the way to do it is my way. *I* remember when *I* told my broker what *I* thought and, of course, *I* was right." You probably know someone who somewhat represents this extreme "*I*" orientation. These people are not going to motivated to invest in something unless it benefits them directly. "What's in it for me?" must be clearly, distinctly, and exquisitely stated. "This is what's in it for you," is the way that you would present any investment recommendation.

"*We-oriented" individuals* are similar to the "affiliation-oriented" person who will be discussed in Chapter 14. Their investment objective typically includes at least some benefit for someone else, such as a vacation home for the family, the children's education, and retirement for them and their spouse. Emphasize the group benefits wherever possible in making an investment recommendation. The regular use of "we," "us," "let's," and so on is a good indicator but not a guarantee that affiliation is the right approach. You'll want to consider other behaviors to verify your suppositions.

INTERNAL VERSUS EXTERNAL MOTIVATION

How a person is motivated is a key to working with them. Some people are internally motivated/motivate themselves while an individual who is externally motivated needs reinforcement from others—some kind of approval or validation from others. These needs can have a large impact on the way an individual makes investment decisions.

Internally motivated people are generally able to make their own investment decisions based upon their perception of the information at hand. However, *externally motivated people* will often need the approval or support of others (e.g., their spouse, family, accountant) before they make an investment commitment. Pushing them to make the decision now, without that approval will only cause problems. Offer to speak with them together with their accountant or spouse while you make your presentation, and you'll have more success. There is an easy way to determine whether an individual is internally or externally motivated. Simply ask how they make an investment decision. An internally motivated person will answer, "I make it myself." An externally motivated individual will answer, "I always check with my spouse/accountant/and so on."

TOWARD VERSUS AWAY

People tend to look either ahead or behind. Some people move through life seeking positive goals, others take the same journey to avoid unpleasantness. While their actions may be identical, their motivation patterns are not and what motivates one, will leave the other cold.

To determine into which category a client fits, listen carefully to his answer when you ask what he likes about his current broker or what made her choose a particular investment. His answer will tell you more than you might expect. For example,

> 1. "I like my present broker because she has provided good service and helps me find the best investments for my retirement account" versus "I like my present broker because, unlike my last broker, she doesn't avoid my calls when I have a question, and she doesn't try to sell me something just because it has a big commission for her."
>
> 2. "I bought this Treasury bill because I don't have to worry about it. I can sleep at night knowing it's not going to miss a payment" versus "I bought this treasury bill because I think it will provide a good safe source of regular income for me."

In each case, both individuals said essentially the same thing, but from the opposite point of view. Thus, while both might buy the same product, they will do so for opposite reasons and must be sold very differently. When explaining an investment to a client with a "toward" orientation, emphasize what it will help them to accomplish. However, when explaining the same product to an "away"-oriented client, emphasize the problems it will help them to avoid.

SIMILARITIES VERSUS DIFFERENCES

Another common pattern can be seen of the tendency of some people to handle new information by *comparing* it with something else they already know and like. Others will *contrast* it with something they already know and dislike.

In our sales courses, we like to try an interesting experiment; we show a group of people three cans of soda pop (e.g., a Coke, a Pepsi, and a Diet Coke) and ask each member of the group what they see. About half tell us, "Three cans of soda, or three cans of cola." The other half give answers like, "Two Cokes and a Pepsi, or two colas and a diet cola, or a Pepsi, a Coke and a Diet Coke." That is, half the group sorts for similarities among the three cans, and the other half sorts for differences between them. These sorting patterns can have a large effect on the success of your sales presentation.

You can determine whether a customer is similarities oriented versus differences oriented by asking what they like about their current investments. If they mention that they bought a bond issue because bonds are similar to CDs, they are probably similarities oriented. When you make a presentation on an investment, compare it with something with which the client is already familiar and which she like (don't automatically assume that anything she currently owns is appropriate; she may have several investments which she hates but doesn't feel she can get rid of).

On the other hand, if she mentions that she bought a bond because, unlike a stock, it provides a dependable source of income, she is probably differences oriented. When making an investment presentation, contrast what you are recommending with something with which she is already familiar but doesn't like.

As you can see, people have different strategies for sorting information about things and making decisions. The patterns that have been presented thus far are but a few of the standard responses which allow you to predict behavior. We have presented the ones that are easily observable and that will give you the greatest personal impact in working with clients. It is important to combine this information with characteristics presented in other chapters.

As an experiment, think of an "ideal" client and respond to the following questions so you can get a feel for the potential ramifications of having this information. Is this person

- Oriented to the past? present? or future?
- Self-motivated (i.e., able to maintain a good work pace without reliance on external sources)?
- Interested in people, places, or things?
- A global or linear thinker?
- Moving toward a goal or moving away from something?
- and so on.

The answers to these questions are important because they literally determine how you must present your recommendations if you are to obtain a commitment from your clients. You can determine it through multiple observations of behavior, in addition to asking certain astute questions to determine any client's motivational strategies.

14

How We Act and React

Have you ever met someone (perhaps a prospect or client) who was caustic, sarcastic, and very aggressive? How about someone who was rigid and would only do things "by the book"? Finally, do you know individuals who are very warm and friendly, and always go along with the crowd?

We all know people who act like that, and we may have even wondered how to deal with them. The fact is that people act the way they do for many different reasons. An important aspect of the art of winning your customer to your point of view centers on your ability to understand and meet the psychological needs behind his actions.

In this chapter you will learn techniques that will enable you to psychologically profile customers within the first few moments of meeting them. It will also teach you how to use that information to meet that customer's hidden agenda of psychological needs as you discuss the products and services your bank has to offer. Fortunately, you don't have to be a psychologist to do this.

POWER—AFFILIATION—ACHIEVEMENT

A Harvard psychologist named David McClelland determined that each of us has three major needs, *power, affiliation,* and *achievement.* Each of us has some *need to feel in control of our lives and our environment (power).* In addition, we are social beings, so we *need to affiliate with others to some extent.* Finally, everyone *needs to feel a sense of accomplishment, or achievement, for a job well done.* However, most of us have at least one need that is stronger than the others and that has a tremendous affect upon how we act and what we purchase.

Need for Power

Do you know someone who always seems to want to take charge of the situation and likes to direct and control others (either directly or from behind the scenes)? Interestingly, there are many reasons why someone may want or need to take charge. The people who take charge because it makes them feel good and/or powerful and/or in control are individual who demonstrate a *need for power.* If they say "Jump," they want someone else to say "How high?"

You see them everywhere, in all walks of life. As clients they like to make brokers do as they're told. These customers are usually very forceful and react negatively to questions or any type of delay (which are often viewed as a personal affront). In a word, they may appear a little like a typical "dictator." However, as you'll see later, they can be quite easy to deal with and often become excellent customers.

Power-Oriented Motivations: People desiring power have a strong desire to take control of others and various situations. They want to be the boss. "Do it my way" and "Follow my directions" are key patterns. In the extreme, they

- Tend to seek the ability to influence, supervise, or control other people.
- Let you know what they want in terms of service and, sometimes, product. Their expectations are frequently expressed as demands (often inflexible) rather than requests.
- They may try to intimidate you with their tone of voice, sarcasm, or real or implied threats if their demands are not met.
- They tend to be most interested in products they perceive as directly or indirectly providing status. For example, to a power-motivated client, municipal bonds may imply status because they are tax advantaged.

Words and Phrases Used by Power-Motivated Clients: You can often recognize power-motivated people by the way they talk and the words they use. Not only is their conversation often self-centered, their voice frequently carries an edge, as though there were no room for compromise. Their conversation tends to center on words and topics like

- "Me," "myself," "I"
- Control
- Power
- Authority
- "Do it my way"
- "I'm the boss"
- "That's *my* decision to make"

Methods for Handling/Selling to a Power-Motivated Customer: Once you meet such individuals, don't just retreat and leave their needs to someone else. They can be remarkably easy to work with. For example,

- Acknowledge their achievements, status, position, and authority.
- Provide symbols of authority such as preferred location.
- Obtain their opinion (preferably publicly).
- Acknowledge their contributions.
- Be sure to emphasize that any purchase is *their* decision.
- Show them how doing what you want will also get them what they desire.
- Involve them in the development of their financial goals and solutions.

In summary, the way to deal with power-oriented customers is to empower them. That is, show them you recognize their intelligence, status, achievements and need for power and meet it. For example,

> "Mr. VanDerbilt, this mutual fund invests primarily in excellent medical research companies specializing in gene therapy and development. While there is a certain amount of risk involved, the potential for extremely rapid growth is also present as the drugs these companies are developing are approved and come to market. This fund was designed for sophisticated investors who understand the risk-reward ratios of investments."

Need for Affiliation

Customers whose primary motivation are affiliation is substantially different from power-oriented individuals. For them, the goal is association with other people. The need to be part of a group and to be accepted by others is of paramount importance on the unconscious level. They like to be around others and feel demotivated and perhaps even depressed when they have to be alone. Hence, their purchasing selections are strongly influenced by what is currently popular and will be accepted by their peer group. They do not like to stand out from the crowd if it will separate them from the group.

Affiliation Motivations: People who demonstrate a strong need for affiliation are driven by their need to be with other people, and are validated primarily by other people. Thus, they

- Like being a member of the team.
- Need to be liked.
- Need acceptance and interpersonal relationships.
- Want/need to work with people.
- Try to minimize conflicts.
- Want to know what are other people doing.

Words and Phrases Used by the Affiliation-Oriented Customer: One way to spot affiliation-oriented people is through their use of terms and phrases, such as

- "We," "us," "let's," "all," and "others"
- "Let's get together"
- "Let's do something for…"
- Group participation
- "What's popular?"

Actions to Take When Dealing with/Selling to an Affiliation-Motivated Customer: These friendly individuals are usually easy to deal with because they like people. As you demonstrate your concern for their interests and needs, you will automatically develop good relations with these clients. For example,

- Thank them for their business.
- Emphasize the popularity of their selected security or service.

- Talk in terms of how their friends will admire their selection.
- Involve them in the development of their financial goals and solutions.

In sum, the way to deal with someone who is highly affiliation oriented is to present them with concepts in terms of the group. Present sales ideas by defining them in terms of other people. Get them involved with the process. Be warm and friendly. For example,

> "Ms. Jones, this mutual fund is one of our most popular investments for children's college funds. I'm confident that your entire family will like both its high projected rate of growth as well as its emphasis on making only blue-chip investments."

Note: One particular type of affiliation-oriented individual (the "social" person) will be discussed in greater detail later in the chapter.

Need for Achievement

Achievement-oriented people place a premium on accomplishing their goals. They respond well to recognition of their accomplishments and often seek products or services that reflect those achievements, for example, purchasing a BMW or Jaguar that reflects their success in business. This can also be seen in their choice of investment products and services, such as the private banking services offered by some institutions to their wealthier clients.

In summary, these individuals want and need a sense of accomplishment. They obtain this from challenging and/or competitive situations. Sometimes this may result in their "competing" with investment professionals to get the "best deal." In such cases, letting them "win" in the end can be key to building a long-term relationship with them, for example, letting them negotiate the commission on one sale (within acceptable limits) until they believe they have achieved a good deal. Achievement-oriented people often share the following characteristics:

- Set long-range, achievable objectives.
- Plan for contingencies.
- Compete against a motivating standard.
- Receive satisfaction from working on a task, as well as its completion.

Words and Phrases Used by Achievers: Like power- and affiliation-oriented people, achievers tend to use words and phrases that identify their needs, for example,

- Innovative ideas
- "Let's plan ahead"
- "Let's get the job done"
- Feeling of accomplishment

Actions to Take with an Achievement-Motivated Customer: The easiest way to help achievement-oriented customers is to

- Recognize their achievements by sending a card or giving them a call when you learn of a promotion or other success.
- Encourage them to consider new ways of achieving their financial goals.
- Involve them in the development of their financial goals and solutions (see financial profiling).

In essence, you can help an achievement-oriented individual by providing recognition of achievements that are meaningful to them. This individual is highly motivated by the successful completion of tasks and can be motivated to purchase rewards for her success. For example,

"Ms. Smith, you mentioned that you have just completed a very successful year and received a substantial bonus. With your retirement already taken care of, this might be an appropriate addition to your investments for that new plane you wanted."

In summary, it should be apparent that each of us has at least some need for power, affiliation, and achievement. At the very least, we need enough of a sense of power to feel that we can control our own lives instead of being controlled by them. Similarly, we all need at least occasional contact and interaction with other people. Too much isolation has long been proven to have very negative effects on our productivity and overall mental and physical adjustment. Finally, everyone needs to feel the sense of competence and closure that comes from completing a task. However, what constitutes too great a drive for power, affiliation, or achievement?

PERSONALITY TYPES

Over the years, psychologists have developed a variety of systems to help understand people's actions. As a result, there are many systems available for profiling someone's behavior, even to the extent of psychiatric evaluation. Here, we will provide a simplified system of categorizing the behavior of others to help you communicate more effectively as well as work with customers' primary behavioral attributes. However, before we present the basis of the psychological profiling system, take a moment and think of the people that you know, or know of, who fit some of the elements of the following descriptions:

- Bill is always "hanging out with the crowd." He bases his sense of self-worth on other people's reactions and perceptions of him. Hence, he is eager to please, and may even appear a "social butterfly." He is very talkative, and tends to be very conscious of the latest fashions and trends.

- Jane always "goes by the book" because "rules were made for good reasons." She rarely takes chances and does not wish to stand out from the crowd. She does not wish to be the leader, but resents whoever does take the lead. She will frequently gossip about people, but will rarely confront them to their face. If a new idea is suggested, she usually has some reason why it won't work and shouldn't even be attempted.

- Jack is a person who is very dogmatic and always has to be right. When he is wrong, he tries to bully his way through, often at the "top of his lungs." He always wants to be in control and is often contemptuous of others. His three most frequently used words are "I," "me," and "myself."

- Samantha is an independent thinker who is respectful of other's feelings and opinions, then makes up her own mind. A natural leader in any group, she is social, polite, and friendly, but not insincerely so. When necessary, she is able to set limits on herself and others.

The purpose of this exercise is to demonstrate how true to life psychological profiling can be. The chances are that you are already thinking of people who fit quite well into some of these categories. In fact, most of us demonstrate at least some of the traits of each of these characters at one time or another, but tend to predominate in one. Each of the following concepts will provide you with additional insights into people that you already know as well as those you have yet to meet.

For the purpose of our profile, we have selected two of Dr. Mc-Clelland's primary response attributes: power and affiliation. High-power individuals tend to dominate social situations and take the lead in any

Figure 14-1 Psychological Grid

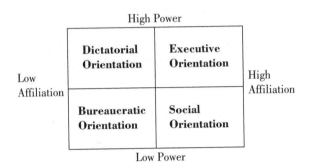

group. Low-power individuals are just the opposite and tend to follow and avoid taking the lead. High-affiliation individuals have a strong need to work and be near others. They tend to be warm, friendly, people oriented, and cooperative. As with power, low-affiliation individuals are also the opposite of high, tending to be more self-centered and withdrawn. They don't cooperate well and may even be hostile.

By combining these two attributes on a grid, it is possible to divide people into groups according to their behavior and underlying needs. Understanding these underlying needs can help you to understand their buying behavior, as well. Figure 14-1 is an example of such a grid and four types of personalities that might result. They are executive, social, bureaucratic, and dictatorial.

THE EXECUTIVE-ORIENTED PERSON AS CUSTOMER/PROSPECT

The *executive-oriented person* is an individual who is an independent thinker, respectful of others feelings and opinions, as well as one who makes up her own mind. A natural leader in any group, she is social, polite, and friendly, but not insincerely so. When necessary, she is able to set limits on herself and others. Because she is affiliation as well as power oriented, the friendliness and warmth of the executive's high power/dominant behavior causes many of her actions to be labeled as assertive, rather than aggressive, by others. Hence, she thinks, "I'm OK, you're OK." Note: In a sense, executive-oriented people really represent something of an extreme, since everyone demonstrates all four tendencies (executive, social, bureaucratic, and dictatorial), depending upon the context.

In many ways, the executive-type person represents the ideal customer. These individuals expect you to understand them, to meet their needs, and to communicate effectively to them just how you will meet those needs. In terms of receptivity, they are willing to listen and are open to new ideas, but will tend to be impatient with "hype." Do everything possible to involve them in the decision-making process while using open-ended questions to determine their needs and simple paraphrasing to verify your understanding.

Be assertive and guide them through the presentation of the product or service you feel will best help them to achieve their financial goal, but do not attempt to oversell or manipulate. They will respond to respect and will return it, with loyalty. Executives are goal oriented and can make decisions.

General Guidelines

Always emphasize the end benefits of their decisions by showing how your product or service will help them to achieve their financial goals. Demonstrate how the features of the solution you have selected correspond to the parameters of their problem. Involve them to the point that the decision that they make is always an "informed decision." For example,

> *You:* "Mrs. Brown, this XYZ stock is both investment grade (meeting your requirements for high quality) and is expected to grow at a rate of 12 percent per year over the next five years (which exceeds your requirement of 8 percent growth). What do you think?"

THE SOCIALLY ORIENTED PERSON AS CUSTOMER/PROSPECT

The *socially oriented person* is an individual who is always "hanging out with the crowd." He bases his sense of self-worth on other people's reactions and perceptions of him. Hence, he is eager to please, and may even appear as a "social butterfly." He is very talkative, and tends to be very conscious of the latest fashions and trends. Because he tends to subordinate his goals to the goals or mores of the group, his is considered a reactive, or passive response. He sees the world from a "You're OK, I'm *not* OK" orientation.

This kind of prospect or customer initially appears to be ideal: he assumes that you have his interests at heart and appears to be easily maneuvered. He is warm, friendly, and easy to convince and becomes easily enthused about anything presented. He can be very talkative!

However, he also tends to have difficulty making decisions, and while he *appears* enthusiastic about a presentation, he will frequently end the conversation by saying that he needs more time (e.g., to talk it over with someone). Socially driven people will often tend to meander and socialize during your presentation and frequently have to be brought back to the subject at hand. When they do listen, they often gloss over the material presented.

General Guidelines

When working with this individual, remember his need for approbation and emphasize benefits that deal with acceptance, esteem, and security needs. Remember that he also needs to socialize. Meet this need, but do not allow it to override the purpose of the call or meeting. Firmly guide him through the presentation and be specific in your recommendations. Don't take his enthusiasm and easy acceptance at face value. Probe for underlying doubts. Finally, rely primarily on closed-ended questions (they will not encourage the meandering that an open probe might), and frequently use summary and reflective statements. This individual can be brought to closure by accentuating how your product or service will meet his needs for safety and for approval from friends and others. For example,

> *You:* "Mr. Jones, insured certificates of deposit are one of our most *popular* investments among people like yourself who are interested in achieving a good rate of return with excellent *safety*. They're very pleased with them."

THE BUREAUCRATICALLY ORIENTED AS CUSTOMER/PROSPECT

A *bureaucratically oriented person* is an individual who always "goes by the book" because "rules were made for good reasons." She rarely takes chances and does not wish to stand out from the crowd. She does not wish to be the leader, but resents whoever is. She will frequently gossip about people, but will rarely confront them to their face. If a new idea is suggested, she usually has some reason why it won't work and shouldn't even be attempted. Of course, like the socially driven person, the bureaucratic individual is an extreme representation. Hers is an "I'm *not* OK, you're *not* OK" orientation.

This customer/prospect tends to believe that investment reps are only out to sell her something she doesn't want or need. However, unlike her more aggressive counterparts, she usually demonstrates this through avoidance behavior such as silence and noncommittal responses. She speaks very little and does not make decisions well.

This individual also has a deep lack of trust and a need to be reassured. In addition, she has both a low self-image and feelings of powerlessness. As a result, she may appear to go along with a presentation but fail to make a decision, for example, by asking for more time and then by being impossible to reach for a follow-up. Where a more actively aggressive person will reject out of hand, this more passive-aggressive individual will avoid confrontation but still fail to cooperate.

General Guidelines

Remember her security needs and stress benefits that will meet them. Don't push. Go slowly and be patient. Take the time to communicate your genuine interest and establish the trust she seeks. It is important to guide her firmly but gently. Draw out her feelings with open probes, pauses, and brief assertions of interest on your part. Emphasize that what you are recommending is the traditional, accepted, prudent solution to her financial need. For example,

> *You:* "Ms. Samuels, a municipal bond is one of the most conservative investments available to meet your need for tax-free income and has traditionally been the method of choice selected to solve this kind of problem."

THE DICTATORIALLY ORIENTED PERSON AS CUSTOMER/PROSPECT

A *dictatorially oriented person* is an individual who is very dogmatic and always has to be right. When he is wrong, he tries to bully his way through, often at the "top of his lungs." He always wants to be in control, and is often contemptuous of others. His three most frequently used words are "I," "me," and "myself." His hostile and unresponsive nature causes many of the dictatorial person's actions to be labeled as aggressive (often with negative connotations). He feels that "I'm OK, you're *not* OK."

This kind of prospect/customer can be very difficult to deal with because he tends to believe that all brokers are corrupt and are interested only in making money, even at their customer's expense. He will often tend to make flat assertions, be sarcastic, argue, and interrupt. He does this because he has strong security and esteem needs and maintains both by trying to keep in control. He is most easily handled by acting assertive but friendly.

Whenever he resists or becomes hostile, you should communicate your desire to understand and your willingness to listen, and to meet his needs (use the "CLAPing" technique discussed earlier). As you successfully communicate your sincere interest in him, his behavior will frequently change from being hostile and aggressive to assertive and less defensive, if not actually warm. It should be remembered that this individual has a strong *need* to trust but fears that he will be "burned" again. How long it takes to win his trust will vary with the customer (and some will never trust a broker). But, once their trust is won, these customers will frequently become the most loyal and the easiest to work with. Once won, another good thing about these customers is that they can and will make decisions.

General Guidelines

Stress the aspects of your product or service that will both meet their financial need and enhance their self-esteem and independence. They need to feel that they are different from, and therefore superior to, others. For example,

> *You:* "Ms. Jones, we are *only showing* this investment opportunity to those *few* of our clients whom we feel have the *investment experience* to really benefit from what it will provide."

When a dictator is upset, let him get it out, then use a series of summary/verification probes to make sure you are on track (CLAP). At first, he may actually appear to escalate his hostility and aggressiveness. However, if you stick with them, that aggressive hostility will peak and drop off to nothing. At this point, dictators often turn into socialites who will take your advice and who can make decisions.

Always be sure you have dealt with the *dictator's* opinions and concerns before bringing your own up, or he will not hear you. Don't let him upset you. Stick to your guns and don't let him overwhelm you. Frequently these individuals really want someone they can depend upon to be in charge. If you cave in, they won't believe in your ability to help protect them from their own bad decisions. To increase understanding and strengthen the relationship, make use of open and summary probes.

Each of us has needs for power, affiliation and achievement. By focusing on a customer's behavior we can easily recognize the relative importance of power and affiliation in their lives and the hidden emotional agendas that affect their buying decisions. Using these needs for power and affiliation (as the two drives which most affect our relationships with others) we have established a personality grid.

Remember that almost no one is a pure executive, socialite, bureaucrat, or dictator all the time. In fact, not only does each of us demonstrate the traits of these four personality types some of the time, it is appropriate to do so. For example, the most effective way to deal with most clients when making decisions is as an executive, personally unswayed by hidden emotional needs. However, when learning a new skill (such as driving or selling derivative products), the by-the-book mentality of the bureaucrat might be safest. When returning home from work to your family, the strong need acceptance and the ability to avoid difficult decisions for a few hours might best be seen in the socialite. Even the personality of a dictator can be very appropriate when one is threatened, such as a soldier in combat. The point to remember is that the personality we show often changes with the context of the situation. Thus, a client who acted like a dictator yesterday may act like an executive today. Deal with each client based upon how they are acting, now, not how they have acted in the past.

15

Putting It All Together— The Profiling Meeting

During the last few chapters we have introduced just some of the information you can obtain during a formal profiling meeting or even just casual conversation if you ask the right questions and listen carefully to your prospect's or customer's answers. In this chapter, we will present an example of a profiling meeting and highlight the information provided by the customer. We have also provided a summary of the prospecting track. During the profiling interview, your questions referring to the track will be italicized,

Step 1: Establish rapport with your prospect/customer and place him or her at ease.

Step 2: Discover customer's needs/goals/problems (e.g., children's/-grandchildren's college, retirement, etc.). Be *concrete* (e.g., Harvard or William and Mary, where specifically do they wish to retire).

Step 3: Prioritize customer needs/goals.

Step 4: Determine the parameters of *each* need/goal. That is,
How much time is needed to reach the goal (e.g., how many years before they retire or before each child reaches college age)?
How much money will they need to achieve their goal (what will the tuition be at Harvard when their children arrive, or how

much money—in today's dollars—will they need to live on when they retire, etc.)?

What steps have they already taken; that is, what investments have they already made with this specific need/goal in mind? *How much do they want to commit to solving this problem*/achieving this goal *at this time?* Do they expect to make additional investments for this goal? When? How much?

Determine their risk tolerance by educating them about the types of financial risks they face regardless of what choice they make (theft, interest rate risk, loss of buying power/inflation, market risk, economic risk, etc.)? With which risk are they most comfortable? How comfortable? Are there any investments they specifically wish to avoid? Why?

Step 5: Once you have established the parameters of each goal/need with the customer, ask if they have any other investments, assets, income, or liabilities—or expect to receive any in the future—that might affect their ability to obtain their goals.

Step 6: Ask for permission to review each of the goals and the parameters of each goal before suggesting any solutions so you can make certain that whatever you suggest will be appropriate. Then review them.

Step 7: Establish an appointment to call or meet again to present/discuss possible solutions to their needs/goals. Then find a solution. Sometimes a client may want an immediate solution to a need. If this occurs, suggest an appropriate one before they leave. At the very least, fill out the paperwork to open a checking account if they do not already have one. Otherwise, thank them for their time and give them a copy of the goals and parameters you have established together. Include your card.

We will begin at the point following your introduction and have asked your customer to sit down. As you read the dialogue, you will explore the parameters of his financial goals and presell the next two sales presentations. You will also note clues provided by the client regarding his sensory orientation, buying motivations, personal strategies, and psychological profile as well as the meaning of several key words that have special significance to this client.

You: "Mr. Jones, how can I help you, today?"

Client: "I'm *looking* for something that will give me a *better rate of return than my CDs.* My neighbor was *telling* me about a mutual fund he has that seems to be doing very well. Do you sell mutual funds? (Too early to tell what his sensory orientation is yet.)

You: "Yes, sir. We offer a wide variety of excellent mutual funds. *Before we go into too much detail on specific funds, may I ask what you want your investment to do for you?*"

Client: "I already *told* you. I want to make *more than I'm getting from my CDs*, right now."

You: "I understand that, sir. What I mean is, *what do you want your money to grow for? What are your financial goals?* For example, some people invest for retirement, or their children's education, or a new boat. What are you investing for? My job is not just to sell you a mutual fund or some other financial product. It is to help you obtain your financial goals. To do that, we first have to determine what those goals are and then understand them together. That's why I asked about your specific goals." (Begin to establish that you are a helping professional rather than just another salesperson.)

Client: "I see. That's kind of personal isn't it?"

You: "Yes, sir. It is. However, while there are thousands of great investment opportunities available, they won't all be good for you. Among other things, the nature of your goal will help determine whether or not your friend's mutual fund will be as good for you as it has been for him."

Client: "Uh huh. Well, I want to make sure my retirement is *safe*, and I want to *see* my children go to college."

You: "That's great. *Excuse me, would you mind if I took some notes while we talk. Your answers are important and I don't want to risk forgetting anything. When we're done, I'll give you a copy. Will that be all right?*" (Get permission to take notes.)

Client: "Sure."

You: "*Do you have any other goals?*"

Client: "I've been thinking about getting a sailboat someday. But I want to make sure that these other goals are taken care of first."

You: "I understand. You mentioned retirement and college for the children. Of the two, which is the greater concern at this time?"

Client: "I'd *say* the children's college."

Note: So far, the customer has given you several pieces of valuable information: (1) he is predominantly *visual* and *auditory* in his sensory orientation; (2) *safety* and a *better rate of return than current CDs* are important to him; and (3) he has three goals, in order of importance, *kids' college*, *retirement*, and a *sailboat*.

You: "Very good. *May I ask a few questions about your plans for the children? It will help us to determine how much money you'll need when its time for them to enter college?*"

Client: "What kind of questions?"

You: "Well, *how many children do you have and what are their ages? Have you an idea of what school you want them to attend?* Things like that." (Make his goal as concrete and real as possible.)

Client: "Oh, all right. We have two children: Carol and Billy. Carol is four and Billy is two."

You: "That's great! *Have you thought about where you'd like them to attend?* Your alma mater, perhaps."

Client: "I don't know. I haven't thought too much about it. I guess I'd like to *see* them go to my old college. But what difference does it make?"

You: "Knowing the school, or at least the type of school, you think they might attend will give us an idea of the costs you'll face when they get there. For example, by the time Carol is old enough to attend, some state schools are expected to cost nearly $30,000 per year, while some private schools may cost three times that. Once we know the type of school and when your children should be attending, we'll automatically know how much you'll need and how long we have to obtain it." (Part of your job is to educate your client about their goals. The profiling meeting often provides an excellent opportunity to demonstrate your professionalism by doing just that.)

Client: "That's interesting. I went to Tufts University, in Boston. I'd like them to go there if its possible."

You: "That's fine. Currently, if Tufts is like most high-end private schools; it costs about $26,000 per year for tuition and other expenses. At the current rate that college expenses have been growing, I would expect them to cost about $53,000 per year when Carol attends and about $55,000 per year when her brother enters. That means we'll need about $215,000 for Carol and $230,000 for Billy if you pay all their expenses. If you like, I'll call the school this afternoon and verify what they expect the cost to be at that time to make sure that our estimate is accurate."

Client: "That's a lot of money."

You: "It sounds as though the figures I've quoted may be higher than you expected. Is that right?"

Client: "Yes. I had no idea it would be so expensive. Did you say a state school would be less than half that cost?"

You: "Yes. Many state schools will be less than half, for residents of the state. *May I ask what steps you have already taken toward providing for the children's education?*"

Client: "Not much. I bought a $10,000 CD for each when they were born."

You: "I see. *Anything else?*"

Client: "Yes. Their grandmother gave each child $5,000 last year. We used the money to buy shares in the XYZ Conservative Growth Fund. Right now, they're each worth about $5,400."

You: "That looks like a good start. *Do you mind if I ask, what made you select the particular CD you chose.*"

Client: "Certainly. I was concerned about *safety*. I worked hard for that money, and *I didn't want to risk losing the money*."

You: "That makes sense. Anything else?"

Client: "I like the bank where I bought it. They've always given me *good service*, and they're *one of the oldest and best known banks in the area*. My family has *used them for four generations*."

You: "Anything else?"

Client: "*I didn't want to risk the stock market*. I lost some money in the crash in 1987 and I didn't trust stocks."

You: "I see. *It looks as though safety is really important to you. Is that right?*"

Client: "Yes."

You: "I can understand that. *What did you see in the XYZ Conservative Growth Fund that encouraged you to invest in them?*"

Client: "Several things. They've been *written up in Money Magazine* as a fund that was *conservative*, yet performed well. Also, because, they invested in a large number of stocks, *I don't have to worry whether I picked the right stock*. They're also *one of the oldest funds on the market* and *have performed well for their entire 30-plus year history*."

You: "*Anything else?*"

Client: "Yes. They only invest in blue-chip stocks and government backed short-term bonds. That should help me *avoid problems*. Also, when I called the fund, they gave me *good service* and answered all my questions."

Note: While explaining why he chose his two investments, your customer has also told you important information that you will need to emphasize when selecting and presenting investments to help him reach his goals: (1) His key buying criteria appear to be *safety, quality, service,* and *name recognition (Money Magazine)* and *a traditional approach* (the bank has been there a long time and his family has used it for four generations, and the mutual fund is old, established and has a long, positive history), and (2) one of his personal strategies is to *avoid problems* (to move away from difficulty). His tendency to seek safety, a traditional approach to things, and to avoid problems, as well as his apparent suspicion about the questions being asked, would appear to indicate certain *bureaucratic* tendencies. However, he is cooperating and is also providing more information than an extremely bureaucratic person might.

You: "Thank you. It sounds as though you've made some very wise investment decisions. One of the things I'm required to talk to you about is investment risk. I'm sure you're aware that there is some risk involved no matter what you do with your money, from leaving it in your safe deposit box at the bank to investing in wheat futures." (To adequately determine a customer's risk tolerance, you will often have to first educate him about risk. Otherwise, they may tell you one thing and mean another.)

Client: "What do you mean?"

You: "Well, look at it this way. If you put your money in a safety deposit box, you risk losing buying power as inflation eats away at it each year. For example, what cost $1.00 in 1950, now costs over $5.00. That's inflation. However, if you invest in a stock and the company has problems, its value could go down. That's called risk of selection. One way to handle that is to buy several different securities in different industries. Thus, if one goes down, its loss may be offset by gains in other areas. That way, we avoid putting all your eggs in one basket. There is also market and interest rate risk. If the whole market goes down, the way it did in 1987, you could lose money if you have to sell at that time. However, if you can wait, you'll notice that the market has more than recovered its former value since then. If interest rate go up significantly, and you have to sell a CD or even a federal bond, you could lose some of your principal as well. The question is, with which kind of risk are you most comfortable and how much can you handle?"

Client: "I want my money to be *as safe as possible. I don't want to lose my principal*, but *I don't want to get killed by inflation*, either. I'm willing to take a *little risk* in the short run if I can see success in the end."

You: "*I'm not sure what you mean by a 'little' risk, Mr. Jones. Let me give you an example.* While good stocks tend to rise long term, in unusual circumstances, even the best individual stock can move up or down by as much as 10 percent in an average day. That means if you bought a stock today for $50.00 per share, tomorrow it might be as high as $55.00 or as low as $45.00 per share, and the next day be back to $52.00 per share. Could you handle that kind of price change?"

Client: "I don't know."

You: "Let me give you another example. If you bought a 20-year government-backed, zero coupon bond today (government backed should be the safest possible) and the interest rate rose just one percentage point, your bond would decline 20 percent. Remember, interest rates have already gone up two percentage points in the last year."

Client: "That's terrible! It *sounds* as though nothing is safe. What can I do?"

You: "As I mentioned before, every investment decision has some risk. The question we need to answer is, with which risk are you most comfortable? For the last fifteen years, college tuition rates have been growing at least two to three times as fast as inflation and that trend is expected to continue. At the same time, the after-tax return on most short-term bonds and CDs has been below the rate of inflation. That means that you must either invest a substantial amount of money or select investments that can grow as quickly as you need them to."

Client: "What kind of investments might do that?"

You: "There are several. For example, you already own a mutual fund that is doing just that. There are also variable annuities, and several other possibilities I'd like to look into. *Have you been comfortable with the performance of your current mutual fund?*"

Client: "Yes. It went down a little at one point, but its done well over the last 30 years and I think it will be okay in the long run."

You: "*Then you would be comfortable with other investments that had the same level and type of risks as a high-quality mutual fund?*"

Client: "Yes." (At this point, you have established a working definition of this clients risk tolerance *for this goal.*)

You: "That's great. Have you considered *how much you would like to invest toward your children's college at this time?*"

Client: "I was thinking about another $10,000 each."

You: "That sounds fine. *Will you be making additional investments in the future for their education?*"

Client: "I was thinking about another $5,000 per year each until they reach school. But now I'm not sure whether that will be enough. If necessary, I can go up to $10,000 per year each."

You: "That's fine. Let me look into this, and I'll get back to you this afternoon or tomorrow with a recommendation for investing for the children's college. Would that be all right?"

Client: "That's fine."

You: "You also mentioned that retirement was an important investment goal. *Have you determined when you want to retire?*"

Client: "I'm 37 right now. I'd like to retire in 25 years, when I'm 62."

You: "Great! Have you thought much about the life-style you would like to enjoy when you're retired?"

Client: "About the same as we have now, only with more travel."

You: "That's interesting. *Have you decided where you'd like to live?* For instance, Florida or Southern California?" (Make their goal as concrete as possible.)

Client: "We'll probably stay here. Our friends are here and we like the area. I designed our house myself and I don't want to think about selling it and moving. At least, not now."

You: "In today's dollars, about how much income would you need to maintain that life-style after retirement? Remember, we assume that your mortgage will be paid off by then and your children out of college. A good rule of thumb is to assume that you will need about two-thirds of what you do now."

Client: "With the house, and the children's education paid for, I'd say we could do very well on about $100,000 per year."

You: "That's fine. What *steps have you already taken to prepare for your retirement?"*

Client: "I have a 401-K plan at work that is currently worth about $340,000. Each year, $30,000 of my salary is automatically placed there. I also have a fixed annuity, currently worth $76,000, growing at a rate of 6 percent. And I have an IRA with another $17,000 in five-year CDs paying 6 percent.

You: "It looks as though you've already made a good start on your retirement goal. *What do you like about your 401 plan?"*

Client: "Several things. *Unlike my other investments, the company matches my donations.* I can also have my *deposits deducted automatically* from my paycheck, without having to miss them. The managers of the plan are an *old, established firm with a long tradition* of solid, conservative growth. In fact, they haven't had a down year in the 45 years they've been in business. They *only buy the highest-quality investments* for the plan."

Note: Your customer has again emphasized tradition, quality, and convenience/service as key criteria when making a buying decision.

You: "That sounds great. *What about your annuity? What do you like about them?"*

Client: "The annuity is *guaranteed* by the insurance company, so I know it's *safe.* It also pays a *rate* that is consistent with those offered on five-year CDs, and the rate is supposed to be adjusted each year to track changes in interest rates in the market, so *I won't lose* if rates rise dramatically. I also like the *tax-deferred* return. That's *one less thing to worry about each year."*

You: "So, basically, you like the safety, convenience, and good tax-deferred return of both investments. Is that right?" (Periodically check to make sure that you have correctly understood his buying criteria.)

Client: "That's right."

You: "What rate of return have you been getting in your 401 plan?"

Client: "About 11 percent."

You: "You mentioned that you have $17,000 worth of five-year CDs in your IRA. When do they mature?"

Client: "At different times. Half will mature this April and the other half, next April."

You: "What made you select CDs rather than something else for you IRA?"

Client: "When I started, CDs were all the bank had available to place in an IRA. Also, the *rates were pretty good* then, and they were *guaranteed.*"

You: "Would you prefer to continue with CDs or, with rates so low, would you rather consider something with a higher rate of return?"

Client: "I don't know. Considering the rate of inflation, I'm not happy with the current *rate* I'm getting. On the other hand, the *principal is guaranteed.* Why don't you *take a look* and *see* if you can find something for me that is *as safe as possible* that gets a *higher rate* of return and *we'll see* about it."

You: "All right. I'll look into it and get back to you later this week, after we've made some progress on the children's educational fund. *What kind and level of risk are you prepared to deal with for your retirement funding? The same as for the children's education?*"

Client: "At least that safe."

You: "*Are you considering making an investment toward your retirement at this time?*"

Client: "Not outside those I've already mentioned. However, I'll get my bonus in a few months, and depending upon what we decide about the children's education, I may put some of it into retirement, then. Otherwise, most of it will go to the kids tuition and that boat I mentioned."

Note: Your client has given you all the initial information you need to help him. You now need to examine alternatives for the CDs in his IRA and review his retirement plans to determine what if any additional steps he will need to take beyond those he is currently taking. Computer software programs are available that you can use to analyze his plan. In addition, your own firm probably has one that it prefers to use.

> *You:* "Let me take this information and run it through the experts in our retirement department, and I'll get back to you by the end of the week with their analysis. Its possible that your current plan will be enough, and if not, they can give you an idea of how much more you'll need to put in to reach your goal. Would that be all right?"
>
> *Client:* "That would be fine."
>
> *You:* "*What kind of a boat are you looking for? Have you picked it out?*"

Client: "Yes. Its a 35-foot, two-masted ketch that sleeps six. Its gorgeous!"

You: "Wow! I can just see you sailing it now. Are you planning on doing any ocean sailing, or will you limit it pretty much to the Great Lakes?" (Make the goal concrete.)

Client: "I haven't decided yet. Mostly the lakes, at first. With their sudden squalls, they can be just as dangerous as any ocean."

You: "That's true. *May I ask how much the boat will cost?*"

Client: "The one I'm looking at will go for about $180,000."

You: "That sounds pretty good. *What steps have you taken so far to obtain it?*"

Client: "I've put about $10,000 a year from my bonus money into a CD each year for the last eight years. If things go well enough this year, I should be able to double that. Right now, the total is around $111,000."

You: "Have considered using some or all of your current savings as a down payment on the boat and taking out a loan for the remainder?"

Client: "Yes I have. While I wouldn't rule that out, entirely, these savings have also provided a handy emergency fund. If I spend them all on the boat and something happens, I won't have any backup."

You: "So, you're saying you might consider a loan, but only if it doesn't leave you without protection. Is that right?"

Client: "Yes. Are you recommending a loan, now?"

You: "No. I'm just exploring possible solutions to your needs. Until I've examined your entire financial picture, I won't know whether a loan is really a good or bad idea. If I understand you correctly, you won't be making any new investments into your boat until you get your bonus. Is that right?"

Client: "Yes."

You: "You mentioned that all of the money for the boat is currently in CDs. What made you choose CDs?"

Client: "Safety and convenience. However, I might be will to consider a conservative mutual fund for half that money, if it will help me get the boat faster. The rest should still stay as an emergency fund."

You: "Thank you. *Do you have any other investments, assets, or liabilities that might affect our ability to achieve these goals? Perhaps other sources of income, or savings accounts, and so on?*"

Client: "My wife also works. Our combined salaries are $210,000 per year. In addition, she also has a retirement plan at work and an IRA, and we own a summer home on the lake outright. It was given to us by her parents when we got married. We have about $15,000 in checking and savings beyond the money I said we wanted to invest for the children's education. The only debt we have is the mortgage on our house—about $200,000 on a $450,000 house."

You: "Wonderful! Do you have adequate life insurance coverage for both you and your spouse, should anything happen to either or both of you?"

Client: "I think so. We have $500,000 coverage on each of us. Half in whole life and half in term."

You: "That sounds like a good start. Listen, we don't sell life insurance. But, if you like, I'll be happy to have our experts analyze your situation and let you know whether you should consider getting more. If you need more, you can just use your own agent. Would you like me to do that?"

Client: "What would that cost?"

You: "Nothing. Before we can help you achieve your financial goals, we have to understand both the goals and your overall financial picture. Then we can work together to help you get what you want."

Client: "That sounds great!"

You: "Let me make a quick copy of my notes for you. Then, I'd like to take just a moment to review them with you to make sure they're accurate. Is that all right?" (Give the original copy of your notes to your client. It's personal and it represents an informal, mental contract between you to work together to obtain his goals.)

Client: "Yes. That would be fine."

You: "You mentioned that you have three goals: kids' college, retirement, and a new boat. Is that right?"

Client: "Yes."

You: "You have two children, Caroline and Billy who you would like to attend your alma mater in 14 and 16 years, respectively. Right?"

Client: "Yes."

You: "You would like them to attend Tufts, and the expected total cost will be in the neighborhood of $445,000. Right?"

Client: "Yes."

You: "At this time, you'd like to invest $10,000 for each child, in something that gets a better rate of return that a CD but which is very safe. For instance, like the high-quality mutual fund you own. Is that right?"

Client: "Yes."

You: "That's great! I'll call you this afternoon or tomorrow with a recommendation. All right?"

Client: "Yes."

Note: Your client has just accepted you as the professional upon whom he will rely for help in solving his children's educational goal. He has just committed to accept anything you call with that matches or exceeds the parameters you have just agreed upon.

You: "Now, your second goal is to retire, here, in 25 years with an income equivalent of $110,000 per year in today's dollars. Is that right?"

Client: "Yes."

You: "You already have an annuity, a 401 plan, and an IRA and are not planning on making additional contributions toward your retirement until you get your bonus. But you would like to look at an alternative to the CDs in your IRA. Right?"

Client: "Yes."

You: "Preferably something as safe as the conservative mutual fund you already own. Right?"

Client: "Yes."

You: Good. I'll also have our retirement specialist review the information you've given me and give you their analysis. Would it be possible for your wife to call or stop by with her retirement information to complete the picture?

Client: "I'll ask her to call this afternoon. I know she wanted to get this organized."

You: "That will work out fine. If she calls this afternoon, I'm sure I can have something for you by Friday. If we could meet then, I could go over our analysis then and also make any recommendations regarding the CDs in your IRA and your insurance coverage at the same time. How does that sound?"

Client: "That will be fine."

Note: Again, you have committed your client to working with *you* to achieve these goals.

You: "And, last but not least, we have your ketch. Thirty-five feet, two masted, and sleeps six. Right?"

Client: "Yes."

You: "It will cost about $180,000, of which you have $111,000 now in CDs. Right?"

Client: "Yes."

You: "Depending upon our analysis of your children's educational and your retirement needs, you will probably add additional funds when you get your bonus. Right?"

Client: "That's right."

You: "Right now, you would consider moving half of it into a high-quality mutual fund, but want to keep the other half in CDs where they can act as an emergency fund until you actually get the boat. Right?"

Client: "Yes."

You: "Sounds as if we're okay so far. Have we missed anything you feel I should know that might affect our ability to achieve these goals?"

Client: "No. That's everything."

You: "That's great! Then I'll look forward to hearing from your wife this afternoon with her retirement information, and I'll get back to you with a suggestion about the boat CDs after we've discussed the children's college and reviewed our analysis of your retirement plans. Would that be all right?"

Client: "That would be great! Thanks for all your help!"

You: "Its been my pleasure. I'll see you and your wife on Friday. Would 6 o'clock be a good time?"

Client: "It's fine for me. I'll ask her and she can tell you if she has a conflict when she calls this afternoon. Thanks again. I'll see you Friday."

In this interview you were able to obtain not only the information you needed to help your client, but also information about the way he thinks, makes decisions, and handles information that will be important when you make your sales presentation to him. Just as important, you have also established yourself as a competent, helping, financial professional, instead of as just one more "get-rich-quick" stock jockey. Finally, you have provided your client with a graphic summary of his goals and current financial picture and committed him to working with you to achieve those goals. Imagine how much easier your sales presentations will be!

V

THE SALES PROCESS

This section likens the sales process to an athletic event that has six distinct phases. First, we prepare ourselves through some type of mental and/or physical practice. We put our best foot forward, begin our winning strategy at the start of the event, go forward or progress through the event, dealing with any challenges or hurdles that may arise (they're part of the game), to cross the finish line or finish the event. Of course, to continue to excel in the future, we analyze our performance and learn from what we did right and what areas for improvement. It is through this process of preparation, doing our best, and self-analysis that continuous improvement can occur and a person can become an Olympian.

TELEPHONE OR FACE-TO-FACE PRESENTATIONS

Some financial consultants prefer to sell by telephone, while others prefer to sell in person. Both work. Each has advantages and disadvantages. The consultative sales process previously described works in both situations. If your manager, or the nature of your relationship with your clients requires you to sell in a specific way, please continue. However, if they do not, examine the following comparison of telephone versus in-person selling:

SELLING BY PHONE VERSUS SELLING IN PERSON

- Selling by phone is more efficient. It can save you time (you can frequently make up to ten telephone sales in the time it would take to make one in-person sales call), travel, and expense.

- Telephone sales are convenient. You can make the sale from any location that has a telephone. In addition, if you are calling from your office, you may have additional data available to answer your client's questions. If you are in his office, you must rely upon what you've brought with you.

- In-person sales are more personal. Whether in your office, or your client's, your bank branch, or the client's home, they enable you to use all of your rapport building and selling skills.

- If your product is complex, or must be demonstrated (e.g. certain forms of insurance and financial plans), or if you plan to make several recommendations at once, it's usually best to make the presentation face to face. Note: The exception is if your client already has experience with the product and wants additional units.

- Some markets are such that you must sell in person to maintain your client base, for example, most insurance. Also, in some countries, securities can only be sold in person.

- Even if you sell in person, always call first, to make an appointment. In addition to being courteous, it guarantees that your client will be there and ready to listen when you arrive.

THE BASIC SALES TRACK

Regardless of whether you make in-person or telephone presentations, the sales call will follow the same basic steps: These traditional four steps are further broken down and expanded within our sales track.

- *Opening*: Here, you set the stage for the presentation by reviewing your customer's need and verifying both your understanding of the situation as well as their desire to solve that need, problem or desire. The opening sequence has three distinct steps:

  Bridge to the previous contact and remind customer of their need.
  Inform them that you have a solution.
  Probe for continued interest.

- *Body of the presentation*: Here, you provide the solution to the customer's problem and explain the appropriate features, advantages, and benefits of the product or service.

  Fortunately, by the time you make your sales presentation, you will have already discovered the customer's buying motivations, his or her key criteria, his or her preference for level of detail, as well as his or her level sophistication during the profiling interview. You will also have already established rapport, which will help ensure that they will carefully listen to your suggestions.

- *Getting commitment/getting the order/closing*: Since your product or service has features that will fulfill the customer's needs and objec-

Figure V-1 The Consultative Sales Track

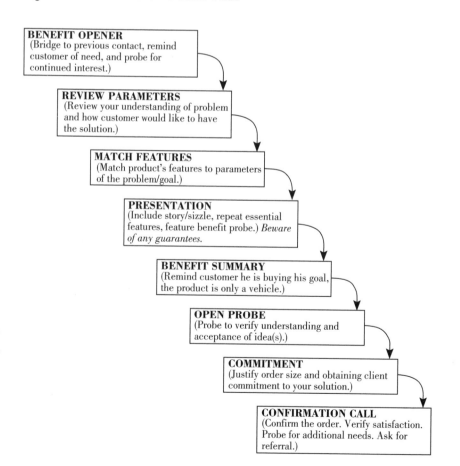

BENEFIT OPENER
(Bridge to previous contact, remind customer of need, and probe for continued interest.)

REVIEW PARAMETERS
(Review your understanding of problem and how customer would like to have the solution.)

MATCH FEATURES
(Match product's features to parameters of the problem/goal.)

PRESENTATION
(Include story/sizzle, repeat essential features, feature benefit probe.) *Beware of any guarantees.*

BENEFIT SUMMARY
(Remind customer he is buying his goal, the product is only a vehicle.)

OPEN PROBE
(Probe to verify understanding and acceptance of idea(s).)

COMMITMENT
(Justify order size and obtaining client commitment to your solution.)

CONFIRMATION CALL
(Confirm the order. Verify satisfaction. Probe for additional needs. Ask for referral.)

tives, this segment of the process can be as simple as offering a customer the product and allowing him or her to buy. However, it is at this point in the sales process that any previously unstated concerns, issues, and objections come up. You'll deal with these issues most effectively by realizing that the customer is merely letting you know what he or she still needs to hear or understand before a buying decision can be made. Essentially, you are learning where you must go for the next step in the process.

- *Follow-up*: This segment includes everything you must do after the sale, including making a confirmation call, answering additional questions, providing service, and getting referrals from the customer so you can expand your business.

Each of these points is further expanded and explained in our sales track, or ideal selling sequence. An overview of the model is provided in Figure V-1 so you can see the logical flow of events. Each of the segments will be explained in greater detail in the following chapters.

CHAPTER

16

Getting Ready
Planning the Sales Call

The next few paragraphs discuss an extremely important aspect of sales. Although it is vital to success, very few brokers give it the attention it deserves. "It" is *preparation.* The vast majority of managers and top producers whom we've polled tell us that planning was an important factor for success.

The statement "People don't plan to fail, they fail to plan" is true in most life situations. It is especially true in sales. While many people become involved in sales at some time in their career, relatively few continue with selling, and fewer still rise to the highest levels of production to become leading producers. Relatively few people pay the "price for success."

Success does have a price in terms of the dedication, preparation, and perspiration that are required to achieve the highest levels of accomplishment.

If you only knew how hard I worked, you wouldn't call me a genius.

Michelangelo

Many brokers try to do everything "off the top of their heads." They barely learn about a product before trying to sell it. Then, rather than striving to constantly improve their presentations and upgrade their knowledge—as one would in almost any other field—they continue to do the same

213

old thing, or convince themselves that they are "naturals" with an intuitive "gift" for sales. Usually these people either drop out of the business or achieve total mediocrity.

SETTING YOURSELF APART FROM YOUR COMPETITION

Unless you have the extremely good fortune of "being the only game in town"—that is, the only investment representative in your particular geographic area—you will have competition. Regardless of your products or services, some competitor will claim to have a better financial product or package at a better price. They will claim to have the best research, advice, execution capability, and so on. Even if your product or service is of equal or better value, you still must actively compete by convincing your prospects and clients to deal with your firm.

Remember: People deal with you and have to trust your abilities. This is especially true if there is the potential of multiple sales—over time or with many products—as will be true for most of your clients. Whenever you are involved in multiple sales, your customer will begin to rely on your judgment, advice, and competence as you deepen your relationship with him. Remember, you are the professional in your field, and your customer will often rely on your knowledge and expertise in the same way he would an attorney or any other professional. In addition, your professionalism will help the reputation of your company and will often provide numerous referral possibilities. *It all boils down to people wanting to deal with someone they can trust.*

It is important for you be able to compare and contrast your product/service with that of your competition. You should know the different features, benefits and advantages of each product. Additionally, you should be able to explain any price, value, and service differences. (When conducting our sales workshops at various firms we are often surprised at how few brokers are able to really differentiate themselves from the competition in other than vague terms.) By identifying the "value that you and your firm brings to the table," you can more effectively stand apart from the competitive crowd.

Each of us places different values on items and we are all motivated by our personal criteria. Hence, what is important to one customer may not be important to another. Surprisingly, *for most people, price is not the key determining factor.* Industry surveys consistently indicated that many people will pay a higher commission or fee if they believe they are getting a better quality product or better service, or if they have a friendly relationship with the sales professional—most people don't go to a discount doctor. While many people do make their own investment decisions and may choose a discount broker, you may still be able work with portions of their overall assets if you demonstrate professionalism and value added.

HOW TO PREPARE AN EFFECTIVE SALES PRESENTATION

The best way to do this is to think of the ideal wording to persuade someone, using the most effective wording you can. After writing your script, practice it a few times. After you've become familiar with the ideal wording, you can throw the script away and concentrate on your customer. This type of preparation allows you to spend your time actually listening to the customer and mentally planning ahead rather than trying to figure out what you're going to say next.

"I don't want my presentation to sound canned," is a common comment from people when they first hear this idea. "Rehearsing something wouldn't let me be natural" is another one. While these are valid concerns, think about some movie or television actors and actresses—ones that are really good. They sound perfectly relaxed and natural even though they are "scripted"—even to the raising of their eyebrows! Their speeches sound natural because they were rehearsed and because those actors and actresses spent hundreds of hours practicing their communication/acting skills. Their careers depend upon their ability to effectively communicate —their characters, the appropriate emotions, the essential meanings of the script. Everything they do is an attempt to communicate. Even though they extensively rehearse, they sound natural. *They sound natural and are effective because they rehearse.*

Preplanning and prerehearsing are the best way to ensure your success.

WORDS THAT SELL—POWER WORDS

Words are powerful tools and can invoke various intellectual or emotional reactions. They are important to consultative selling because your word choice may invoke positive or negative, unconscious reactions. Certain commonly used words can actually the customer to back away. For example, a salesperson saying "I want to sell you something" may cause you to mentally grab your wallet and protect your money because you know that they want your money. "I have something that will meet your needs" puts you in a different mind set. Listed below are words that "sell" and words that "unsell."

Words That Sell = Words to Employ

Understand	Proven	Health	Easy
~~Guarantee~~*	Money	Safety	Save
New	Love	Discovery	Right
Results	Truth	Comfort	Proud
Profit	Deserve	Happy	Trust
Value	Fun	Vital	You
Security	Advantage	Positive	Benefits

*A dangerous word in the financial services industry. Use with extreme caution, or eliminate, as we did, entirely.

Words That Unsell = Words to Avoid

Deal	Cost	Pay	Contract
Sign	Try	Worry	Loss
Lose	Hurt	Buy	Death
Bad	Sell	Sold	Price
Decision	Hard	Difficult	Obligation
Liable	Fail	Liability	Failure

THE CONSULTATIVE SALES TRACK

Our suggested presentation format is actually more comprehensive than others. It expands the four basic areas of opener, body, commitment, and follow-up into eight discrete steps and increases the overall effectiveness of the presentation. *These eight steps are introduced here and will become the focus of the next five chapters.* Our recommended sales approach appears in Figure 16-1.

The *benefit opener* reminds the prospect/customer of his or her need, and probes for continued interest. *Reviewing the parameters* of the need/problem actually begins the consultative sales process. These parameters were elicited during the profiling interview. Reviewing these parameters ensures that nothing has changed since that interview and verifies your complete understanding. This also reinforces the need in the customer's mind.

Figure 16-1 Consultative Sales Track

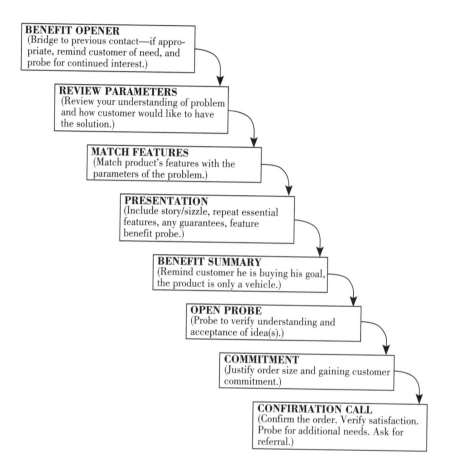

The final step in the opening sequence is to provide an overview of how the *features* of the selected product will solve your customer's need/problem and continues the process of obtaining customer commitment to any solution that meets or exceeds his or her requirements. The opening sequence is covered in Chapter 17.

The *presentation* includes the story/sizzle surrounding your product, as well as a repetition of the essential features, benefits, and advantages to the customer. Chapter 18 explores this area.

The *benefit summary* reminds customers they are buying something that will fulfill their goals; that is, the product is the best vehicle for them to get what they want/need. An *open probe* is then used to ensure that all the customer's pertinent concerns and questions have been answered. Both reinforcement the customer commitment to accept your solution. Chapter 19 deals with this area.

Dealing with customer questions and hesitancy is the subject of Chapter 20. In it you'll learn that the questions customers ask are often the keys to getting their commitment to accept your solution(s). The next step consists of obtaining the customer's *commitment* by justifying the order size and then asking for the order. Details are in Chapter 21.

The final step in the Consultative Sales Track is Chapter 22's *confirmation/follow-up call*, which confirms the sale and reminds the customer that a wise purchase was made, while asking for referrals and completes the commitment process. This chapter also deals with follow-up and handling problems.

Part of the reason for the effectiveness of our consultative sales track is that it truly takes into account the needs of the individual customer. Remember, you will have already qualified and profiled the person *prior to* making the presentation and will then make the presentation by using the person's primary thought process as well as their individual buying motivations. This approach, coupled with the suggestions immediately following, make this model both unique and extraordinarily effective.

PRESENTATION FORMATS

The first step in adapting your presentation to virtually anyone is the realization that *not everyone should receive the same presentation.* Consider customers with two extremes in background knowledge about your product or service:

The Highly Sophisticated Buyer Versus the Very Unsophisticated Buyer

Highly sophisticated buyers already know what they want and are generally familiar with industry jargon. If you were suggesting options, you should feel free to talk about spreads, straddles, and LEAPS. (See Chapter 23 for additional options commentary.) Sophisticated customers can handle that type of information and would be insulted if you tried to explain the basic concepts to them. However, *very unsophisticated buyers* would probably be totally confused by all the jargon, might feel intimidated, and would almost certainly need explanations that were more simplistic.

What works for one person may not work for the other. The key is to pay attention to their questions and then match their sophistication level. Also, watch their reactions. If you see a confused look on the customer's face, you may be presenting unfamiliar material. There may be other reasons for such a reaction, including not perceiving how some feature would be of benefit, daydreaming for a moment, trying to remember a sales point you had made, thinking of a concern, and so on. (One of the reasons for having a rehearsed presentation is that it allows you to pay close attention to the customer rather than to what you are going to say next.) Also note that even a sophisticated customer may not be familiar with certain aspects of your material. If they knew *all* the answers, they might not be using your services.

The two extremes regarding customer sophistication levels should cause you to modify your basic presentation to match their level of knowledge. If you prepare two presentations—one for each extreme—you should be able to match the vast majority of people who fall somewhere in between. The amount of detail you will provide is also dependent upon the particular person you are dealing with. Again, we find it helpful to prepare for two extremes, thereby having the ability to match virtually anyone.

The "Give Me the Highlights" Versus the "Give Me All the Details" Buyer

"Give me the highlights" buyers want product ideas given in summary mode. Equivalently, they want the headlines, not all the story details. They could become quite bored (and resentful) if they are given too much unnecessary information. Such a person can be either sophisticated or unsophisticated. Remember that industry and firm compliance standards indicate that enough information must be provided to allow the customer to make an informed decision. Therefore, especially with prospects or new clients, you must go beyond the mere highlights when dealing with topics such as risk and suitability.

On the other hand, *"give me all the details" buyers* want as much information as they can get. Such people seemingly want to know everything about everything and wish to absorb all of the product knowledge available. Of course, they may be highly interested in one aspect of the presentation and only want a summary of other parts.

KISS AND THE THREE-LEVEL PRESENTATION

The best way to make a presentation is to *allow the customer to determine both the level of sophistication and detail that is being presented.* This is

Figure 16-2 KISS and the Three-Level Presentation

Features	Level I	Level II	Level
A	?		
		?	
			?
B	?		
		?	
			?

easily accomplished using our *KISS and the Three-Level Presentation*[1] *method.*

KISS is the acronym for *keep it short and sweet.* It initially assumes that a headline/summary presentation is preferred, but it allows for the customer to determine the sophistication level and the detail levels at each point.

The presentation actually contains three distinct levels of detail with built-in checks and balances in the form of verifying questions to the customer. The customer's request for additional information determines whether you go forward or provide additional detail on the current point. The customer's request also provides an indication as to the degree of sophistication you should employ for that phase of the presentation. Graphically, it is represented by Figure 16-2 and is expanded in the text that follows.

KISS

Keep it short and sweet ensures that your ideas are presented with an appropriate level of detail. Most financial salespeople oversell. Consequently, more sales have been lost from overselling and providing too much information than from providing too little information. Yet some salespeople insist on trying to tell the client everything they know about the product as well as their philosophies on life. Most customers find such laborious presentations boring: they are certainly inefficient and generally ineffective.

[1]Originally developed by Steven Drozdeck and introduced in *What They DON'T Teach You in Sales 101,* by Drozdeck, Yeager, and Sommer (New York: McGraw-Hill, 1991).

The Three-Level Presentation

As you know, customers are interested in what the product will do for them as individuals. They are interested in the key points as applied to their individual needs and goals. Anything extra that you present is usually unnecessary and potentially detrimental to the customer's acceptance of your solution. Therefore, make your presentations as simple as possible. Present only what is necessary. If your customer needs additional information or explanation, then and only then do you present more. However, if your customer accepts the first level of the presentation, then that is all you provide.

For the sake of the example, pretend that you can divide the main body of a mutual fund presentation into five distinct parts: (1) details on the mutual fund company, (2) their competitive edge, (3) technical details, (4) economic and market commentary with risk and reward, and (5) various fund services.

Each of the areas should have three levels of potential commentary. *Level I* represents the headline version in three or four sentences of each of the five key ideas. This is followed by a question to verify client understanding and acceptance. The client can say yes or no.

If the Client Says Yes. If the client both understands and accepts what you have said, you then continue to part 2 of the presentation (the competitive edge, in this example) and provide another headline comment. You continue providing the headline version as long as the client gives you positive responses. If the client is sophisticated and knowledgeable, it should be possible for you to give the entire presentation—regardless of what you are selling—in less than two minutes.

If the Client Says No. If, at any headlined segment, the client needs more information, you should be able to provide additional information. You merely explain the headline in additional detail (*Level II* is perhaps 8 to 12 sentences) and probe for understanding and/or acceptance. If the client says yes, return to the headline level for the next segment. (It is important to realize that clients can need additional information on one topic but be quite knowledgeable in other areas. By regularly returning to the headline level, you avoid talking down to the client, a practice that usually generates very negative reactions.) If the client still needs additional information and says no to your question probing for understanding, then be prepared to give a lot of detailed information as you enter *Level III*. After explaining that aspect in detail, you again go to the headline level for the next major point.

This approach ensures that you present only the appropriate amount of information to the client. Where additional information is needed, it is given. If none is needed, you have quickly and efficiently made the pertinent points and can quickly gain client commitment. Make note of where the client was knowledgeable and where he was not. In future presentations you will then automatically provide the appropriate level of detail. If, for example, the client generally asks technically oriented questions, you can then provide more technical information for that client than for others.

PRECALL PLANNING

It is important to be as prepared for your sales presentation as possible. The precall planning form in Figure 16-3 was designed to allow you to more effectively plan your presentation. By preidentifying the key features, benefits, and advantages of your product/service, you are mentally preparing yourself for success. You may only have to do it once or twice if you represent a small financial product line, but you may prepare a number of these forms if you are responsible for a variety of products. Remember that the value of this form of preparation is that you make your sales presentation in the most effective manner. The precall planning forms allow you to quickly review the optimal ways of presenting a particular product and remind you to take the needs of the particular customer into account.

PRESENTATION TYPES AND METHODS

Thus far you have only been introduced to making a verbal presentation. Telling someone information is important. It is also important to involve their other senses of sight and touch. The most effective presentations involve sight, sound, and touch/do aspects. (See Chapter 4.)

   According to Albert Mehrabian, 55 percent of our communication is through posture, gestures, and facial expressions; 38 percent is through our tone of voice; and only 7 percent through words themselves.[2] These percentages have proven themselves valid through scores of other studies that also indicate that 85 to 93 percent of communication occurs below the conscious level of awareness. Therefore, in a face-to-face presentation you are able to deliver 100 percent of the message, while a telephone presentation allows you to deliver only 45 percent; and a letter only 7 percent.

- *Sight*: Visual aids such as charts, pictures, and illustrations help a person paint a mental picture of the advantages of the product/service to them. Sometimes merely jotting down figures with your pen or, better

[2]Albert Mehrabian, *Silent Message* (Belmont, CA: Wadsworth, 1971), pp. 248–257.

Figure 16-3

Precall Planning Form
(condensed version of our standard form)

Customer: _____

Needs/objectives: _____

Special needs: _____

Product to present: _____

Initial need statement to generate interest:

1. Benefit opener
2. Probe for accuracy
3. Review parameters of problem/need
4. Match features

Presentation:

1. Refer to specific product
2. State specific features and benefits and relate to need(s).

	Feature	Benefit	Advantage
A.	_____	_____	_____
B.	_____	_____	_____
...			

Note: Not every customer is interested in every feature. Probe regularly for acceptance.

If customer has questions or concerns,

1. Probe to get objection as specific as possible.
2. Rephrase objection in question form and/or CLAP.
3. Provide appropriate information.

Possible Objections	Appropriate Response

Getting Commitment:

1. Justify order size.
2. Request commitment.

yet, getting the customer to write things down reinforces your points with a visual image. You increase the impact of your presentation when you involve the various senses.

- *Sound*: The words you choose must be supported by your intonation and level of excitement. Prepare for both what you want to say and how you want to say it.

- *Feel*: Whenever possible try to instill a positive feeling with the product or service you are recommending. This is partly accomplished by emphasizing the benefits the customer will receive and the sense of accomplishment for making inroads into the solving of a financial need.

Depending upon your recommendation, you may wish to give your customer some information about the product or company that will make them feel proud they own it. For example, a few years ago, the Ford Taurus was designed by getting input from thousands of factory workers, engineers and car owners. Whenever possible their suggestions were incorporated into the design. This gave each person on the assembly line a sense of "ownership" and "pride in workmanship." Of course, Taurus car buyers, were pleased that so many good ideas were incorporated into the vehicle. How the Taurus was designed became an occasional topic of conversation with friends and associates—increasing Taurus sales and the pride of ownership even further. Brokers were certainly pointing out this fact to their clients.

Pride of ownership and positive associations are helpful in any sale. If something is beneficial, let the customer know. "Whenever you see someone buying medical supplies or baby products at the grocery store or pharmacy, they are contributing to Johnson & Johnson." The whole idea is to provide customers with something they will both remember and be proud of. This creates an emotional attachment to the product. Having this information is also useful for dealing with "buyer's remorse" (regret at making the purchase or, using a euphemism, "postpurchase dissonance").

BUYING MOTIVATIONS

As was shown in Chapter 12, people have unique reasons for making their decisions. While some people are motivated by price, convenience, and quality; other people are persuaded by variety, reputation, and service. Therefore, your sales preparation should include how to describe various product features, advantages, and benefits in terms that a client can most fully appreciate. For example, if a customer places a high premium on convenience, and you are selling a money market fund, it would be wise to relate as many features to the benefit of "convenience" as possible. "This fund," you might say, "lets you withdraw money at any time through either checks or a debit card. This makes it very convenient for paying bills or accessing your money."

The following list represents words that are often used by customers when they describe what they want—from or in a product or service, from a sales professional, from a company they will do business with. Your job is to take the features, benefits, and advantages of your product and be able to relate them to as many of the words as possible. Preparing yourself in this manner will allow you to more easily relate to the customers psychological buying motivations.

Customer Motivation Words

Convenience	Reliability/dependability	Safety
Popularity	Service	Suitability
Quality	Integrity	Unique
Selection	Relationship	Traditional way of doing things
Price	Value	What many other people are doing
Ease of use		

We've found it useful to prepare a grid of various products and services and have brokers describe the features, advantages, and benefits of various products and services relative to customer motivation words. Figure 16-4 will clarify what we mean.

Figure 16-4 Features, Advantages, and Benefits of Various Investment Products

	Mutual Fund	UIT	Muni	Annuity
Convenience				
Popularity				
Quality				
Selection				
Price	Volume discounts			
Etc.				

NEGOTIATION

If you were selling for a different industry you would expect certain clients to negotiate with you regarding price, delivery time, quantity, and so on. In the financial services industry, you may, depending upon firm policies, reduce the fee on a sale and provide some additional services such as a portfolio review for free. For the most part, there is a limited amount of negotiation for the typical retail customer. However, this is not true for larger corporate clients. Your firm may be able to offer numerous additional concessions (beyond price) to get the business.

Even though you are not in an industry that traditionally negotiates with customers, you must be prepared to do some price, service, or quantity negotiating anyway, especially on larger or multiple sale orders. Again, your sales manager will let you know what the parameters are.

MENTAL REHEARSAL

One final, but extraordinarily important, element in planning the sales call is the value of mental rehearsal. *We are what we think we are, and we do what we regularly imagine, that is, what we program ourselves to do.* It is wise to mentally practice giving your presentations—practicing what you are going to say and how you will respond to a series of situations. For example, you may want to mentally rehearse explaining your product or service to people at different levels of sophistication. How might you explain a difficult concept to someone who doesn't have a high level of sophistication? How would you answer specific questions?

The more you mentally rehearse, the better you will perform. What you mentally rehearse is what you will probably do when faced with a real-life situation because it creates a "mental model." Failure to mentally prepare yourself for different contingencies may mean that you have to "wing it" later. Of course, if you "wing it," you may not get the results you want.

Mental rehearsal is so powerful and effective that it is regularly employed by athletic teams, actors and actresses, attorneys, and everyone who wishes to insure consistently high performance. It works! Numerous studies have shown the power of mental rehearsal.

All great successes and all failures rehearse! The difference is that the successful people/ "professionals" mentally see themselves effectively dealing with situations. They anticipate difficulties and see themselves overcoming those difficulties. They practice "success" in their minds, and they mentally succeed. On the other hand, those people who fail typically imagine the difficulties and envision themselves becoming overwhelmed and defeated. Mentally, they stop at the first signs of difficulty. Their mental map stops, and they mentally practice failure (or at least they practice not succeeding.) Then, when encountering a similar situation in real life, they unconsciously follow their own self-defeating programming.

> Our actions, reactions and attitudes follow our personal, mental images. We can choose our images. What have you been choosing?

Remember, *"People don't plan to fail, they fail to plan."* Pre-thinking and rehearsing what you will say and how you will say it can make a tremendous difference in your success rates. Prepare a script choosing the most effective words you can think of and practice that script. It is only through thorough preparation and practice that you will know the most effective words, phrases and descriptions of any product or service. You'll also know where and how to place emphasis and tonal changes.

Remember, your livelihood is dependent upon your persuasive ability. Even if you are confident about something, people will not follow your advice unless you *appear* confident, and enthusiastic, and knowledgeable. By learning to make your presentation at different levels of sophistication, you increase your ability to be effective with many people. Essentially, thorough preparation allows you to take a general script or presentation and modify it for different people—modifying the amount of information and the sophistication level of that information while taking into account different personality styles. This allows you to individualize your presentation and make it highly persuasive. This practice allows you to become "purposely successful" rather than "randomly or accidentally successful." Eventually, you will do all the right things intuitively and will rise to the heights of the sales profession.

17

Ready, Set, Go
Opening the Sales Call

BENEFIT OPENER
(Bridge to previous contact, remind customer of need, and probe for continued interest.)

The first few moments of the sales call communicate your agenda to your client. A remarkable number of sales are lost right here because the financial advisor fails to choose his words based upon the client's point of view. Hence, instead of leading the client toward solving a problem, some brokers begin by building additional barriers or sales resistance. For example, "The last time we spoke you had $25,000 to speculate with. Is that still the case?" This statement is perceived, perhaps unconsciously, as the broker looking for a commission. Examples of the correct way are provided later. Your opener must accomplish several things:

- You must remind your client of who you are (especially for new relationships).

- You must provide a rationale for the call that creates enough interest for him to continue the call. This is accomplished by reminding him that he has a financial problem and that you have a solution.

- You must probe to determine if your client is prepared to deal with the purpose of the call at this time.

Reminding your client of your relationship and the purpose of the call is relatively easy. Use a bridging statement to connecting the current call to an earlier discussion of his needs. For example,

> "Mr. Smith, this is John Brown at Paine Webber. The last time we spoke you mentioned an interest in increasing your retirement nest egg (reminds the client of who you are and bridges to an earlier statement). Is this still your primary interest? (probes for validation of his assumption of the client's goal) I think I may have found just what you're looking for. (I have a solution to your problem.) "Do you have a minute?" (probes for acceptance)

ADVANTAGES OF THE BENEFIT OPENER

The primary advantage of the benefit opener derives from the fact that the opener tells your client your objective. When you use a benefit opener, you tell your client that the primary purpose of your call is to help him achieve his goal (college tuition, etc.). For example, "Mr. Jones, the last time we spoke, you mentioned that your primary objective was obtaining sufficient funds to pay for John's college tuition. Is that still the case?" *This reminds the client of the fact that you are a professional who has called to help him solve a problem* (namely, his son's tuition), rather than a "salesman" calling to solve your own problem (i.e., higher production credits). This difference is the reason why benefit openers create far less sales resistance than non-benefit openers. Here are several examples of nonbenefit openers, followed by alternative benefit openers:

> If you are selling stocks,
>
> *Nonbenefit*: "Mr. Jones, this is Mary Nicholson at Prudential Securities. How are you? The last time we spoke you said you wanted to invest in a good-quality growth stock." (This clearly communicates the sales nature of the call.)
>
> *Benefit*: "Mr. Jones, this is Mary Nicholson at Prudential Securities. How are you? The last time we spoke, you indicated that

your primary concern was saving for your children's education. Is that still the case?" (Tells the client that you are calling to help him solve their tuition problem.)

If you're involved in banking services,

Nonbenefit: "Mr. Black, this is Bob Smith at Bank America. How are you, today? The last time we spoke, you said that you had a $25,000 certificate of deposit coming due at your bank this Friday." (This clearly indicates to the client that the purpose of the call is to spend his $25,000 for him.)

Benefit: Mr. Black, this is Bob Smith at Bank America. How are you today? The last time we spoke, you said that your chief concern was generating enough income to live on, now that you are retired. Is that still the case?" (Tells the client that you may be able to help him obtain more income to live on.)

If you are selling insurance, you might say something like

Nonbenefit: "Mr. Johnson, this is Anita Andrews at Home Life. How are you? Last week you mentioned that you only had $100,000 coverage of life insurance. Is that still the case?" (Tells the client that you want to sell him life insurance, for your benefit.)

Benefit: "Mr. Johnson, this is Anita Andrews at Home Life. How are you? Last week you mentioned that you were concerned about how to protect your family in the event of your death. Is that still the case?" (Tells the client that you are ready to help him solve his problem.)

What if you are selling something like mutual funds?

Nonbenefit: "Mr. Brown, this is Phil Malloy at Citibank Investment Services. How are you? When we last spoke, you said you had $20,000 coming due, that you would like to invest in a mutual fund. Is that still the case?" (This tells your client that this is a sales call and that your primary interest is in getting at his $20,000 dollars.)

Benefit: "Mr. Brown, this is Phil Malloy at Citibank Investment Services. How are you today? When we last spoke, you said that you wanted to find a way to fund your retirement that would provide both current income and a hedge against inflation. Is that still the case?" (Reminds the client of the specific nature of his problem and implies that you have a solution.)

Since the first things you mention communicate the impression of what you're most interested in, these brokers have to decide whether they want to create the impression that they called because they were interested in the client's money (i.e., making a commission) or in helping him. In reality, each broker may have had their client's best interests as their only concern, but the nonbenefit openers created a vastly different impression. The primary advantage of the benefit opener derives from the fact that it tells the customer what your objective is—to help them achieve their goal.

PROBING

Each of the previous examples included a probe to verify that the need still existed. Basically the customer, can say "Yes" or "No." If "Yes," you can continue. If "No," you ask questions about the current situation or need or reschedule the call. In either case, you have the information you need to continue the conversation or to go towards a different agenda. Also realize that the possibility exists that the situation or need has already been taken care of. The customer's circumstances may have changed, they may have spent the money, may have already purchased another product, and so on. It is as important to probe during the opener as it is to do during the rest of the sales call. Only by probing throughout the call can you get confirmation of goals, permission to continue, and commitment to participate. Also, probing questions are among the best ways to involve your customer in the call.

> **REVIEW PARAMETERS**
> **(Review your understanding of the problem and how customer would like to have the solution.)**

Here you review the customer's specific goal or problem and verify the need for a solution. A brief review of the previously established parameters of the solution continues the process of leading to customer commitment. (The information about acceptable parameters was obtained when you profiled the customer.) This brief review helps ensure that your customers will realize that you really do understand their needs. It also provides them with the opportunity to give you additional information that could help you solve their problems. Meanwhile you are verifying your understanding of the situation.

You are also committing the customer to buy anything that meets or exceeds the parameters you have jointly established for a solution to their need. Additionally, the client may not always remember all the agreed-upon parameters. This is a good reminder for them, too.

MATCH FEATURES
(Match product's features with the parameters of the solution.)

After you have reviewed and verified the parameters of your customer's need, you match each parameter with the corresponding feature of your product or service. In doing so, you powerfully demonstrate the logic of your choice by showing how each feature of your product or service meets, or exceeds, the corresponding parameter of the customer's need. Continuing our example of the insurance agent,

> *You:* "I have a safe investment offering a return about 25 percent greater than the bank, and which will allow you to have greater investment flexibility than a standard savings account. In addition, your daughter will have the money available in 15 years, but you will always have access to it in case you need it for other reasons. Does that sound like something you'd be interested in?"
>
> *Customer:* "Of course!"

What is the customer going to say: "No"? Of course, they will want to hear more because you have exceeded their expectations. (Note: If they did say "No," you would return to profiling and find out why.) At this point, your customer has again committed himself and must listen to your presentation. This technique is similar to, but much more powerful than, the traditional "trial close."

At this point, you have completed the opening sequence. By following these basic steps you ensure that it is appropriate to go to the next step— the sales presentation. The opening sequence increases customer commitment by reminding the customer that he has a need that he wants solved. You demonstrate your professionalism and desire to help by verifying your understanding. Finally, it allows you to discover any last-minute changes in the situation before you become involved in making a presentation that may no longer be appropriate. (It is as important to probe during the opener as it is throughout the rest of the sales call to elicit confirmation of goals, assent to continue, and commitment to participate. Involve your client in the call as early as possible.)

Here is an example of the entire opening sequence. The product is Buy-Sell Insurance. The client's is a partner in a small business. (Ideally, this presentation should be made to both partners.)

"Mr. Rogers, this is Lisa Ballinger at Metropolitan. How are you today?"

"FINE, THANK YOU."

"Great! The last time we spoke, you stated that you needed to find a way to protect your business in the event that either you or your partner should die. Is that still the case?"

"YES, IT IS."

"I think I may have the solution to your problem. Do you have a moment to hear about it?" (Note: Probes for commitment to listen, now.)

"YES."

"Before I tell you what I have, do you mind if we take just a moment to review the parameters we discussed. I want to make sure that I'm on track."

"THAT'S FINE."

"Good. If I have it correctly, you said that the two of you are equal partners and that the firm's current market value is approximately $2 million dollars. Right?"

"THAT'S RIGHT."

"You also said that if something happened to either of you that it you both wanted to be able to run the business your own way, without interference from possible heirs. Am I right?"

"YES."

"In addition, you said that it would take at least a year to find and train a replacement. So, you would need to not only be able to buy out the other's share from the estate, but also replace the lost services. Correct?"

"YES."

MATCH THE FEATURES

Having reviewed and verified the parameters of the client's need, Lisa can now match the features of the product or service which she is selling.

Match each parameter with the corresponding feature of your product or service. In so doing, you powerfully demonstrate the logic of your choice by showing how each feature of your product/service meets, or exceeds, the corresponding parameter of the problem.

She continues:

> "You mentioned that you needed to be able to buy out your partner's share of the business (or vice versa) for $1 million. We have a policy that will not only enable you to do that more cheaply than your current plan, it will also automatically grow with your business to cover its increasing value. How's that sound, so far?"
>
> "GOOD."
>
> "Second, you said that you would need in the neighborhood of 12 months of protection while one of you sought and trained a replacement manager. Your current coverage is only $400,000. It sounds as though you will need at least $500,000, plus additional funds to cover your lost production for the time spent searching and training. We can provide you with $750,000 worth of coverage for just a little more than you are paying now for $400,000. Sounds pretty good, doesn't it?"
>
> "GREAT, SO FAR."
>
> "Would you like to hear more?"
>
> "YES."

At this point, your client virtually must listen to your presentation and has virtually bought the entire package! During the profile presale, he committed to buy anything that matched his parameters (see "Profiling"). You have just matched or exceeded them. When he asks to hear more, he has already bought it in his own mind.

Remember: Matching your product's features to the parameters of your client's need becomes a powerful trial close.

18

Implementing Your Strategy
The Body of the Sales Presentation

The opener reminds your client that he has a problem that you can solve. Reviewing the parameters starts you both at the same point and begins gaining client acceptance. Matching the features to the parameters begins the building of a powerful case for your product or service.

The purpose of your "presentation" is to introduce and justify the product or service that you've selected as a solution. Your presentation leads the client through a process of understanding and identifying with your product/service as a solution to his goal. It then moves him to the close, where he formally "owns" your solution before you accept the order.

> **PRESENTATION**
> (Include story/sizzle, repeat essential features, feature benefit probe.)
> *Beware of any guarantees.*

Ideally, your presentation will move the client through a series of commitment probes (sometimes called the "yes set") that will assist him in accepting your solution. To make your presentation effective there are certain key data that you must provide. Just which information you should include will vary with the product or service that you sell. However, in all cases, the data should be sufficiently complete to enable your client to make an informed decision. (The concept of complete information and investors making informed decisions is an extraordinarily important issue. Virtually all financial services regulatory authorities—SEC, NYSE, NASD, OCC,—are highly concerned about this issue. Compliance, full disclosure, and a host of other important topics are covered in Section VI.) Concern for the customer should be paramount in all sales presentations. Sales professional use the consultative approach because, in the long run, any approach that does not consider the customer's needs first will have limited success.

Unfortunately, many people think about the presentation as that moment in which they are making a product recommendation and trying to gain buyer commitment. On the other hand, professionals consider the actual recommendation as only one small aspect of the presentation. Consultative selling includes the profiling process, the opening, dealing with customer concerns, and the follow-up as equally (or even more) important parts of the presentation. This is one of the reasons they are at the top of the ladder of success.

You will want to include the data necessary to validate your selection of the given product or service as appropriate to solve your client's problem. This is particularly important, because every investment decision you ask a client to make involves some risk. Remember, even putting his money in a vault incurs the risk of inflation.

You can be sure that the client has enough information for that informed decision by matching the parameters of the problem. Then give enough of a story about your product or service to provide the "sizzle" necessary to help him to emotionally identify with it.

SUPPORTING DATA

Supporting data should include, but are not necessarily limited to, the features which correspond to the parameters of the client's goal/problem. They should also include any identifying information and any information that might be thought of as "negative." Such information is very important so that the client is not "unpleasantly surprised" when finding this out for himself. It's better if your clients hear such information from you.

The following data should be included:

1. Name of the product/service.
2. The relative safety of the product or service. For example, a bond's rating by S&P or a stock's rating by your company, Moody's or Value

Line, and so on (investment grade, good quality, etc.). Does this product/service fit within your client's risk tolerance for this goal? Is it FDIC insured?

3. The compounded rate of expected growth of capital, if any. For example, a research report on a stock that indicates an expected earnings growth of 15 percent per year. Will this growth rate enable the client to meet his goal within the required time frame?

4. The dividend paid, if significant or requested. For fixed-income products, such as corporate bonds, coupon, current yield, yield to maturity, and yield to call.

5. Call data for fixed-income products. When and under what circumstances can a client expect to lose his ownership? When is the maturity (day-month-year)?

6. The issuing authority, especially for fixed-income securities.

7. The ability to pay interest and dividends.

8. The price of the security/service. For bonds it is useful to be aware of the price in yield to maturity basis points as well as dollars.

9. A complete description of the bond summarizing all features should be given before asking for the order.

THE STORY AND THE SIZZLE

Sizzle has been defined, by some, as the story the client will remember after the sale. It consists of data that will enable the client to emotionally identify with the product and, if possible, become excited about owning it in addition to believing that it will help solve his problem. In short, the story and the sizzle have three main purposes:

1. To support, or justify, the figures you provide when discussing your product/service's features

2. To help your client to emotionally identify with your product or service

3. To provide a supporting story that your client will remember after the sale

For example,

(1) Champion International is the largest owner of timberland in the world. The company owns 6 million acres of timber, roughly equivalent to the entire state of Rhode Island and half of the state

of Massachusetts, or (2) AT&T is the owner of Bell Labs, the world's premier research and development facility. Bell Labs has produced an average of one patent per day since 1906.

The company's annual report, your firm's research reports, and so on provide valuable information that can usually be translated into "sizzle." Also, *Research Magazine* provides special brochures and videos highlighting certain companies. See Appendix for information on this service.

FEATURE-ADVANTAGE-BENEFIT PROBE

When you present the essential features of your product to your client, it is important to keep him involved in the process and to help him see the connection between his problem and your solution. To do this you need to connect each essential fact with the problem, demonstrating how that product/service fills the parameters of the problem. Then probe for acceptance. For example,

> "Mr. Jones, this certificate of deposit is FDIC insured, providing the safety of principle to maturity that you were interested in for the down payment on that house. Don't you think?"

> "Mrs. Smith, the projected 12 percent growth of this stock should more than provide the growth that we need for your son's college fund. Wouldn't you agree?"

These examples connect the solution with the client's objective, demonstrating the logic of accepting your solution and making the suggested purchase. (See Chapter 20 on closing techniques.)

Caveat We would like to offer a caveat regarding the sale of securities. Many of the young financial consultants with whom we have worked over the years have gotten caught up in the image of being a "broker." They get so excited about a given stock or bond that they are selling that they actually begin to believe that the specific security is really important (even to the customer). We would suggest, that with certain exceptions that is not true. Here's why:

If we could give you a free vacation in Aruba for two weeks, all expenses paid (shows, hotel, meals, etc.), you might get excited. You now have only one problem, getting there. Obviously, you would immediately call your travel agent and tell her the parameters of your problem (destination, dates, level of comfort, speed and safety required, and how much you are willing to spend). She would then check and call back with a recommendation for your transportation. As long as her recommendation meets, or exceeds, your parameters, would you really care what it is? Of course not! All that you are really interested in is your destination, Aruba.

The same is true of most investors. They are interested in their end goal (retirement, tuition, etc.) As long as your recommendation meets or exceeds all their agreed-upon parameters, it doesn't matter what it is! This is why you carefully determined the parameters within the profiling segment and why you verified the parameters in the opening portion of the sales process. (See Chapter 17.)

INDIVIDUALIZING YOUR PRESENTATION

Once you've prepared your presentation and know what you want to say and how you want to say it, you can devote your mental energies to dealing with your customer's needs and making appropriate adaptations within the presentation based upon their reactions to what you are saying. Such adaptations and enhancements include all the psychological needs discussed in the previous section. Your presentation becomes stronger because you can carefully listen as well as respond to any other subtle clues, such as shifts in body language.

BUYING SIGNALS

Your client will often provide "buying signals." These may take several forms:

- Ownership questions
- Positive statements that can be "built" upon
- Some pauses

Ownership Questions

When these signals occur, build on them and move toward the close. Sometimes these signals will appear before the you have completed your presentation. If this occurs, reinforce them and radically shorten your presentation. However, be sure that you include any essential data. Then move to the close. You should not automatically assume that your client is ready to place an order simply because of a buying signal. Here are examples of ownership questions:

"When will I receive the first dividend?"
"How long until the sale settles?"
"When will I need to transfer the funds?"

Here are examples of clients' positive statements that you can build upon as you close:

"I like the safety of certificates of deposit."
"Several of my friends own this mutual fund and they are very pleased with it."

Always listen for buying signals. Make mental note of them. Client buying signals let you know what the client is most interested in. You will use this information during the closing sequence by highlighting and reviewing them. This is much more effective than merely presenting a "laundry list" of features, advantages, and benefits and hoping that the overwhelming amount of evidence will cause the client to buy.

BUILDING MOMENTUM

As you explain the various features of your product or service to your customer, make sure that you periodically ask questions to verify their acceptance of your explanation. This serves the threefold purpose of (1) building a series of "Yes" responses, (2) allowing any concerns to be brought to light right now, rather than sometime later, and (3) helping to ensure that your recommendation continues to be appropriate.

Building a series of "Yes" responses is an excellent way to build a positive attitude in your customer and help ensure the customer's acceptance of your idea or solution. As a customer says, "Yes, I like that," or "Yes, that makes sense," and "Yes" (to something else), it becomes psychologically difficult to say "no" to the solution. Each time the customer says "Yes" he or she is making a minimental purchase. Using the KISS and the Three-Level Presentation method, you get a "Yes" at each juncture. The cumulative effect of the consultative sales approach is the customer's willing acceptance of your ideas. All your actions, even your basic attitude and philosophy, are customer centered. Building positive momentum by developing a "yes set" assists the customer in gaining and maintaining enthusiasm for your solution. It allows the final decision to be more readily accepted and helps deal with some people's natural reluctance to make commitments or to change.

If your customer says "No" or "I'm not sure" to one of your statements, you realize that you should spend additional time on that segment of the presentation. Depending upon the statement, a "No" could mean that a particular feature is not meaningful to the customer, or that she disagrees, or that she does not see the value of your suggestion. The important point is that you have the opportunity to address her concern and get it out in the open. Failure to address the concern might cause the customer to mentally focus on the one point of disagreement and not pay attention to anything else you are saying.

Preview of the Closing Sequence

Traditionally, dealing with customer objections is handled after attempting to close the sale. Our sales process takes a different approach by having any questions, comments, concerns, or objections brought forth *before* final customer commitment is obtained. Also, remember, the customer has already committed to this solution many times prior to reaching this point.

This approach is both more consultative in nature as well as substantially more powerful and persuasive than standard approaches. It is more consultative because your ongoing concern is meeting the customer's needs and ensuring that your product or service is appropriate to those needs. Dealing with questions, comments, concerns, or objections before trying to gain commitment also deepens the customer's trust in you because of your continued demonstrated concern with their needs. This process is substantially more powerful and persuasive because once all questions have been answered, there is every reason for the customer to buy. In fact, not only would it be illogical, it would be irrational for the customer to say "No." (Some clients will, of course, say "No," but that will be dealt with separately.)

CUSTOM FITTING THE SALES PRESENTATION

The consultative sales model we've presented works in the vast majority of instances. It works because it is simple and takes many factors into consideration. We strongly recommend that you get into the habit of preparing your presentations using this format. Doing so will allow you to maximize your probabilities of success.

There are many things you can do to make any presentation even more powerful (as shown in the previous chapter). They include:

- Using visual aids such as brochures, slides, pictures, graphs, and so on. The adage "A picture is worth a thousand words" is very true in sales. Consider using computer graphics.
- Using visual, auditory, and kinesthetic language as appropriate.
- Involving other significant parties in the conversation.
- Incorporating personality styles and buying motivations.

DIFFICULTIES TO ANTICIPATE

We are rarely given an ideal situation where everything goes perfectly. In most sales situations you should expect a few minor difficulties or annoyances, such as unexpected interruptions in the form of visitors or phone calls, running out of time, not having an answer to a question, having to check with a product specialist or sales manager on some product detail, and so on. No matter how well you prepare, these trivial things will occur at some point in time. Many of these difficulties will be taken care of over time as you learn the habits of each customer and you become accustomed to such day-to-day occurrences.

An important point to remember is that despite any of these interruptions, you can deal with almost anything. If you've established rapport and demonstrated a professional "I care" and "I'm here to help" attitude, then you are someone with whom they want to work. In life, and in business, it's hard to find someone who really cares. However, if such interruptions occur too often, some clients may consider you and your firm unprofessional.

PRESENTATIONS TO GROUPS

You may find yourself in a situation where you must make a presentation to numerous people, such as when presenting your firm's products and services to a corporation or an investment club. (Subsequent presentations will usually be made to one person who represents the group.) Some decisions are only made by committee, but there is usually one person in charge. The question is, "Who?" Very often the person doing the talking is not the person in charge. Pay attention to who the other members of the group tend to turn toward to get an opinion. Pay special attention to whose opinion is listened to very carefully by the rest of the group. Chances are, that's the person in charge and the one you should be directing your presentation toward. However, you must still make sure that you include everybody. Here are some rules of thumb for making a presentation to a group:

- Try to establish rapport with as many people as possible, but concentrate on the person in charge.
- Look at each individual for 3 to 5 seconds to maintain eye contact.
- Use visual aids that can be easily seen by everyone.
- Carefully plan your opening.
- Use words in all three sensory modes—visual, auditory, and kinesthetic—but concentrate on auditory and kinesthetic because the visual people are already taken care of by the visual aids and your sales literature.
- Have extra copies of any handouts or literature.
- Rehearse your presentation.
- Pay attention to who the group members look to as the decision maker.
- Direct additional efforts at that person.
- Be prepared for questions from anyone at anytime.
- Expect that someone will try to show off his knowledge, sometimes at your expense.
- Always keep in mind that you are probably one of many brokers competing for the company's business.

(Additional comments on presenting to groups have already been presented in Chapter 7.)

The best suggestion that we can make for group presentations is to take a course in public speaking. There are many valuable speaking techniques and the speech-making practice sessions would be invaluable. The time you spend becoming a polished presenter will reap you numerous commissions.

Your presentation begins while you are profiling because the customer commits to a solution which meets or exceeds his parameters. It is presenting a solution to a problem you elicited during profiling. The consultative selling sales sequence is designed to regularly verify your customer's needs and build a positive attitude which will lead them to acceptance of your proposal.

Since you are constantly placing the customer's needs first, you are maintaining and deepening the levels of rapport and trust. The most effective presentations are those which involve the customer's senses—visual, auditory and kinesthetic. That is, show, tell and do—all while building a sense of excitement with the realization that the problems will be solved.

19

Hurdles and Challenges
Dealing with Objections, Questions, and Concerns

As in any athletic event, we expect certain hurdles and challenges as part of the game. They are not considered negative or something to be avoided; they are something to be anticipated, planned for, dealt with. So too is dealing with your customer's objections, questions, and concerns. They are an expected, normal, part of the sales process.

In this chapter we will deal with some specific strategies for dealing with both objections and stalls. This will eliminate most "resistance" that you may encounter. *Resistance* is reluctance to buy. Most resistance comes from the fact that clients see financial salespeople as trying to impose a sale on them, and financial salespeople see their relationship with clients as adversarial. In consultative selling, the relationship is consultative—working together to meet the client's needs. The broker is an "insider," not an outsider.

In the minds of most sales professionals it would be unthinkable to have a series of sales presentations in which someone did not raise a question, express a concern, disagree with something, or employ some sort of delaying tactics. All these difficulties are so common that they are considered "part of the sales game." In fact, they are so common that entire books have been written on this one subject. Unfortunately, these are given a negative connotation by being labeled as "rejection." As you are learning in this book, *the easiest way to deal with resistance is to avoid it in the first place.*

Consultative selling's emphasis on finding and presenting solutions to customer's prestated needs avoids much of the traditional "resistance" that occurs when products or solutions are offered without deep concern, or understanding of, for the customer's real needs. Our strong emphasis on effective profiling and "the customer must come first" substantially reduces "resistance."

While the sales process outlined in this book does significantly reduce the amount and intensity of resistance because of our emphasis on rapport building and in-depth profiling, we are not aware of any process that eliminates it entirely. Many people postpone decisions and maintain their current status. While this is not a problem for certain sales situations, it can often become a problem when people or companies are asked to make a large (relative to the customer) commitments in time, money, effort, or changing the way they are doing things. Since you are involved in large-ticket, intangible sales you'll find yourself facing this situation with regularity.

We are changing the sales sequence from the traditional method where objections are dealt with after the final arguments or an attempt to gain commitment has been made. We have found, for the reasons provided later in the chapter, that it is better to deal with the customer's questions, comments, or concerns before the close.

OPEN PROBE
(Probe to verify understanding
and acceptance of idea(s).)

WHERE ARE WE WITHIN
THE SALES PROCESS?

At this point in the sales track, you will have just completed the benefit summary and probed to verify the customer's understanding and acceptance of your idea(s). Here you will give customers breathing room by encouraging them to ask questions or bring up concerns. This step is a vital part of consultative selling because it helps ensure that your recommendation is the correct solution for this problem. If you fail to address (or allow for) specific concerns, the customer may consciously or unconsciously feel pushed and back away from the sale—even though your proposed solution is just what they need. It is absolutely vital to remember that most decisions are made on an *unconscious level*. Failure to address a customer's concern can easily create a defensive response and negate everything you've said. This step, the open probe, will allow any unresolved issues/questions/concerns to be brought up. In fact, it is important to encourage the customer to bring up any and all issues that she may have.

In some traditional methods, financial salespeople actually attempt to avoid or bypass this area. As a result, customers often later feel that products have been pushed down their throats and suffer buyers' remorse. It's almost as if their unanswered questions fester until they grow out of proportion. If your customers aren't asking questions and giving comments, concerns, or objections, unstated, potentially unrealistic expectations can remain. Then, even if the product performs to specifications, it can still fail in the customer's eye because of these unrealistic expectations.

Benefits you'll obtain from employing the consultative sales approach include

- Better customer relationships
- Customers feeling as part of the problem-solving process, rather than being pushed
- Elimination, or at least reduction of, buyer's remorse
- Bringing out problems before you ask for a commitment
- Allowing the customer to "own" the idea
- Increasing your effectiveness

In essence, you should welcome these questions, comments, concerns, and objections because you are being given the information you need to more fully satisfy your customer's needs and thereby make the sale. As you will see, most of the time, an objection is a direct indication of some important point that has not yet been adequately addressed. If you don't address it now, you will have to do it later. However, if you do address it now, you will make obtaining a commitment from the customer that much easier.

THERE IS NO SUCH THING AS RESISTANCE!

It is important to realize that there is no such thing as "resistance." There are merely situations in which customers do not fully appreciate the benefits of the solutions presented to them (see Figure 19-1). Another reason for resistance might be that you were missing a vital piece of information and have therefore not taken something into account. While the idea that there is no such thing as resistance could be considered heresy in some

Figure 19-1 Causes of Customer Resistance

Lack or loss of rapport

Failure to listen

> . . . on your part
> . . . on the customer's part

Customer not knowing you are listening

Failure to ask questions

> . . . on your part
> . . . on the customer's part

Failure to determine actual/hidden needs

Lack of understanding

> . . . on your part
> . . . on the customer's part

Not appreciating benefits

> . . . on your part
> . . . on the customer's part

Inappropriate solution for the problem specified

Client's perception of you as commission driven

sales circles, we find it useful belief because it places the responsibility for effective communication on you. It forces you to take responsibility for the outcome of your representation and reduces the tendency to blame outside influences.

Stephen Covey's *The 7 Habits of Highly Effective People*[1] emphasizes the need to take total responsibility for one's actions rather than being a "victim" of circumstance. This applies to our discussion of resistance when we take the responsibility for the sale upon our shoulders.

Over the years we've heard too many financial salespeople make statements such as, "The prospect just wasn't ready to buy" or "The customer didn't want to be convinced." Over the course of your career, you will hear statements similar to these used as an excuse for a sale not being made.

---

[1] Steven R. Covey, *The 7 Habits of Highly Effective People* (New York: Fireside Book/Simon & Schuster, 1990).

Most of the time these and similar statements are used to hide the fact that the broker just hadn't uncovered some vital piece of information earlier in the helping process. They are placing the responsibility for the lost sale on the prospect or client rather than on themselves. One will tend to hear these statements from mediocre financial salespeople, while true professionals don't need these excuses. They're too busy making sales.

It would be ridiculous for us to suggest that it is always the brokers responsibility for not making the sale. Yet we find it very useful for our professional development to make the assumption that *if a sale is ever lost, there is something going on that we are not aware of.* This approach places the responsibility for the entire sales process on you, the sales professional, because you are responsible for the following:

- Gaining rapport
- Determining customer goals and the products needed to reach them
- Identifying customer psychological motivations
- Preparing, packaging, and presenting the best solution product or service in such a way that matches the client's psychological mode
- Uncovering any hidden agendas
- Providing suitable follow-up

Using this approach, the vast majority of things that can go wrong are taken into account as part of the consultative sales process. Professionals take responsibility for all aspects of the communications process. As a result, fewer errors or surprises occur and more sales are made.

RESISTANCE—OBJECTIONS—STALLS

Resistance occurs when someone feels pushed to do something that she believes is not in her best interest. It's the response you have when your needs are not being met or when someone is trying to get you to do something against your will. It is a normal and appropriate response to the situations listed. *Resistance rarely occurs when our needs are being met, when we feel that something is good for us, or when we believe we are getting a good deal. It only occurs when some vital, internal criterion is not met.*

An important point to remember is that *people do not resist themselves.* When you make a presentation based upon the customer's needs, objectives, and criteria (i.e., using the consultative sales approach) and structure your sales presentation based upon their thought patterns, it becomes quite difficult for people to "resist themselves." As we've said before, if there is resistance, it is because something was not communicated clearly.

Proper qualifying and profiling can also be a great help in avoiding resistance by clearly establishing the parameters of the desired solution to an identified need. By answering the following question before you ever present a solution, you can easily avoid a great deal of resistance.

1. Is the prospect or customer really committed to obtaining a solution to her need at this time? Does she really want it? Note: The customer may want it but not realize that she can have it.

2. Do she have the resources to follow through on her commitment at this time without jeopardizing other important goals?

Failure to answer these questions before presenting a solution has resulted in a great deal of frustrating and unnecessary "resistance" for a great many people.

Objections are a verbal form of resistance and should be considered opportunities to discover additional customer needs, questions, or concerns. Objections can occur for a number of reasons, including

- The customer failed to understand a key point.
- The customer failed to understand how something would be beneficial.
- The salesperson's failed to adequately convey the benefits.
- A key piece of information was missing.
- The customer just didn't hear something said.
- The customer has a different understanding or belief about something.
- The customer had a need that was previously unstated and not taken into account by the broker.
- The customer has a need that was previously stated but either forgotten or assigned the wrong priority by the salesperson, and so on.
- The wrong solution was presented.

Objections can provide you with valuable information necessary to help your customer meet their needs. Without having the basis of the objection brought to light, a financial salesperson might offer something inappropriate for the customer. It could be something that does not fully satisfy their need(s), or the customer might not understand how what is being offered could fulfill his need(s) and objectives. Typical objections include

"The price is too high."

"It won't do what I need it to do."

"Now is not the right time to do it."

Each "stated" objection may actually be covering a "hidden" objection. For example, "The price is too high" may actually mean "I can't afford it." "It won't do what I need" may really mean, "I don't understand how it works." This will be covered in greater detail later in the chapter. Whenever you get an objection, you must deal with it by asking clarifying questions.

Objections are often an indication of a customer's key criteria and can provide a very useful indication of what it will take to obtain their commitment. Essentially, an objection often lets you know what you must do to convince them. Therefore, instead of resisting the idea of handling objections, welcome them.

Traditionally, brokers, like most salespeople, have seen objections as something that must be beaten down; that is, they want to "overcome" the objections. This, almost by definition, is confrontational—even when done in a smooth, polished manner. By employing consultative selling techniques, you explore the issue at hand by asking questions, and either allow clients to come to the appropriate understanding that their concern is unwarranted, or you will realize that some other product or service may be more appropriate for them. However, once an objection is expressed, you have the opportunity to deal with the issue and any remaining barriers to the sale. Welcome objections!

Stalls are merely ways to postpone making the final decision to buy. Our definition relates it to "customer hesitancy" and "procrastination." The most common stalls include:

"Let me think it over."

"I have to talk to my spouse/accountant/attorney/somebody."

"Let me check my finances," and so on.

Each "stated" stall could actually be covering one or more "hidden" stalls. For example, "Let me think it over" may be a polite way of saying, "It's too expensive" or "I can't afford it." (Responding effectively to stalls is also covered in greater detail later in the chapter.) Basically, when you get a stall, you must deal with it by asking questions. Unfortunately, "stall" usually has a negative, emotional association for some financial salespeople and certain authors. For example, the customer owes me this sale and now they're "stalling."

A *limiting condition* represents a specific requirement that must be fulfilled, such as client about to make a large purchase, not having enough money, needing their money back on a certain date, and so on. It is something that is part of the equation and cannot be compromised.

Some stalls are absolutely valid, in that some people must mull things over in their heads, or talk to another decision maker, or review their finances before a decision or commitment can be made. However, it is also true that many of these statements are merely automatic responses designed to postpone the buying decision. By asking certain questions you can discover which category the stall falls under. If it is a necessary or limiting condition, rather than a postponement, then you should allow them the opportunity to do what they must do; otherwise, you may generate feelings of resentment. For example, many people make joint decisions with their spouses. In such cases, it would be unreasonable for you to insist that a decision be made by only one of them. Of course, you would take such necessary conditions into account in future situations and ensure that both parties were present during any sales presentation. However, if their stall was merely an automatic response designed to postpone the buying decision, then a different procedure should be employed. This is all covered later in the chapter.

Real professionals always try to leave the customer with a positive feeling. In other words, never "slam the door" on a customer who may later make a purchase. Treat people well so they come back rather than going away and telling all their friends about their dissatisfaction.

Win-Win or No Deal

Your internal beliefs—win-win or win-lose—are unconsciously reflected in everything you say or do, including: your body posture, speech pattern, vocabulary, emotional reactions to situations, and how the entire presentation is made. A win-win attitude, in which the customer must get a good deal and you and your firm are fairly compensated should be evident through all aspects of the presentation.

One final point is the fact that a win-lose attitude generates a tremendous amount of self-destructive stress. You already know many of the negative results of stress, but did you know that over 75 to 80 percent of work-related illness and absenteeism is due to stress and that most job burnout is a direct result of stress? The effects of stress and specific techniques to manage stress are addressed in Section VII, Chapter 27.

It is better to lose the sale than to lose your relationship with the customer.

Techniques for Handling Stalls and Objections

Whenever a customer begins to "resist" you, it is important to realize that some issue is not being met and that you must drop your agenda of closing the sale for a while to determine what is going on. For example, if you were making your presentation, you might stop the presentation and go back to profiling the customer to verify a key point. Failure to do this inevitably increases the resistance and, at best, results in a breakdown in the conversation. At worst, it results in the loss of the relationship. Remember that in consultative selling *the agenda is always to help the customer*. Occasionally you will have to shift your focus of attention from making a presentation back to questioning to ensure that the customer's needs are being met. One of the best ways to identify the causes of resistance while getting useful information for the consultative sales process is using the CLAP (clarify, acknowledge, legitimize, probe) technique introduced in Chapter 4.

Responding Having successfully determined the nature of the customer's resistance, you must now respond to it. Overly long answers tend to be given by individuals who are nervous and unsure of themselves, so remember KISS (keep it short and sweet). If, in the customer's perception, you appear nervous or defensive, the customer may wonder what you are nervous about and whether you have something to hide. This can quickly undermine the rapport you have built through CLAPing.

Example:

Take the case of the little boy who asked his mother where he came from. His mother became extremely embarrassed and provided a detailed answer that included a complete description of how babies are conceived and born. The boy looked increasingly confused throughout the discussion and his mother became increasingly uncomfortable as her "lecture" progressed. Finally, when it was over and she "probed" to see if he was satisfied, he said, "Gee, Mom, that's wild! Johnny comes from Chicago."

Two points are made by this story: (1) make sure you actually know what is being asked, not what you assume is being asked and (2) if you see from their responses that you may be on the wrong track, stop and CLAP again so that you can deal with the real question.

When responding to an objection, make sure of the following:

1. That you are providing the appropriate amount of information. Remember the principles behind KISS and the Three-Level Presentation.

2. Mentally check yourself to ensure that you are appropriately matching your customer's level of sophistication.

Probe Again   Once you responded to your customers' objections, it is important to prove again to determine, first, if they have understood and accepted your response, and second, if they have any further questions or concerns. Once this has been accomplished, you may return to your agenda of helping them toward a solution and can continue with the balance of your presentation if you feel that it is still appropriate.

Standard Responses for Stalls and Objections

If you went to a clothing store and the clerk asked, "Can I help you?" the chances are that, like most people, you would say something like, "No. I'm just looking." This automatic response occurs despite the fact that you were shopping for clothing. Many people have these automatic responses when faced with potential sales situations or when asked to make a decision. Comments like, "Let me think it over," "The price is too high," and "I don't have any money" are the norm in many cases. As a professional you should have an automatic, "off the top of your head" response for these common stalls. By doing so you appear confident and can provide an opportunity to explore the reasons behind the statement. Here are some responses that you might consider using.

Ideas for Dealing with Customer Hesitancy and Objections

There are a few objections that salespeople hear over and over again. In most cases you can easily handle these objections by adopting a curious attitude and asking additional questions. Remember, in most cases you will get good, useful information that you can use now or sometime in the future. Always do your best to assist your customer to accept a solution, but be gentle. Preserve the potential of the long-term relationship. (Remaining curious and asking additional questions—using the CLAPing technique—is a useful response for almost any objection. Also, be very careful of your voice tones and inflection. The slightest hint of anger, frustration, or sarcasm will undo all that you are trying to accomplish.

"Let Me Think It Over" "I can appreciate your need to think it over. What exactly do you need to think about?" Or "In my experience, sometimes needing to think it over is an indication that I didn't fully explain something. Would you be willing to share with me what I should have explained more fully?"

At this point one of two things can happen: (1) the customer really does need to think about it (perhaps it is an important part of his decision-making strategy), or (2) you will discover which "piece of the puzzle" the customer is missing.

If part of a customer's decision-making strategy is a need for time, then there is nothing that you should do about it. Merely build that into your future conversations by saying something like "Why don't you think about this for a couple of days and I'll get back with you then." This way, you have beaten the customer to the punch.

You might now add, "Is there any additional information I can get you in the meantime?" If there were any unstated concerns, they'd probably come out now. The customer is psychologically "off the hook" about making an important decision and will often give you the real reason. Hence, you will probably get the information you need to make the sale right then or when you next speak to the customer.

"Send Me Some Literature" "I'd be happy to send you information. So that I send you only the information you specifically need, please let me know what you want." Again, the customer will provide you with information that represents their key motivations. Some people must see things before they can make decisions. Others need to hear from others. Regardless of the customer's visual or auditory orientation, you should take her needs into careful consideration.

"I Have to Talk to My Spouse ... Accountant ... Attorney ..." Fair enough. Many people do have a need to discuss major items with an advisor. If this is the case, you will probably be wise to encourage a meeting with the other person. At least you will be able to present the full information in the most favorable light. Remember that your customer will probably not remember most of what you said. Your customer is, therefore, not the ideal person to be making the presentation for you to that advisor. The advisor, without adequate information, will usually recommend that the product or service not be purchased.

Many other people use this objection as a way of postponing the decision. By questioning the customer about exactly who she needs to talk to and what she needs to talk to that person about, you *may* train your customer to make a decision on a more timely basis, which will increase your efficiency in future sales with this person.

Most of the time you can avoid this situation by asking, during the profiling interview, whether another person will be involved in the decision making process. If yes, then you know what to expect. If, however, the answer is no, then you may wish to explore the customer's comfort level and work a bit harder at the commitment stage (see next chapter). Special note: Male brokers have an unfortunate tendency to assume that a married, female client must discuss an investment with her husband. This is a bad assumption to make because (1) many women make their own decisions, and (2) such an assumption often generates unnecessary resentment on the client's part.

"The Price Is Too High" (the yield's too low, the commission is too high, etc.)   At this point the customer has probably already indicated a positive acceptance of your idea. However, there is a question regarding value received versus price paid. Your job is to determine "high in comparison to what?" Also remember that you've already determined the price level in the profiling segment. If their expectations about cost are too low, you will have already begun an educational process to help bring their expectations more in line with reality.

You should be able to do an analysis of features and benefits versus cost. It is also helpful to know precisely what your competition is charging. If this becomes a common objection for you, make sure that you can justify the higher price in terms of better product value, higher levels of service, product reliability, and so on. Then, realizing that some of your competitors are offering similar products or services at lower prices, you actually make the higher price one of your selling points; that is, you bring up the fact that your product costs more because it is a better product.

Very rarely is price the total concern. Many people are quite willing to pay a higher price if they feel they are getting superior returns in other areas. Price may not be an object if the customer's primary motivation is to feel good. Other people may be willing to pay a higher price if they know that the service they will receive will be superior. Finally, some people may say the price is too high just to find out how your react. After all, experience has shown that not everyone is totally honest in their statement of objections. *In all cases, react by exploring what they mean by their objection and how they made that determination. Get specific information and use the CLAPing technique to gain more information.*

"I Don't Think This Is for Me" "What makes you feel that way?" or paraphrasing, "Sounds like it doesn't meet your needs." You will probably receive another important piece of information about the customer. Take that information and factor it into your subsequent conversation. Of course, you may discover that the customer is right and that the product or service is wrong for them. At that point, be a professional and recommend that they consider something different. You will have made a friend who will give you referrals and who will come back to you when the time is right.

"I Want to Shop Around" "Sounds like you want to see what the competition is offering. Is that the case? What specifically are you looking for?" The same logic described in the previous questions applies to this one. When you find out why, you will get the reason behind the excuse. In many situations it is perfectly reasonable to do comparison shopping for CD rates, annuities, municipal bonds, and so on. Trying to push a person into an immediate sale will only generate resentment.

You can even encourage people to shop around if you have a good product. It shows you have confidence and implies that additional shopping would merely be a waste of their time. The chances are they will not want to go searching. However, as part of your own preparation you should have done any comparison shopping yourself, so you can give the customer the benefit of your own experience. You could say something like this: "I can appreciate your desire to shop around for the best value. Of course, being in this business, I've already done that for you and can tell you what is available from our competitors. Would that be helpful?" Your attitude will determine whether this statement is believable or not. Be careful, because it could sound like you're trying to prevent them from seeing your competitors.

Another response could be: "When you said you wanted to shop around, what was it that you wanted to compare? . . . features? . . . prices?" At this point you are receiving key information about their criteria and may be able to uncover a hidden objection.

You will find out the basis of the stall. It is vital to realize that some people do need to spend time mulling it over in their head, seeing whatever else is available, and so on before they can make a decision. Be careful not to push too hard because you would risk the loss of rapport.

"I Just Don't Know" "What do you need to know that would make a difference for you?" Gather information and incorporate it into your response.

WHERE DO WE GO FROM HERE?

Once you've discovered the cause of their objection and uncovered the initial reason for their discomfort, it is important to probe further and discover if there are any additional hidden objections or agendas. There probably will be. For example, many people will say that they don't like a product or some portion of a product instead of admitting that they can't afford it at this moment. Unless you discover the hidden objection, you may be spinning your wheels trying to provide product-oriented information.

As a rule of thumb, once a customer raises a third objection (after you've dealt with two others), you should consider the possibility that there is a hidden reason that the customer is currently unwilling to share with you. The hidden reason may also be hidden from the customer—he may be uncomfortable and may not know why. At this point, it may be worthwhile to address the issue diplomatically by saying something like, "I'm getting the sense that there may be something of even greater concern on your mind. It would help me tremendously if you would share that with me because there may be numerous options available to us, depending upon the nature of your concern." Or "I'd really like to do business with you and help you satisfy your needs. However, it seems that I missed something significant that we should probably try to work together to solve."

In both situations, allow the customer to talk. Does it always work? Of course not. Is it worth trying, especially if nothing else seems to be working? Definitely! This will again be addressed in the next chapter when we discuss, "The sale begins when the customer says 'No.'"

If the customer continues to say "No," and if she is a large enough account, continue checking with her. Sometimes situations change. An excellent example of persistence is how Bruce Goldner obtained one of his largest accounts. He had a client who had a small account with him. The client also had $1.75 million in municipal bonds at another firm. Although Bruce tried as hard as he could, the client would not let Bruce manage the large position. Bruce's only strategy was to continue to send sales literature and tax-advantaged income ideas on a regular basis. For three years the client did nothing. One day, he asked Bruce to transfer the account to Bruce's firm. Of course Bruce was ecstatic. After getting the bonds in house, Bruce eventually asked him why he had finally transferred the bonds after three years.

His comment, "My other broker died." The point is, don't automatically give up just because someone says "No."

Dealing with objections is merely a way of further determining customer needs. Whenever someone offers an "objection" she is offering you valuable information that you can use in the sales presentation. Objections are *not* something to be overcome, as is taught in the traditional sales approaches; they *are* something that must be dealt with in the pursuit of customer satisfaction.

Recognize the possibility that what a customer says, initially, is not necessarily what is really meant. You must probe, clarify, and further explore the meaning behind the objection. Many times you will be able to deal with the concern in an easy manner. Also, many times you will have to determine whether what you are offering is appropriate for this customer, at this moment in time. If not, postpone or decline the sale. It is almost impossible to believe how much goodwill you will generate (and how many compliance problems you will avoid). If the customer insists on buying, as they often do, you have to reexplore the appropriateness of the product. (The suitability of a product for a particular client is essential. If you are unsure, check with your manager. We address the issue of suitability generally in Section VI and address suitability and compliance specifically within Chapter 25.)

Consultative selling and customer satisfaction go hand in hand. There is no conflict, there is only concern on your part, that the customer fulfills his objectives. It is only through helping your customers achieve their goals that everyone wins.

20

Crossing the Finish Line
Closing the Sale: Completing the Helping Process

As a financial sales professional, your sole reason for being is to help your customers solve a problem or meet a need. However, unless you complete the process by closing the sale for the product or service they need, you have not fulfilled your purpose.

In a sense, every aspect of your discussion with your prospect or customer has been a prelude to this point. From the initial meeting where you established rapport, to the discussions and questions determining needs and motivations, and through the presentation—all was designed to discover a need and obtain the customer's commitment to the solution (See Figure 20-1). You actually gained initial commitment to a solution during the profiling segment while you were discovering the customer's needs. The customer's acceptance of your solution is his placing an order with you. Our sports analogy of "Crossing the Finish Line" means that both you *and* your customer arrive together. Another way of thinking about it is that you are the coach and you have assisted your customer to arrive at the correct decision.

Gaining customer commitment to a solution should be the logical conclusion of everything that has previously occurred. When employing the consultative sales approach, there is virtually no need to push the customer (as is done in traditional sales approaches). Instead, you *lead* the person to

Figure 20-1 Consultative Sales Track

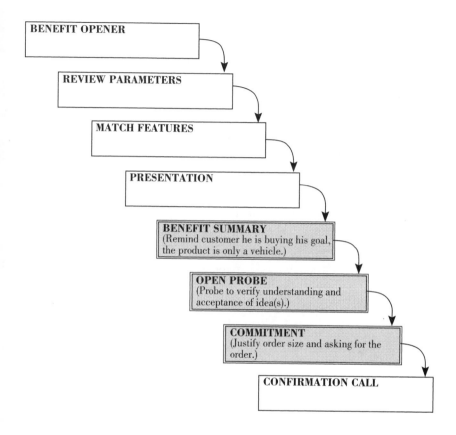

BENEFIT OPENER

REVIEW PARAMETERS

MATCH FEATURES

PRESENTATION

BENEFIT SUMMARY
(Remind customer he is buying his goal,
the product is only a vehicle.)

OPEN PROBE
(Probe to verify understanding and
acceptance of idea(s).)

COMMITMENT
(Justify order size and asking for the
order.)

CONFIRMATION CALL

the appropriate conclusion. This creates a positive, win-win situation that is very helpful for referrals and repeat business. It brings closure to his or her need and reinforces the long-term sales process.

REASONS FOR NOT ASKING FOR THE ORDER

Many traditional salespeople actually dread asking for an order. Most of these people do not have an effective approach to assisting customers and, as a result, are essentially uncomfortable about the entire sales process. (If you find yourself associated with a company that employs the "hard sell," and if it makes you uncomfortable with either the process or with yourself, you may be wise to search for a different company.)

The biggest problem that many people have is actually asking for the order at the end of the sales process. There are numerous reasons for this, including

- Fear of rejection, that is, the customer saying "No"
- Conscious or unconscious realization that their solution is less than ideal and that they may be pushing something that isn't wanted, isn't needed, and the customer is unable to afford (the definition of the traditional salesperson)
- Lack of rapport with customer
- Being unaware of the customer's actual needs, thereby offering a solution that is "a shot in the dark"
- Being unaware of the customer's psychological profile and buying motivations; consequently, not really knowing how to make the presentation in the most effective manner
- Having hidden something from the customer, perhaps by bypassing or disregarding a concern.

For these reasons and many more, some individuals avoided asking for the order even though:

- It was their job.
- It was the way they got paid and promoted.
- It was how they were measured.
- *It was why they were hired* (hired to sell).

The consultative selling approach offers a better solution in which the customer's commitment is the only logical course of action.

It is important to realize that most customers will not ask to place the order themselves. For most people, spending money and making a commitment or a change are difficult. During your presentation people are *not* mentally saying to themselves, "I hope this broker asks me to buy some stocks. I can't wait to buy. Please ask!" Psychologically, it is easier for customers to say yes to you than it is to request that you please take their order. Furthermore, most customers fear change (even though it may be positive) and must be motivated to actually get off the fence and make a decision. A primary function of your job is to help them in that process through motivation and persuasion. Otherwise, all your efforts will potentially have been a waste of time.

In summary, financial salespeople avoid asking for the order for many reasons, including the belief that people neither can, nor should, be influenced; the potential for displeasing the customer; and the rejection that may result from asking ("If I don't ask, they may not buy, but they won't reject me, either.").

In general, fear of asking for the order is ridiculous. Ask yourself, "What is the absolutely worst thing that can happen if I ask for the order?" The customer is not going to throw eggs at you; you won't be thrown out on your ear; no one will laugh at you. The very worst that can happen is that the person says no—giving you the opportunity to find out why and perhaps uncover a previously unstated need or concern. When you find out the reasons, you will also discover key motivations that can then be addressed.

"To Ask or Not to Ask. That Is the Question."

Of course, the other side of the coin is that you can choose not to ask for the order and be relegated to mediocrity or, using a euphemism from modern business, eventually "terminated." It is unfortunate that some people will allow themselves to be fired rather than put their egos on the line. Of course, they won't see it as black and white as this. There are usually many other reasons or excuses such as "I wasn't cut out for sales," "The market wasn't good," and so on. All may be contributing factors, but the responsibility still lies with the individual—you. Again, if you employ the sales process recommended by this book, problems like the ones previously outlined will usually be bypassed. The pages that follow provide a specific procedure to follow that ties together many of the things you have already learned.

> **BENEFIT SUMMARY**
> (Remind customer he is solving his need, buying the product is only a vehicle.)

Before asking for the order, it is important to summarize the links between your product's features and the benefit(s) sought by your customer, that is, their buying motivations and investment parameters. This provides a final reminder to the customer of why he is purchasing the product and prepares him for the commitment/closing stage. *If your presentation has been effective, customers virtually have to agree. When they do, they have effectively bought your product again.*

> **OPEN PROBE**
> **(Probe to verify understanding**
> **and acceptance of idea(s).)**

We introduced this step in the previous chapter. It is here that you want to discover any objections that the customer may have. If an objection exists and is voiced, then you should deal with it immediately and probe for more information. If the customer gives you another "Yes," probe again and continue with the commitment process.

We cannot overemphasize the importance of probing for acceptance and understanding throughout your presentation. The last time you bought a car, even if you knew all there was to know about it, you probably asked questions before you bought it. Why? If you're like most people, it was because you wanted to be reassured that you were doing the right thing in making that particular purchase. Given the price of that investment, you could not afford to be wrong. Your customers are no different. They have a psychological need to be reassured that they are making the right choice.

> **COMMITMENT**
> **(Justify order size and ask for**
> **the order.)**

A Purchase Should Be the Next Logical Step

The customer's purchase of your product or service should be the logical conclusion of your discussion. You have carefully reviewed the benefits to be received and made sure the client agreed that the product or service will fulfill a particular need. You have been doing this throughout the presentation and have already addressed any questions, concerns, or objections the customer may have had. Remember, you are offering a solution to help him, not asking for a commission to help yourself.

Justifying the Order Size

Many financial salespeople believe that you should always ask for the biggest order you can get. While sophisticated customers know how much they can spend for your product or service, as well as how much they need, it is still your responsibility to suggest an order size that is appropriate. If you don't do this, the customer may feel that you don't really understand her needs or that you are grabbing for her wallet. In either case, you may lose all the credibility you have so carefully built up. If you have profiled your customer effectively, you already know the appropriate-size order to suggest.

You may think the worst thing that can happen when you ask for a big order is that the order size will be reduced by the customer or that you won't get the order at all. In actuality, the worst thing may be that you *will* get the order! Failure or refusal to pay, cancellation of the entire order, law suits, and so on are some of the extreme responses. Loss of rapport and confidence and the potential of the long-term relationship are the more common consequences. The few times when someone places an unusually larger order, are offset by the negative effects from the majority who are annoyed by this unprofessional sales tactic. However, in most cases your only indication will come from loss of the client, fewer referrals, and so on. For example,

> A prospect/client reveals that she has $25,000 to invest. The broker assumes this is the tip of the iceberg and suggests that she buy 1,000 shares of XYZ stock at $25 a share. The client agrees. Later the market corrects, and at the broker's trial it comes out that he put his customer's entire liquid net worth into one stock. The broker has demonstrated that he was not competent, ethical, or professional, and certainly did not "know his customer."

If you have properly profiled your customer, you will know

- Her financial needs and goals
- The funds she has available/committed for the purchase a solution to her need/goal
- Her risk tolerances for investments relative to those goals

With such information, you can make order-size recommendations that are balanced and appropriate. As a result, your recommendations will not meet the kind of resistance that is generated when customers feel you are using them. Ideally, you will work with your customers to establish their goals and the parameters of each of those goals. If you do this, the order size will always be correct, and your customers will find it far more difficult to turn down the order.

The simplest way to verify and justify an order size is to refer to that parameter that you developed jointly during the profiling session and *repeated at the beginning of your sales presentation* (during the "review parameters" stage). For example, "Ms. Brown, a few minutes ago you indicated that you wanted to spend up to $5,000 for Mary's (the child) education at this time. Is that still correct?" (Unless your presentation was extremely good, or very bad, your customer should stay with the parameters that you established during profiling and reiterated during the review of the parameters.)

At each of the previous steps you are hopefully getting a "Yes" response. The "yes set" helps the customer build enthusiasm for the purchase and deal with tendencies to postpone needed decisions.

You've already gotten customer acceptance numerous times.

+	The benefit opener confirmed continued interest.	Yes#1
+	You presented the review of the parameters and customer wants to hear more.	Yes#2
+	Responses to the probes following each part of the presentation were favorable.	Yes#3+
+	You handled all the customer objections and concerns.	Yes#4+
+	Customer agrees with multiple summary of benefits.	Yes#5+++
=	You gained commitment.	**YES!**

By the time you get to the close, your customer may have said "yes" (or its equivalent) 10 to 20 times!

There are stylistic differences in how you present the summary as well as in how you ask for the order. The summary should be coordinated to the approach you have taken in the sales presentation. That is, if you were using visual aids, continue to do so. The idea is to have a smooth transition from the presentation segment to the gaining commitment segment.

THE SALE BEGINS WHEN THE CUSTOMER SAYS "NO"

One thing consistently said by the people we've interviewed, and by most of the really good sales books, is the value of not taking the initial "no" for an answer. At least ask, "What specific reasons do you have for not making this purchase?" It all comes back to realizing that the product/service you recommended was, in your best professional opinion, right for this customer and this moment in time to help solve his problem. If nothing else, you deserve to know what happened so that you can avoid such situations in the future. You may also discover what you missed in your original profiling session so that you can avoid similar situations in the future, and perhaps reopen a sales discussion with a new understanding of the client's needs. A good way of thinking about it may be that the client's rejection of your proposal (assuming you have made all reasonable efforts to discuss it and that, based on the new information, your original proposal is no longer viable) is merely the basis for a new discussion on a different idea.

In many cases, there is some underlying, previously unstated, concern that hasn't been addressed or wasn't adequately answered in the earlier phases of the conversation. The customer feels uncomfortable about something and you ought to find out what it is. You should be quite curious at this point because of all the preliminary work you've done with this person. You still have the customer's interest as a primary concern allowing you to continue to go forward. You are trying to help the customer solve a problem. The customer needs your services. Continue to maintain the professional, consultative attitude.

Also remember that many people dislike, or fear, change. Surveys have shown that only 20 percent of people are "change accepting" and that 80 percent of people are "change rejecting." These statistics would indicate that most people do not like the thought of change and, at least on an unconscious level, will avoid it. Given this realization, it may become your responsibility to motivate and persuade your clients do what is best for them. You must be positive in your mind that you are right and very open to the possibility of unstated objections that may be in the way and that might actually negate the validity of your recommendation.

THE BEST CLOSE

The best close is one that is very consultative and follows the format outlined earlier. By reminding your customer of his need, and the parameters of its solution, and then demonstrating how your solution will resolve his need, you can make an extraordinarily persuasive case. You don't have to rely on "mere techniques" or efforts to "pressure" the customer.

The best closing techniques also involve as many senses as possible. Recall how people process information using the visual, auditory, or feelings mode. Also remember that in the preparation stage we suggested that you prepare presentations so that all senses were employed. The same logic applies to obtaining customer commitment for your solution to his need.

Personal Performance Analysis

This analysis will be expanded more fully in Chapter 26 when we offer a specific method for analyzing your performance. For now it is wise to keep track of the number of times you make a full or partial sales presentation, as well as the number of times you actually ask for the order. Your sales will increase dramatically the moment you pay conscious attention to asking for the order. Most people are amazed at how rarely they say something like, "I'd like to place an order for this annuity . . . this bond . . . this policy. . . . this whatever." Remember, *you can't help your customer unless you ask for the order!*

You've already justified the size of the order—now ask for it! No wishy-washy, "sorta-kinda" stuff—go for it! Ask for the order! If you do that, you will win with regularity. If you don't do it, you've wasted your time and energy. Your willingness to ask for the order will determine your level of sales success. If you have been employing the consultative sales approach throughout your discussions with customers, then, assuming that there were no questions, comments, concerns or objections that would prevent a purchase, this is the right product/service for this person at this moment in time! If the solution is appropriate, it becomes your duty to employ all your persuasive skills to assist the customer to make a decision. This is a "soft" method that produces a compelling response.

The Dartnell Corporation found in a survey[1] that 90 percent of (sales) reps quit selling before the prospect was ready to buy, despite the fact that 80 percent of sales are made after the fifth contact. They found

48 percent of salespeople quit pitching after the first contact.			
25 percent	"	"	second contact.
12 percent	"	"	third contact.
5 percent	"	"	fourth contact.
10 percent	"	"	fifth contact or later.

By discovering the customer's needs, getting acceptance that any solution that meets or exceeds his parameters will be purchased, and then making a persuasive presentation that emotionally and intellectually proves your case, the gaining commitment stage is relatively simple.

Regardless of the logic, some people will still hesitate for a variety of reasons. If the reasons come from the human tendency to procrastinate making a commitment, then you have some tools to assist them in "doing the right thing" for themselves. If the reasons come from hidden, previously unstated, information, then you may have to rethink your solution. In either event, you maintain the relationship and the attitude that you are there to assist the customer. You remain and enhance your professional standing.

[1]As reported in "Hang In There, Baby," *Sales & Marketing Management*, December 1993.

21

Getting Better and Better
Postsales Analysis, Duties, and Responsibilities

In profiling we set up the parameters of each goal and, therefore, the rationale for the next few phone calls. This chapter concludes this section on the selling process for each of your client's goals. You will discover that what you do after the sale is made is potentially as, or even more, important than the sales process itself. It is here that you will consolidate the long-term relationship with your customer. It is after the first sale that you have the opportunity to fulfill additional customer needs in the process known as *account penetration.* Postsale follow-up will enable you to get referrals that will further promote your business. It is also postsale that you *analyze your own performance* and advance your professional skills.

Consultative selling emphasizes that appropriate follow-up and customer service are vital to long-term customer relationships. In fact, 100 percent of the sales managers we've polled indicated that these areas were very important for success in sales. This chapter also allows you to focus on both your customer's and your own continued development. Continuous improvement—on a personal and professional level, and for every business—is essential for long-term success. But how do you improve?

Professional, consultative selling places heavy emphasis on continuous improvement in every sense of the word. Coupled with ongoing concern for your customer's well-being, you, as a professional, more quickly increase your business.

CONFIRM THE ORDER

Once your customer has accepted the order, make sure you are both clear on the points of your agreement by reading it back to them. Then tell them that you will call back shortly with a confirmation of the sale. For example,

> "Ms. Sprect, let me make sure I have all this down correctly. We're going to buy 5 units of the Corporate Income Fund 554th Monthly Payment Series. The price per unit is $996 for a total investment of $4,980, plus accrued interest. Is that correct? I'll give you a confirmation call later. Thank you."

It is always important to verify your order in some manner to ensure that no misunderstandings occur. Make sure that you actually read back to the client what you write on the order ticket. This avoids having to go to your manager with comments such as

> "I marked buy for sell, now I don't feel so well."
> "I meant 100 shares, not 1,000"
> "I should have bought the Jan 50 put rather than the Jan 50 call."
> "I have to bust a trade. I bought ABC Industries instead of ABC Corp."
> "I entered a limit rather than a market order, and the market really moved."
> "Wrong stock. Wrong price. Bad day."
> "Hi boss, do you have a sense of humor?"

Always call back with the confirmation because

- That's what a professional does.
- It will enable you to reinforce the customer's decision to buy.
- It will enable you to confirm the cost of the transaction (so the customer can put the check in the mail).
- The confirmation call is the ideal time to ask for a referral (more on that later).

Confirming the sale/order is also an excellent way to reduce the anxiety experienced by many customers when they have just made a major purchase. Of course, this is not necessarily true for smaller sales, yet remember that people still like to be reassured. For example,

> "Mr. James, this is Bob Bennet. I'm just calling to confirm that we were able to obtain the XYZ stock at 23 and 7/8 per share. For 1,000 shares, that works out to $24,212, including commissions. Congratulations. I think we've made an excellent start on building your retirement fund. Wouldn't you agree?"

Must you absolutely do this? Of course not! Is it wise to follow-up on a sale with a confirmation call? Absolutely!

Buyer's Remorse—Revisited

After any purchase, most people are anxious about their decision and wonder whether or not they did the right thing. In other words, they are often scared and second-guess themselves. Depending upon the purchase, friends and family members may tell them that they didn't need it in the first place; they paid too much; there are better products available; they have a friend in the business; the service is inferior, or no good; or the market is about to go to a place otherwise known for its extreme warmth. If any of these things occur, and they often do, your customers now may have their confidence shaken, perhaps severely. "What did I do? What did I do?" is what they might be saying in their head.

As you can well imagine, once doubt is planted in someone's head, any concerns are magnified. Such concerns, left unchecked become "buyer's remorse"—where customers are sorry that they bought it in the first place, they are unhappy with their brokers, and they think themselves foolish and may begin to panic.

Buyers remorse, even if the customer is unable to return the item (because of the nature of the product or a "no-returns" policy—especially with respect to stocks, commodities, or options) may come back to haunt you. When people are dissatisfied they will tell 9 to 15 friends about their problem, their financial salesperson, your company, and your product line. In essence, one dissatisfied customer gives a lot of negative publicity. As you know, *it is extremely difficult to overcome a bad reputation and extremely easy to get one.*

This is not to imply that everyone suffers from buyer's remorse. Most people remain satisfied with their purchases. However, there are also many people who second-guess themselves and put themselves in such a negative mental state. An experienced broker can often spot the likely candidates of buyer's remorse. For example, you might say something like this to a socialite client: "Most of your friends will congratulate you on your purchase. Of course, a few people may not even be aware of the overall value that you received. If someone you talk to isn't sure or wonders about this product/service, please refer them directly to me. I'll be happy to give them the same great service you have received while providing them with all the additional information they require. How does that sound?" (This may result in a referral.)

While buyer's remorse happens occasionally, customers often find themselves with new questions or concerns that they had not previously addressed. This becomes one additional reason for the confirmation call. It allows you do quickly deal with any issues quickly as well as to reinforce the point that the customer made a good purchase. A confirmation call, therefore, allows you to

- Verify the order.
- Reassure the customer.
- Deal with certain causes of "buyer's remorse."
- Perhaps, get additional referral business.
- Increase the customer's confidence and trust in you.
- Verify and reinforce satisfaction.

REFERRALS

There are only three ways to increase a base of customers: beat the bushes for new customers, hope you have someone respond to an advertisement and either calls you or walks in, or obtain referrals. Asking for a referral is often the single easiest way to obtain new customers. However, like closing a sale, the biggest problem in asking for a referral is doing it. The reasons we most typically hear for not asking for a referral are

- Fear of rejection
- Embarrassment over what the customer may think
- Fear of inconveniencing the customer
- Forgetting
- Fear of being considered unprofessional

Yes, asking for a referral *may* result in rejection and failure to get the referral. This is especially true if you ask ineffectively. However, *failing to ask for a referral will almost guarantee not getting one.*

Caldwell Banker, the real estate sales chain, indicates that a full 85 percent of customers polled would provide a referral if asked. However, very few customers were ever asked. Surveys within the financial services industry yield similar results.

It is possible that a customer will feel inconvenienced if he is asked for the name of someone else you can help. However, placing untested assumptions upon a customer (i.e., assuming they will actually feel inconvenienced, rather than complimented) is, at best, self-defeating. Your customer may not feel that way at all. In addition, remember that you have just helped her solve one or more of her problems. Many people will actually feel indebted to you and would be grateful for a chance to repay that "debt."

If someone has just done you a favor—has helped you out of a dilemma and helped you get what you wanted—how would you feel? Chances are, like most people, you would shake that person's hand and say "Thank you" and wish to return the favor. Chances are, also, that you've had some one help you in the past and that you felt grateful. Finally, the chances are that you've recommended a particular store to one of your friends because of something that happened that you liked. In each of these cases, the chances are that you would have returned the favor by giving the sales professional a referral if asked. This is also true for financial services.

Forgetting is the most common reason for not asking for a referral. Try to constantly remind yourself to ask for a referral. (There will be a series of suggested "referral request statements" offered later in this chapter.) The key to getting referrals is to *remember to ask!* We know many brokers who tape a sign to their phone that says: "Ask for referrals." We know of other sales professionals who don't consider it a successful day unless they've obtained three referrals.

As you know, referrals are the easiest source of new business. Regardless of what you sell, getting referrals is an excellent source of new business. There are many star performers who obtain over 80 percent of their new business in this manner. Satisfied customers will let their friends and associates know about you, but you must let them know that you both accept and want referrals. It is surprising how many people would be absolutely pleased to give you a recommendation. (Remember that when people are dissatisfied they will voluntarily tell 9 to 15 friends about their negative experience. You owe it to yourself to take advantage of the times when they are happy and satisfied.)

Here is a story that we originally presented in *Consultative Selling Techniques for Financial Professionals*. We repeat it here because the situation is so common (although the numbers not as dramatic). During our training sessions, we've heard many variations on the story.

A very successful financial consultant did not make it a practice to ask for referrals. However, after attending a seminar on getting referrals, his manager asked him to try obtaining a referral from one of his clients. The broker called a client to whom he had recently sold $800,000 in municipal bonds. When he asked her if she knew anyone else he could help, she said, "Oh my heavens! Do you accept referrals? I didn't think you did. So, every time you sold me a bond, I told the other five girls in my bridge club, and they made the identical purchase. When they asked me if you could help them, I said I didn't think you accepted referrals. I just told them to call your firm and open an account."

This broker was not a happy man. By failing to ask for a referral, he realized he had lost commissions on an additional $4 million in long-term municipal bond sales (that is over $80,000 in lost commissions), never mind the additional products he might have sold.

The possibilities for getting referrals are endless. Sometimes just saying that you appreciate their business and hope that they tell their friends to please visit your office is enough to gain referral business. However, always remember that obtaining referrals is one of the keys to success. There are basically two types of referrals: *active referrals,* when the person comes to you based upon the recommendation of one of your satisfied customers, and *passive referrals,* where you contact them based upon the recommendation of one of your satisfied customers.

MAINTAINING GOOD SERVICE

A major factor in receiving referrals is providing good service. Many brokers take their customers for granted. This doesn't work in personal relationships, and it certainly doesn't work in business relationships. While they were still prospects, you promised them the sun, the moon, and the stars if only they would become customers. "You will get the best service possible," you promised. Then they became customers, and the honeymoon was over. The salesperson failed to live up to all the promises, and the customer became some other broker's prospect and was wooed away.

As you periodically keep in touch after the initial sale, try to upgrade your value to the customer. You can do this by periodically calling to find out how they are doing, whether the customer has additional needs, sending them product updates or information on new products. All these show that you care.

Changes in Life Style

Changes in life style or personal circumstances may require modifications in their portfolio or create opportunities for additional products and referrals. For example, the birth of a child may provide the opportunity for a savings program for the education, a uniform gift to minors account, referrals to the grandparents who may wish to establish their own programs, transfer of certain assets to the child's lower tax bracket, trust accounts, and so on. (This is more fully covered in Section VI.) Other common situations which require multiple financial readjustments include

Divorce	Inheritance/bonus	Marriage
Death of partner	Layoff	Illness
Job change	Lawsuit	Retirement

The key point is: Unless you keep in touch with your clients, you may never know.

It may seem like time, money, and effort that could be better spent somewhere else, but remember that you are developing your referral business. You will be constantly keeping your name in front of the person and occasionally reminding him or her to keep you in mind. Where appropriate, you should consider sending birthday and holiday cards to your customers. It won't be too long before you are considered a close associate and perhaps a friend of the family. Many high-level sales professionals strongly recommend this approach. They attribute much of their success to maintaining good service and keeping their names in front of others.

ASKING FOR REFERRALS

The best way to obtain referrals is to ask for them. Start with friends, family members, associates, and anyone else who has an interest in seeing you do well. Make them conscious of your desire to expand your business. Some of the ideas presented earlier in the book are also applicable here.

The traditional approach to asking for referrals would be to say something like, "I'm pleased that I was able to assist you and would welcome the opportunity to assist some of your friends or family members. Who in your (choose one) neighborhood, club, church, profession, family might I be able to contact?" For certain types of business this approach may be very effective. However, in financial sales, this approach can cause several problems:

- Unless customers really understand your products/services, that is, sophisticated customers, they are not competent to know who else might need such a purchase. (Until customers come to you, many probably had no idea which specific product is an appropriate solution to their need.)
- It does not utilize the customer's information base of people who have similar goals or problems to solve.
- You would also immediately be labeled a "salesman"—with all the potentially negative connotations associated with that label. Unfortunately this triggers customers' natural sales resistance.

If you were to go to your doctor with a sore throat, you would expect her to diagnose your problem and prescribe a solution. You would not expect her to ask you if you know anyone else who could use some penicillin. You are not competent to diagnose or prescribe. But you might know someone who would be interested in finding a good doctor. Your customer is no different. If he knew who needed a specific solution, he wouldn't have needed you to tell him that he needed it.

When asking for a referral, it is important to recognize that giving referrals will be good for the customer as well as for you. You want to let the customer know that you can also help her friends solve similar problems. For example, "Mr. Jones, I think we've done a good job of taking care of the kids' college education, today. Wouldn't you agree?" (If he agrees, he has just admitted that you have done him a service and he "owes" you one in return.) "Can you think of anyone else with college-bound children, whom I might be able to help the same way?" (While he might not be competent to determine who needs a particular financial product, he certainly knows who has children that they are planning on sending to college.) *Always think of additional ways that you can assist your customer or a referral of that customer.*

In speaking to customers, it is the authors' experience that asking specifically for family or friends can be threatening to the customer because it may be considered intrusive. By describing the kinds of problems you have helped them solve (such as college, retirement, security, etc.), the request for referrals becomes less threatening and still triggers associations that will make it easy for the customer to think of names. The reason for this is that we sort people in our memories by the interests or problems we share in common with them. We generally don't have a mental insurance file. For example, if you ask anyone for the name of someone he knows who needs a good insurance agent he is likely to respond with, "I have no idea." But, if you ask him who he knows who has children to send to college, or who is concerned about saving for retirement, or even who would like to save up to buy a 60-foot, two-masted sloop, he can probably give you many names, and a good insurance agent might help each of them. The difference occurs because *these are goals, or problems, that they are concerned about.* They've discussed them with friends, family and associates with similar concerns. Hence, they can easily recall the names of those with whom they share these goals.

Cards and Letters

Another method is to send out a nice card or letter that says something like

> From time to time you may meet someone who has a need for our services. I would appreciate it if you would give them my name.
>
> It has been a pleasure working with you, and I am looking forward to assisting you in the future.
>
> Thank you again for any assistance that you may provide.

Make sure you enclose a few of your business cards for distribution. This is not as effective as asking outright, but it does let the customer know you appreciate his business. Often, sending a handwritten note saying, "I just wanted you to know that I appreciate your business and am looking forward to continuing to work with you in the future," goes a long way.

Asking for Advice

People love to help others if given the opportunity. If you ask someone for advice, he or she will usually give it with pleasure. Why not ask some of your customers for advice on how you might get additional customers? They'll probably think of several ways that you haven't considered. They become mentally attuned to search for opportunities for you, and some of them are going to give you great ideas. Of course, they automatically become referral sources. One idea that almost everyone comes up with is recommending you to any friend or associate they can think of. We know of brokers who ended up with too many referrals because their customers/friends were so busy prospecting for them! Many people would love to help you if you merely allow them the opportunity and are appropriately appreciative.

Effective Networking

Maximize your networking system. For example, did you ever think of inviting a few of your customers and their advisors or friends to a private seminar on the changing conditions of the financial services industry or the economy? The information may be able to help them in their business.

You can invite customers to special seminars that would be of interest to them and require only that they bring a friend. Your customers will get to know each other, and you will become a center of influence. You can do the same thing at a customer's home—sort of a "Tupperware party" for financial advice. Your customer invites a few friends over to his or her house for a private seminar that you will conduct. Because you are there, you are deemed a member of the group of friends and will probably obtain a few accounts.

Each of your current prospects or customers can be considered the center of her own network of friends. Just join five or six networks. Even if you were only able to convince a small percentage of your customers to hold these private seminars, you would still make numerous contacts.

If you allow people to assist you, they will love you for it. Being extremely referral-conscious is probably the easiest and most effective way to increase your business. It only works for the sales professional who is doing an excellent job. Perhaps this is one of the many rewards for doing the right thing for others—they return the favor.

It is frequently, although not always, true that the most successful people succeed because they deserve to—they pay the price for success.

POSTSALE FOLLOW-UP

In addition to a confirmation call, which offers a host of benefits, there are often times when you will meet again with your customer to fulfill your ongoing responsibilities. This is especially true when dealing with corporate/business accounts. Depending upon the product, some typical postsale responsibilities include

- *Checking* on the order. Many other departments may be involved in setting up a employee stock purchase plan.
- *Conducting educational seminars* on taxes, gifting, and so on.
- Providing individual *financial counseling.*
- *Offering additional products and services.* Some products have different options available that the customer may not have wanted (or may not have known he wanted), such as cash management, when the pur-

chase was first made. For example, your follow-up with the customer and employees may uncover additional opportunities to help.

Offer your customers information on new business opportunities, different ways of using their products, business ideas, and information on what is happening in the industry. Always remember that, as a sales professional, you are an important source of information for your customer regarding matters within your industry. You are a recognized expert. Your customers rely upon you for financial advice and services.

Follow-up provides goodwill between you and your customer. By making sure the customer is satisfied, you are laying the foundation for a productive and positive business relationship. By meeting with a variety of people, over time you will discover other needs and additional ways to assist your customers. This is especially true when dealing with corporations. You become a valuable corporate asset and the person who receives most, if not all, of that customer's business. This is what happens when you establish strong relationships through consultative selling. Follow-up is also important because so many brokers fail to do it. It can really make you stand out from the competition.

Follow-up, account penetration (sales of additional products to the same customer), and service are not one-time things. All are provided on an ongoing basis and should be incorporated into your daily or weekly activities calendar. There are many ways to provide ongoing follow-up meeting with the customer. Three important tools available to you are phones, the mail, and a fax machine. Consider using these business tools to

- Send holiday or special-occasion cards.
- Send birthday cards. (Everyone, it seems, sends holiday cards and most people get quite a few. However, people tend to get birthday cards only from select friends and family members. If you were to only send one card a year to your customer, make it a birthday card.)
- Phone your customer whenever you've thought of a new way for him to increase business or benefit from using your product line, such as a new portfolio review service, or with market changes.
- Mail clippings on items of interest to your customer. It may not have to do with what you sell, but it does show that you care.
- Write congratulatory notes to people who have received awards or been promoted. *When working with corporate clients, remember to acknowledge people besides your one or two contacts within the company. Your*

corporate contact/or customer may be promoted, may leave or be assigned new responsibilities. Someone else may become your new point of contact. Wouldn't it be nice if you already had a good relationship with him or her?

- Prepare a brief monthly or quarterly newsletter. Remember, that you want to keep your name in front of your customers. This is, of course, subject to manager/compliance approval.

- Occasionally send product literature on new products and services you have available.

- Give a phone call if you learn something useful about one of your customer's competitors (although not if that competitor is also one of your customers). If your firm produces a relevant industry report, send that to your customer.

Remember to keep you customers informed and keep your name in front of them. Your competitors will.

As you help your customers achieve their goals they will help you achieve your goals.

NOTHING IS AS PERFECT AS IT SEEMS

Nothing is as perfect as it seems in most aspects of life. These next ideas on how to handle *complaints* deal with those times when things do not go perfectly well, when something goes wrong, when someone may be having a bad day and takes it out on you.

Complaints happen, are a normal part of business, and should be expected. There are two categories of complaints to consider: those you can anticipate and those that are unusual.

Complaints you can anticipate include those times when

- The confirmation was late.
- The quantity delivered was more or less than was ordered.
- Accounting error(s) appear on a bill. (Being charged too much or being charged for something not purchased tends to upset some people.)
- The product doesn't perform as promised:
    The company goes bankrupt.
    The stock goes down.

You can undoubtedly think of a another dozen reasons why someone might complain. The point is, all these can be anticipated, and when they occur, you can quickly get on the phone and resolve them.

Make sure you don't spend too much time fixing problems and putting out fires. Make sure what you are doing is worth the efforts involved. Delegate responsibility whenever possible or appropriate to your sales assistant. Let the customer know what is being done, who is handling it, and when you will follow up with that person. It gives your sales assistant more status in your customer's eyes and involves the SA in your business.

Always ask yourself if you are making the most productive use of your time. If the account potential is worth your time and effort, then, by all means, give it whatever it is worth. Often inappropriate amounts of time and energy are devoted to customers who complain the loudest, even though their account may not warrant such service.

Only by recognizing the value of your time and taking an objective look at account potential can you make such decisions. Even then, especially in the early years of your career, or until you know the policies of your company, check with your sales manager or boss. Advise your customer of the situation and let them make the decision (or take the heat). If you don't deal with a reasonable (or unreasonable) customer complaint, the now angry customer may even complain to the president of your company, not only about the problem but about you. On the other hand, if you devote an inordinate amount of time to fixing problems, you may not be making enough sales and put your job on the line. If you are unsure about how to handle the situation, ask your manager.

Remedial Action

The best remedial action is avoidance of the problem in the first place. But mistakes will happen. Certain unavoidable things sometimes occur and your company will probably have a policy for dealing with them. These policies may include

- Rebates or refunds
- Busted trades
- Discounts on future purchases
- Apologies

As Leslie Brokaw says, "In the wake of a botched job, the right combination of explanation, apology, and compensation can make a world of difference to your customers—and to your business's chances of success."[1]

Whatever the policy, inform your customer and indicate how it is your desire to avoid such situations in the future. Mistakes, once or twice, are often tolerated. Don't let them become a habit.

QUESTIONS THAT GENERATE FUTURE SALES AND KEEP YOU UP TO DATE

Getting new customers is only half the battle. The other is finding more ways to help your current customers in what is called account penetration. Many customers have more needs than are ever discovered by their broker because their needs change. This is true of virtually every broker that we've ever met or even heard about. The best brokers realize this and are constantly searching for ways to more completely satisfy their customers' needs. They are constantly asking additional penetrating questions and presenting additional ideas. As a result, they uncover needs that the average financial salesperson never even imagines exists—with a corresponding increase in compensation.

You'll be amazed with the results of the following experiment. When you are involved in sales, ask the following questions of about 20 of your best accounts, and you'll undoubtedly be amazed by their answers.

The Key Questions

How many times were you ever asked questions, similar to the following, by salespeople you have dealt with? What additional needs/opportunities might they have discovered if they had asked these questions?

- Can you possibly think of a couple of additional ways that I may be of help to you?
- What could you have used that I failed to offer you?
- Is there anything that I might be able to do for your company? Who should I contact to offer my financial services?
- How, specifically, may I better serve your needs in the future?
- Are you aware of the full extent of our product line?
- What could my company do to earn more of your business?

[1]"The Model Damage-Control Letter" by Leslie Brokaw, *INC.*, January 1994, p. 73.

Pick the questions that seem best and adapt them to your own style. Then, ask 20 of your accounts. The very best sales professionals are constantly asking these or similar questions. We are sure that you'll find the answers both educational and rewarding.

SELF-ANALYSIS AND DEVELOPMENT

You know the value of being prepared and constantly improving your product knowledge as well as your knowledge of the industry. It is equally important to analyze your personal performance after the sale. It is only by getting ongoing feedback, performing constant self-evaluation that you can hope to continuously improve. Since increased personal performance translates to higher income and enhanced career opportunities, these self-evaluation procedures are worth your attention. Combined with the information in subsequent chapters you'll be able to maintain ongoing motivation. We also suggest that you regularly perform a self-critique or evaluation on your sales performance. Experience has shown that this is always valuable and necessary if you are to enhance your performance. It is important to constantly refine your presentations and neutralize or eliminate bad habits.

FEEDBACK FROM YOUR MANAGER
OR PEERS

If you really want to improve, allow another broker to provide you with feedback about your performance. They'll hear things that you are doing which have already become habitual even though you have been giving yourself a self-critique. They'll also be able to offer alternate ways of saying things or making your presentation which will enhance your overall professionalism. Use them to stay out of a rut. That broker will also become a member of your personal support group and will start to have a vested interest in your success.

VI

THE ART AND SCIENCE OF MONEY MANAGEMENT

There are basically only two ways to make money in the financial services industry: (1) serve more clients and (2) increase the amount of assets you manage from the clients you already have. To accomplish this, you must have excellent interpersonal communications skills *and* be perceived as quite knowledgeable.

Acquiring excellent interpersonal communication skills and obtaining more clients have been the subjects of much of this book. Expanding the assets you manage (account penetration) has already been partially addressed in the chapters on financial profiling. It will be more fully explored in this section as the investment and resource pyramid concept is expanded beyond a mere profiling tool to that of ongoing asset management, a Dynamic Investment and Resource Allocation™ method. This section deals with such other important issues as

- Developing and explaining an investment philosophy.
- Surveying the three primary market forecasting tools.
- Explaining economic concepts to your clients in layman's terms.
- Assessing changes in market conditions.

- Assessing changes in client's personal conditions.
- Assessing investment strategies used by mutual funds and annuities.
- Analyzing options.
- Renewing industry rules and regulations.

22

"So, How Do You Pick Stocks?"
Developing an Investment Philosophy

You must occasionally explain complex topics to prospects and clients so that they feel comfortable with your recommendation and your level of expertise. To reiterate this key point: *you must be perceived as professional.*

This chapter has three primary goals:

1. Provide overviews of a stock/portfolio selection process that, with minor variations, is employed by most portfolio managers.

2. Provide an effective way of verbalizing this process to your clients.

3. Add value to your own investment philosophy.

In addition to having a good deal of knowledge about your products and services *you must also be able to provide a logical rationale for your solutions you recommend for their needs.* As a broker you may offer portfolio management services provided by yourself, your firm, or outside money managers such as mutual funds, fixed and variable annuities, and wrap accounts. Investors may ask you a series of technical questions that they will reasonably are expect you to answer. Thus, you should anticipate questions about dividends, growth rates, and safety, and so on. However, sometimes questions will be more complex. For example, a client may read something about Fed funds, inflation, the CPI, the GDP, fiscal policy, relative strength, momentum, and so on, in *any* of the financial periodicals and ask you to comment on what they read. "How does _____ affect me?" they might ask. Explaining these topics and answering their questions in simple terms can be difficult.

For example, explaining specifically how money managers manage money can be a difficult task. In reality, the vast majority of customers will be satisfied with a brief, almost vague explanation that makes them feel confident that their money is in knowledgeable, sophisticated hands. However, there are also many sophisticated customers who may wish to know, in much greater detail, the approaches, strategies, and investment philosophies that will be applied to their funds. These customers will not be satisfied with a vague explanation and could even find such an explanation potentially insulting. Certainly, they might choose another broker if you cannot answer such "simple" questions. For instance, read the following dialogue and determine how the client might feel:

> *Client:* "How do money managers find the right stocks? What do they do that makes them so special?"
>
> *Broker:* "They use sophisticated methods to find excellent potential situations using computer evaluations and relying upon the expertise of their portfolio managers who have been in the business for over 20 years."
>
> (Actually, this answer would probably satisfy most people.)
>
> *Client:* "Please be more specific about their stock selection process."
>
> *Broker:* "I don't know the exact process, but its quite sophisticated."
>
> *Client:* "Well, do they use the "top-down" or the "bottom-up" approach?"
>
> *Broker:* "I'm not too sure what you mean."
>
> *Client:* "I'm sure you can call the money manager and ask. By the way, what is your personal investment approach?"
>
> *Broker:* "I buy low and sell high."
>
> *Client:* (Chuckling) "That's what we all try to do. But how exactly do you determine what to buy and sell?"
>
> *Broker:* "I listen to our analysts, who are among the best in the world, and follow their recommendations. After all, they are paid to watch the market."

If you were the client, would you want this person as your broker?

If this were a sophisticated client, do you think he or she would deal with this broker?

Many brokers are appropriately taught to follow the advice of their analysts, portfolio managers, investment strategists, or senior people. "You do the selling and leave the managing to us" is the essential message. That's fine, as long as the broker doesn't have to explain anything beyond the basics. It also makes the broker completely dependent upon the people providing the advice. Brokers are not hired to analyze; they're hired to assist clients attain financial goals. Some brokers have "paralysis from analysis" and spend most or all of their time "studying" the market without coming to any conclusion, thereby accomplishing nothing. While they're analyzing the market, they are not helping clients. A "good mix" is needed between total reliance on the analyst(s) and doing it by yourself. Irrespective of what "mix" is right for you, you must be able to explain what the analysts suggest or what you suggest when the client asks, "Why?" or "Tell me more."

Most money management firms identify the basics of their investment philosophy within their sales literature. However, if not, you can always request that information from the fund by writing or calling. Here are two examples of a firm's investment summary: "We take a 'top-down' approach to the management of balanced portfolios, analyzing market and business cycles to determine which segments of the equity and bond markets will offer opportunities for price appreciation. . . ." A different money management firm says, "Our approach to the management of balanced portfolios emphasizes the 'bottom-up' identification of equity securities with potential for earnings growth, with the fixed income portion of the portfolio intended to limit overall portfolio volatility and to provide a stable income stream. The allocation of assets between equities and fixed income is based on our analysis of relative values within the financial markets."

It is important to be able to verbalize your own investment approach and philosophy beyond, "I listen to what our research analysts recommend"—the basic defense of many brokers. Such a statement is unacceptable to the vast majority of sophisticated and moneyed investors. Similarly, "The mutual fund managers are continually searching for the best opportunities" (undervalued situations, total return candidates, etc.) is equally unacceptable to sophisticated clients because it is too vague and doesn't answer the question regarding the criteria or methodology they employ. Regardless of whose money management expertise you are recommending, it is important to be able to describe their approach with an appropriate amount of detail (refer to the KISS and the Three-Level Presentation comments in Chapter 16).

PORTFOLIO MANAGEMENT STRATEGIES

There are two primary methods of portfolio management:

1. The *top-down approach*, which with economic and fundamental analysis and sorts through the data to eventually discover a series of viable stocks
2. The *bottom-up approach*, which starts with an individual stock and then ensures that the recommendation is justifiable for various reasons

As will be explored more fully, each is further modified by the portfolio manager's investment goals, such as total return, special value, undervalued, growth, and so on. Regardless of the investment goals, the top-down and bottom-up approaches have proven themselves as excellent investment strategies.

STOCK SELECTION METHODS

Stock selection procedures can generally be grouped into three primary schools of thought: *economic, fundamental,* and *technical.* A fourth school, *quantitative,* is becoming increasingly popular because of the increases in computer speed and sophistication. Each school of market forecasting and stock selection has its advocates and each works some of the time, but none are infallible. As you will see later, it is incumbent upon you (or the portfolio manager) to take the best from the various approaches. This chapter merely provides an overview of the process.

Before explaining the "top-down" and "bottom-up" approaches for portfolio selection, it is important to have a more complete understanding of economic, fundamental, and technical analysis. Michael Gayed, author of *Intermarket Analysis and Investing: Integrating Economic, Fundamental, and Technical Trends*, N.Y., Simon & Schuster/NYIF, 1990, provides the following definitions.

> Successful investing depends on the ability of investors to determine the market trend and direction of future price movement. . . . There are three schools of market analysis: economic, fundamental, and technical. Each advocates a unique methodology devised to help anticipate, and capitalize on, potential profit opportunities.

Economic Analysis

Economists are concerned with the business outlook, inflation, employment, and the economy at large. They study the statistics published by the Department of Commerce, the Department of Labor, the Federal Reserve Board (Fed), and the Bureau of Census, among others. Economists carefully analyze the Fed's monetary policy to project the future course of business activities. By analyzing the economic indicators, economists can forecast inflation, the housing market, the rate of unemployment, the household savings rate, corporate profits, and the economic cycle. . . . Studying the cyclical behavior of these economic indicators can help investors anticipate major turning points in business and in financial markets.

Careful analysis of the economic aggregates [statistics] can enhance investors' understanding of the impact of the business cycle on the stock and bond markets. This, in turn, can lead to improved awareness of the risks and rewards associated with the different stages of the cycle.

Fundamental Analysis

Analysis of fundamentals is, by far, the discipline most widely followed by professionals in the investment community. . . . By performing an in-depth analysis of the balance sheet, they claim, investors can assess the financial health of a corporation and its long-term potential. Fundamentalists' techniques are considered of great value in forecasting earnings, dividends, and sales growth. By analyzing financial statements, they identify liquidity, profitability, leverage, and market-related ratios as key to ascertaining a solid financial position. . . . Fundamental analysis is an effective way to deal with security risk and helps ensure the soundness of the overall investment decision.

Fundamentals serve as the catalyst that propels the trend of stock prices. Rising earnings and growing sales of a particular company should lead to financial growth. When investors are alerted to those improving fundamentals, buying demand for stocks expands, which pushes [stock] prices upward.

Fundamental analysis of industry groups is also important for the asset allocation process and active money management. Awareness of the groups' characteristics and typical behavior during the different phases of the business cycle helps identify leadership and avoid poor performers.

Market/Technical Analysis

The "market-timing method [technical analysis] utilizes studies of the internal market dynamics. It is helpful in measuring the relative performance among the various market sectors. Market timers [technicians] rely on statistical analysis to assess the prevailing trend. This method's thrust is based on comparative studies of the price momentum that propels strength or weakness in the broad market as well as on comparative studies of different industry groups and individual stocks.

One of this method's greatest strengths is its ability to track the flow of money that results from the continuous shift in the supply and demand forces characterizing intermediate and long-term market dynamics. By analyzing the industry groups' price momentum and the market averages, the quantitative method helps investors detect the changes in the market trend. Such analysis uses the concept of rate of change, momentum oscillators, and investors' psychology to determine evolving strength or weakness in financial markets. It is, indeed, the school that concerns itself with market trend perspectives; it relies heavily on comparative techniques to uncover the internal dynamics that help propel prices along a well-defined course. In addition, market timing techniques can help detect major turning points in the general market, industry groups, and individual stocks.

In essence:

All of these disciplines of market analysis have one goal in common: To identify market trends and anticipate important turning points. . . .

The Top-Down Stock Selection Process

To help you verbalize the portfolio selection (and management) strategies employed by most money managers (including your own firm's portfolio managers, mutual fund managers, etc.) we have provided two levels of explanation. The first level provides a brief overview of the entire process and should be sufficient for use with the vast majority of investors. The second level is more comprehensive. It is offered as a more sophisticated explanation as well as some useful ideas that you may wish to incorporate into your own investment approaches. It is not meant to be complete and is only a summary of our *Market Strategies* course.[1]

The Top-Down Approach—Level I   Essentially, the top-down approach involves an analysis of the current economic and political situation to determine which industries may be positively or negatively affected by anticipated events. For example, when new homes are generally being built, the roof and wallboard, construction, and lumber industries are among those positively affected. Conversely, when interest rates are high and we are experiencing a recessionary environment, new home sales decline and these industries are adversely affected. By analyzing major economic trends, economists attempt to identify various industry groups for possible purchase.

An analysis of industry fundamentals such as sales projections, production, available inventory, and corporate profitability further refines the process and identifies those industries that can be expected to do well in the foreseeable future.

Some money managers also analyze relative performance (how well an industry group is doing versus other industry groups or the market averages) in terms of potential price appreciation. If the statistics provide a positive valuation, then there is an increased probability that the industry group will remain attractive to many investors.

Having determined which groups have positive economic, fundamental, and, depending upon the manager, technical justification, individual stocks are selected from the best groups. The criteria for stock selection vary from manager to manager and are also partly dependent upon the investment objectives of the portfolio. Considerations such as price, dividends, sales, inventories, market niche, management expertise, profitability, overall financial structure and situation, and how a company compares to its competitors are carefully considered. While there are dozens of other factors that may be evaluated, the main point is that each portfolio manager or portfolio management team goes through an exhaustive process to find the best possible stocks for their portfolio and uses a particular manager "style." A brief definition of various investment manager styles follows:

- Value   The value manager reviews the universe of stocks searching for undervalued stocks based on fundamental and/or technical criteria.

---

[1]The Market Strategies course was originally developed by Steven Drozdeck while he was the manager of professional development for Merrill Lynch & Co. The industry and stock selection procedures presented in the course have been taught to over 15,000 brokers. Currently the course is taught to brokers at various financial firms.

- Growth   Growth managers look for companies whose sales, earnings, etc. are expected to grow more rapidly than other companies within the same industry.

- GARP (growth at a reasonable price)   Value and Growth criteria are considered. These managers typically do not focus on dividend yields like the Value managers, nor will high PE multiple stocks be considered like a traditional Growth manager.

- Contrarian   "Out-of-favor" securities are preferred.

- Sector rotator   These managers seek to identify and overweight those sectors of the stock market that are expected to perform well and underweight those that are expected to lag the market. (This is more fully explained in the Model Portfolio.

- Active asset allocation   These managers believe that allocating assets "optimally" among a broad asset range (stocks, bonds, cash) is much more important to portfolio performance than individual security selection.

- Income/yield   These managers take a bottom-up approach, concentrating on stocks with high dividend yields or dividend growth rates, lower than average PE ratios, and fundamentals strong enough to allow for capital appreciation.

- Core   These managers create portfolios which replicate the sector weightings of particular market index (e.g., Value Line).

- Indexing   These managers try to replicate the performance of a market index by purchasing all or a representative sampling the stocks within the index. Broad diversification is accomplished.

There are, of course, many variations on each of these approaches. Some managers prefer to make stock purchases within industry groups that are currently out of favor (therefore, lower priced or undervalued) and, it is hoped, therefore realize greater long-term price appreciation. Other managers look for "special situations" such as companies that have new technologies, a new patent on a drug, a manufacturer who is the best, or only, "game in town," and so on. These managers hope to find these special situations before other investors draw the same conclusions.

A funnel with a series of filters is a good analogy. (See Figure 22-1.) Each filter (step in the process) narrows the field of candidate industries or stocks. Eventually, a small number of stocks meet all the criteria and are

Figure 22-1 The Top-Down Approach

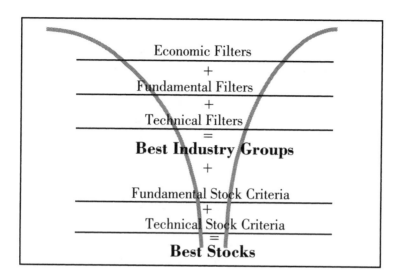

Economic Filters
+
Fundamental Filters
+
Technical Filters
=
Best Industry Groups
+
Fundamental Stock Criteria
+
Technical Stock Criteria
=
Best Stocks

chosen for the portfolio. This is an ongoing process that eventually takes profits, it is hoped, in previously purchased stocks and replaces them with stocks that have not yet made their move.

This rather simple explanation reviews the top-down approach used by most professional money managers. Conceptually, it makes sense and helps ensure an ongoing, objective evaluation of the portfolio. This is also the value added that the money manager brings to the table. On the other hand, the bottom-up approach begins by looking at a particular stock (or industry group) that has outperformed the market. The portfolio manager then compares that stock to its competitors and reviews the performance of the stock's industry group and the overall strength of the economy. Stocks are usually selected from those industry groups that have performed well during periods of market weakness. The expectation is that they will do substantially better (at least during the initial stages) than other stocks/industries at the early stages of a bullish market.

These two comprehensive stock selection methods should be contrasted with the method employed by some financial salespeople that encourage them turn to a more senior/knowledgeable person and whisper, "I have a client who wants growth. What do you like?" (We've actually observed this occur with a client actually sitting at the broker's desk. We wish we had a picture of the client's face as he looked at the person he was considering as his broker.)

"How Do You Pick Stocks?" "How Do They Pick Stocks?" "How Does the Mutual Fund Manager Pick Stocks?"   If you were asked how you (or the particular money manager that you are recommending) picks stocks, you might reply, "How do I/they pick stocks? In essence I/they use the top-down approach, which initially examines economic trends and then chooses industry groups that have the highest probabilities of benefiting from the anticipated economic environment. From these industry groups individual stocks are then chosen which meet key criteria, thereby finding, in their professional opinion, the best of the best." (Remember the KISS and the Three-Level Presentation approach introduced in Chapter 16. You can always present additional information if you choose or if they request by verbalizing some of the information contained in the upcoming Level II explanation.)

Another way of explaining your investment philosophy is as follows:

> "Our firm's specialists analyze the economy and make recommendations of industry groups expected to do well during the current economic cycle. I try to find several diverse industry groups that look particularly promising among those they recommend.
>
> "Our fundamental analysts examine individual companies to determine their overall strength and the quality of their management. Based on their recommendations, I look for companies in the industry groups I've selected that they feel are not only financially sound and well managed, but that are also undervalued.
>
> "Next, I check with our technical analysts to find out how each of these stocks is expected to perform in the near and intermediate term. From those results, I select the three or four stocks I recommend."

The Top-Down Approach—Level II

This more comprehensive explanation incorporates everything that was previously stated for Level I (we'll avoid as much redundancy as possible) and significantly expands the amount of material presented.

There are two processes that are normally employed: *industry and group selection* and *individual stock selection*. As stated before, these explanations merely provide an overview of the process that is normally taught in our 8-to 14-hour Market Strategies Course. Note: We have used some standard industry terminology (jargon) within the explanations. This chapter is designed to give the "flavor" of the process, not to "teach" it.

Industry and Group Selection

Economic Analysis

Economists look at the characteristics of the major industry sectors that have acted in a similar manner with each other during various stages of the economic cycle. Certain industry groups have their greatest *relative* strength during the early stages of a bull market, while others have their greatest relative strength during a bear market. That is, some groups are weakest during a bear market while others are weakest during a bull market. For example, profits for basic industries depend upon overall industrial capacity utilization. Approaching the peak of an economic cycle, shortages and back-orders tend to develop for steel, aluminum, and so on, because other (non–basic industry) manufacturers have used up their own stockpiled inventories for their own manufacturing purposes. Therefore, companies in the basic industry group may benefit from increased prices

Figure 22-2 The Top-Down Approach

Economic Filters
+
Fundamental Filters
+
Technical Filters
=
Best Industry Groups
+
Fundamental Stock Criteria
+
Technical Stock Criteria
=
Best Stocks

due to supply shortages near economic peaks. These industries, therefore, have their best relative performance in late bull and early and middle bear markets, which usually coincide with economic peaks. The basic industries have their worst relative performance during early or middle bull market when other industries—coming out of a recession—look more attractive to the investment community. Hence, by studying the current political, economic, monetary, and interest rate cycles you can determine which industry groups have increased probabilities of success due to economic reasons.

The rebuilding of America's infrastructure, cutbacks in military spending, and/or the development of new markets in Europe and Asia affect which major market groups will be positively or negatively affected by the resultant reallocation of assets. These additional factors are incorporated into our current place within an economic cycle. The analysts then superimpose the stock market cycle on to the entire process.

In summary, the stock market is a leading economic indicator itself and generally begins a bull market cycle during the latter part of an economic recession. At that point, certain industry groups can logically (due to economic and fundamental reasons) be expected to outperform the market during this initial phase. As the economy expands, other industry groups achieve favored status and have their best relative strength. Eventually, the economy starts to peak, and even though the economy is still seemingly strong, the stock market begins its bear market cycle in anticipation of upcoming economic weakness. During bear markets, different industry groups begin their upward rotations.

Fundamental Analysis

Simultaneously, yet independent from economists, fundamental analysts are also analyzing the state of American business. However, they examine factors such as inventory turnover ratios, sales projections, return on equity, and a host of other company and industry figures that indicate the financial status of individual corporations and of different industries. From these analyses, they determine which companies and industries should have the highest probability of success and which companies they will, therefore, recommend for long-term purchases.

Fundamental analysts promote companies that are expected to outperform the market due to the company's increasing financial strength, enhanced competitive position, introduction of a new product line, and so on. If numerous companies within a particular industry are expected to do well, then the entire industry is considered strong.

Model Portfolio

The economic and fundamental information is analyzed and a model, or ideal, portfolio is developed. Such a portfolio provides an overall strategy of how large amounts of money should be diversified and weighted. For example, it suggests how a larger percentage of assets within a broad-based portfolio should be placed in industry groups that have a higher probability of success during the next year due to economic and fundamental reasons. It further suggests that lesser amounts of money be placed within industry groups which do not have the same probabilities of success. This is all done to, it is hoped, outperform a broad-based market index such as the S&P 500.

While the economy and the market go through their cycles, the portfolio weightings will change as industries come into and fall out of favor. As the economists and fundamentalists make their adaptations, these changes are reflected within an updated model portfolio and individual portfolios are modified accordingly.

Technical Analysis

An analysis of industry and group rotation often occurs next. In general, industry groups in an uptrend tend to continue going up until certain parameters are reached/violated. Industry groups in a downward trend continue until they reach oversold conditions and begin a turn-around situation. Using technical analysis it is possible to divide the market into various categories of relative strength (strength-weakness relative to the overall market) and momentum (power behind the market move). Portfolio managers then look for industries in the beginning or middle of uptrends (avoiding overextended situations) or those that have completed their bottoming process.

The End Result of Industry and Group Selection   Taking all these factors into consideration, we find industry groups that have economic, fundamental, and technical justification. These industry groups have the highest probabilities of success within the stock market. It is from these industry groups (which slowly but surely change as the environment changes) that the best stocks, on both a fundamental and technical basis, are chosen.

Stock Selection Method

Fundamental Analysis of Individual Companies

This phase examines a series of key criteria used to compare all the stocks within a particular industry group. However, the weightings you give to cer-

Figure 22-3 The Top-Down Approach

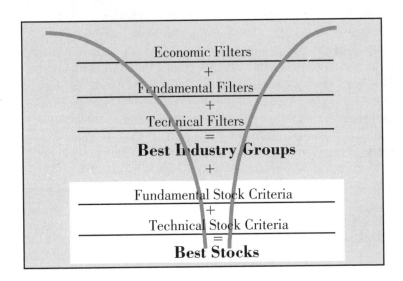

tain criteria will vary depending upon (1) the individual clients' needs/objectives, (2) the portfolios' objectives, and (3) the overall market climate.

The key criteria used to compare companies often include

- *Earnings per share (EPS) growth rates* in the past, present, and anticipated future. Searching for companies that have/are/will outperform their competitors. EPS is a key determinant of market success.

- *Return on equity.* This is a good way to measure a company's overall managerial efficiency. Ultimately, a company got to where it is and will get to where it is going based upon the abilities of its management. Search for companies that have a better return on equity track record than their competition.

- *Optionability.* The possibility of using options as a hedging tool is highly valuable due to increased portfolio management flexibility that can be employed when and if necessary. This flexibility can often make the difference between success and failure. *Only the most conservative option strategies should be employed for the vast majority of portfolios.*

Other comparative measures, such as dividend and dividend growth rates, long-term liabilities as a percentage of capitalization, percentage of stock held by institutions, book value, market to book value, and overall market value should also be considered. The cumulative effect of all these statistics will help determine which companies have the greatest relative attractiveness. (Note: These are companies within the most attractive industry groups.)

Portfolio strategists and managers will give different weightings to various items of financial data depending upon the portfolio's objectives. Managers searching for "value" have different criteria than those portfolios trying to achieve "growth," "income," or "total return." Some funds and portfolio managers specialize in special market niches—such as technology, health care, and so on—and therefore may favor different criteria. The criteria used in the stock selection process depend upon the portfolio's objectives.

Publications such as *Standard & Poor's, Value Line, Morningstar,* and *Moody's* all offer a wealth of fundamental information. Furthermore, magazines such as *Business Week, Fortune, Forbes,* and *Financial World* also offer numerous tables that allow you to compare one company with another.

Technical Analysis of Individual Companies

The last major sorting/culling stage is an examination of the performance of these companies selected via the fundamental analysis filters. Using technical analysis, four key criteria are employed when looking at the chart patterns. These same criteria are constantly monitored for change. (Any broker can easily review these criteria by using various technical chart services. We use *Current Market Perspectives* by S&P/Trendline in our courses.) In our opinion, the four most important technical criteria provided are

- Support-resistance
- Relative strength
- Volume
- Stock price relative to the 150-day moving average

Other criteria are also employed in the final selection process, and their weightings are partly dependent upon the portfolios'/investors' objectives. Only companies that have good chart patterns are selected. Note: Many managers do not use technical analysis at this, or any, stage.

The Net Effect

Companies which have good fundamental figures, stories, and chart patterns are chosen as candidates for final selection. Each of these stocks is within

an industry group that has good economic, fundamental, and technical justification. In summary, this organized and objective method quickly identifies the major opportunities within the market. (Special situations—new
products, take-overs, etc.)—are identified by a separate group of analysts
and are not part of this process.)

ECONOMICS IN ONE EASY LESSON

Upon hearing the word "economics," the majority of the populace and many
brokers become glassy-eyed, break into a cold sweat, and remember being
introduced to mountains of technical data and complex charts. These brokers may relate to the following, humorous definition of economics.

> Economics is a process whereby a person is able to turn out, with
> prolific fortitude, indefinite strings of incomprehensible mathe-
> matical figures, calculated with micromatic precision from vague
> assumptions, which are based on debatable figures taken from
> inconclusive data, carried out through forms of problematical ac-
> curacy by persons of doubtful reliability and questionable men-
> tality, for the avowed purpose of annoying and confusing a hope-
> lessly befuddled group of key personnel who never read the
> damned reports anyway.
>
> Anonymous

Unfortunately, because so many people feel this way, they do not avail
themselves of the information that is readily available and so important to
understanding the dynamics of the various markets. The next subsection attempts to partly rectify this situation by providing the basics of economics
in lay terms so that any broker can explain most economic concepts to their
clients. Remember that it is important to be able to explain complex topics
in simple terms. This economic explanation would be the equivalent of the
Level I Explanation of the "Top-Down" approach.

The "Ripple Effect" in the U.S. Economy
—*For Those Who Never Studied Economics*[2]
"Economic forces are constantly expanding and/or contracting.
The effects of these forces partially explain why economic recov-

---

[2]A reprint of an article written by Steven R. Drozdeck.

eries and recessions occur. When a pebble is dropped in the middle of still water it creates a series of ripples which expand in ever widening circles. Eventually, the ripples extend across the sides of the container where the "bouncing-off effect" causes new ripples to go in the opposite direction canceling out some of the secondary ripples from the pebble. Back and forth they go till the water is calm again, and a new pebble is dropped. This analogy can help explain our economic system.

To explore the "ripple effect" more fully, let us break into an economic cycle just as an improvement in business conditions is about to begin. The economic news has been poor. The number of people who are unemployed is constantly increasing. They, by definition, are spending as little as possible which means that sales figures are generally poor. Stores have "inventory liquidation sales" in order to bring in some cash to improve their overall financial position. Businesses depend upon constant cash flow in order to meet their weekly money needs—payroll, advertising, rent, etc. Because of their poor cash flow position, these businesses will order only the minimum of inventory needed to sell to their clients. Other businesses, who supply the retail stores, are in a similar position and keep their production and their payrolls minimal.

The government might try to stimulate the economy by reducing taxes or making interest rates go lower and credit more readily available. Some people, having more money in their pockets, and able to borrow money at low interest rates, begin to spend money on appliances, cars, clothing, etc. This makes more money available to businesses as sales are increased. These stores have to order more merchandise to replace the items that were sold. Since this is simultaneously happening for hundreds of thousands of stores, they will order from their suppliers, who must now increase production to fill new orders. Additional workers are hired to fulfill the orders—who now have more money to spend and further increase sales. It may take more than a year before the entire economy feels the effects of the initial governmental attempt to stimulate sales. The process goes a bit further. The suppliers must order from their whole salers who must order from their own suppliers. Most companies will benefit from the increase in economic activity.

As employment increases and credit remains available, many individuals will purchase or build new homes. As construction of these new dwellings begins, the construction industry—workers and suppliers—receives economic benefit. Eventually, after many new homes have been built, the appliances, furnishings, carpets, etc., industries develop increased cash flow. The process continues. . . .

Some companies have to order new, more efficient machinery to fulfill their current and anticipated production requirements. The suppliers of these machines receive benefit. These companies, as well as individuals, are borrowing from the bank in order to make their purchases. Unless the government is printing new money (which is inflationary), the banks will to have less cash available to make loans. (Remember that millions of people and companies are trying to borrow at the same time.) As less cash is available, the banks will charge higher rates of interest (due to the laws of supply and demand). At first, the money is borrowed and spent anyway, which causes increases in economic activity, *and* higher interest charges. Eventually, the interest rates will become high enough to reduce some additional borrowing. By now employment has increased tremendously. Most people have jobs, and companies need additional workers. In order to attract workers, these companies must offer more attractive salaries to their new and current employees. The increased salary expense is passed on to the consumer in the form of higher prices. Now, even though some people have more money to spend because of increased salaries, it takes more money to purchase new items. Interest rates are still going up so some people must cut-back on their spending.

The manufacturing companies which are now paying higher salaries, have higher debt because of the money they borrowed for new machinery; and are paying higher interest rates; and are also making fewer sales. They are making products faster than those products are being sold which means that their stockpile of unsold items increases. It also costs money to maintain and store those items, so their profits decline further. It gets to the point where it is unprofitable to produce more items because those items are not being sold fast enough. Therefore, production is reduced. Unless sales increase again, these companies will have to lay-off some of their workers to reduce their overall expenses.

Some workers will be laid-off and, as a result, will tend to spend money less freely than they had previously and overall sales become slightly lower. Meanwhile, mortgage rates are increasing with other interest rates and fewer people order new homes. This is also true for various companies who can no longer afford to build new manufacturing plants. The construction industry is negatively affected. Fewer construction workers are needed and some people are laid-off. The companies that service the construction industry also experiencing a turn-down in business. The same response. The negative aspects of the ripple-effect are beginning to be felt. Nationwide sales are reduced and less production is needed. The ripple-effect expands. Unemployment increases and people spend less. As this occurs, confidence in the health of the economy erodes and spending is reduced. Less spending, still. Loans are still being paid-off from previous purchases at relatively high interest rates. With reduced sales and personal income, this further reduces spending. Yet, because of a lesser demand for credit, interest rates now start to decline. The government begins to make more money available in order to stimulate the economy so the effects of the already beginning recession are relatively mild. The process continues until prices and interest rates become low enough to motivate some people to start spending again and a new economic upturn begins.

Of course, the above explanation is grossly oversimplified. However, it does explain some of the basic economic forces and their effects. The economy is in a never-ending cycle whose complexity is staggering. Everything happens for a reason, and to everything there is a season.

A question that is often asked is: "Why doesn't the government allow the economy to expand indefinitely by further stimulating the economy before the negative effects of the "ripple-effect" have a chance to take hold?" The government cannot do this without allowing another major inflationary cycle to begin. The negative effects would be disastrous."

23

Dynamic Investment and Resource Allocation Method

In Chapter 11, the Investment Pyramid was introduced as a financial profiling and asset allocation tool. This chapter will expand the use of the investment pyramid for periodic account reevaluation based upon market changes as well as changes in the client's personal situation. Additionally, the chapter will address such topics as

- Choosing the right type of investment vehicle
- Asset reallocation as a result of market changes
- Changing client circumstances
- Suitability of products based on client objectives

Resource apportionment is a new investment concept which employs the investment and resource pyramid as a dynamic method for portfolio management. Figure 23-1 shows an expanded version of the pyramid and includes various investments as well as other financial resources, such as equity in a business and vested retirement benefits. When dealing with your client's total financial picture, it important to include assets not traditionally considered by others. The *Dynamic Investment and Resource Allocation™ method* that was developed as part of our market strategies course conceptually demon-

Figure 23-1 The Investment/Resource Pyramid

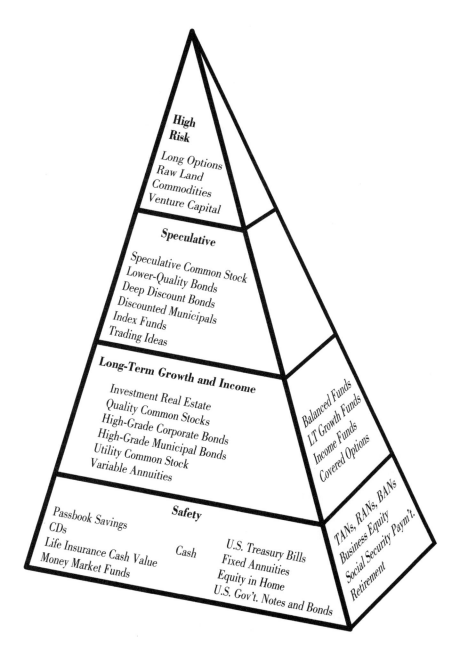

strates how changing personal and economic/market circumstances must be considered as we make needed changes within the client's portfolio.

Importantly, the entire process can be used as a sales tool with your clients to help them easily appreciate how you will manage their money. In essence, it helps them understand your own investment philosophy and provides the rationale and setup for any portfolio changes that you may recommend in the future. As you will see, this is an extremely important part of the consultative selling process and allows you to stand far apart from your competition and be perceived has highly sophisticated.

PRIORITIZING KEY INVESTMENT OBJECTIVES

Figure 23-2 is taken from our Investor Review Form™ and shows how you might merge information on your prospect/client profiling form with the concepts of the investment pyramid. Various investor objectives are ranked in order of priority. Each objective is assigned a percentage of the portfolio and the appropriate level of risk is assigned.

Depending upon the size of the portfolio, each investment objective can be fulfilled by a particular type of asset. Very large portfolios can have

Figure 23-2 Key Financial and Investment Objectives

	Rank	Pct of $	Low	Med	Above Average	Specific Products
Retirement income			L	M	AA	
Financial independence			L	M	AA	
Increase current income			L	M	AA	
Hedge versus inflation			L	M	AA	
Estate building			L	M	AA	
Children's education			L	M	AA	
Long-term growth			L	M	AA	
Speculation			L	M	AA	
Other			L	M	AA	
Other			L	M	AA	

Particular investment areas requiring special attention:

a separate investment and resource pyramid for each objective. For example, an investor with $1 million available (equivalently a mini-institution for most brokers) to invest may wish to accomplish a variety of goals, including

- Allocating $100,000 each to the three children with different investment objectives for each
- Placing $300,000 in a retirement account with protection of capital being the investment goal
- Placing another $100,000 in the same or a different retirement account with growth being the investment goal
- Placing the last $300,000 into a general investment account trying to achieve a broad mix of objectives

This person may require a six different allocation strategies—one for each of the monetary allocations. Depending upon the ages and educational needs of each of the three children, different asset allocation strategies might be employed. One child might require a greater safety orientation if college and grad school will be attended shortly. A younger child may have a larger percentage of assets allocated to growth vehicles.

Different Folks, Different Strokes

It seems that everyone has his or her own "asset allocation strategy" available on any computer. Unfortunately, most seem to give a person's age as the greatest (and, in some cases, only) weighting. Of course, age is an extremely important criteria that must be taken into consideration, but other key factors include

- Net worth
- Annual income of client and spouse
- Money available or due from other sources, such as retirement distribution or inheritance
- Discretionary dollars available
- Annual estimate of excess spendable dollars available for potential capital replacement or capital additions
- Size of current retirement plan(s), anticipated future value of plan and amount of money currently vested
- Number of children whose education may be funded

- Other possible long-term expenses such as caring for aged parents (or other disabled people)
- Risk tolerance—intellectual and emotional
- Whether additional assets may become available (such as a separate portfolio held by the spouse or by the client)
- Investment objective(s) of the client
- Investment goals of the portfolio
- Economic conditions within the United States and our trading partners
- Market expectations in and out of the United States
- Inflationary expectations
- Interest rate projections
- Economic, military, political, and social stability in and out of the United States

While the list is certainly not all inclusive, it does highlight some of the additional factors which must be taken into consideration when creating and managing an investment and resource pyramid.

Figure 23-3 shows how the shape of a pyramid may change for

1. Different individuals based upon age, resources, and other factors just listed
2. Changes in investment/resource structure and composition due to economic/market expectations
3. Varying investment objectives

1. Different Individuals Based Upon Age, Resources, and Other Factors *Pyramid I* may represent younger persons who have the time and money to recoup potential capital losses. Hence, they have a narrower base/foundation devoted to safety and have a higher percentage allocation devoted to products with increased risks. Of course, factors such as lesser amounts of money, lower earnings potential, or psychological disposition to risk may suggest that a different pyramid strategy/shape is more appropriate. Young individuals with little money, low earnings potential, and a risk-adverse posture (as well they should be for the circumstances described) ought to be putting the vast majority of the money into the safety area and would therefore choose pyramid IV. On the other hand, a wealthy individual with excellent earnings potential (possibly with multiple port-

Figure 23-3 Investment/Resource Pyramids

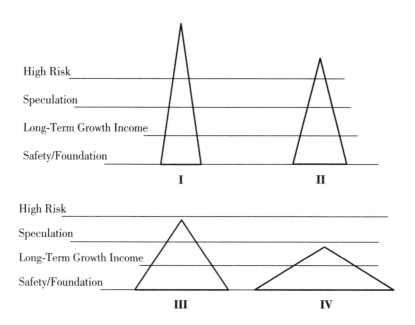

folios) may lean toward higher risk investments. "Different strokes for different folks."

Pyramid II may represent people in their thirties, who are beginning to expand their investment base—perhaps with equity in a house—and may have lesser amounts of money in the high risk area. As above, different personal and financial circumstances might suggest different resource apportionment strategies.

Pyramid III may represent middle-aged couples who may only choose to speculate as a hedge versus inflation. The value of their retirement plan (and whether they're vested) may constitute a large portion of the foundation. Also note that, for most investors, the time available to recoup from a financial loss is reduced. Financial disasters may totally and irreparably destroy a person. Remember that the foundation should constitute diversified resources. Here, additional portfolio insurance may be taken in the form of long term index put options (see chapter 24 for additional ideas).

Pyramid IV emphasizes the safety aspect and would typically apply to elderly individuals who have to have the majority of money in the foundation and whose long-term growth and income portion may be as a hedge against inflation. This pyramid could also be appropriate for college students wishing to fund grad school or young couples just starting out and trying to build a strong foundation.

2. Changes in Investment/Resource Structure Relative to Economic/ Market Expectations Different types of financial assets are considered here, including stocks, bonds, mutual funds, annuities, and commodities. When reviewing the following comments, take into account that a person's investment/resource allocation is more than just a portfolio of common stocks. Too many brokers limit their own thinking and reposition only a limited number of financial assets. As major changes in economic or market conditions develop, it is important to look at the "total picture." Refer again to Figure 23-3.

Pyramid I represents a portfolio strategy within the latter part of a bull market when "speculation" is the name of the game. This is a very dangerous time within the market because speculative excesses are quickly corrected. Therefore, note how money remained in the foundation and the long-term growth and income area (rather than putting most/all of the money in the higher-risk categories.) Be ready to take a pyramid IV approach as we go through the market "topping process" and begin any corrections.

Pyramid II can be a portfolio during the early to middle stages of a bull market when economic and market conditions look favorable. Again, note the conservative emphasis.

Pyramid III is for those times when we are unsure of economic or market events: more safety, less speculation. Pyramid III is also for those individuals wishing a less speculative posture than described in the pyramid I commentary.

Pyramid IV is for economically uncertain times, or within bear market or economic recession. Note that monetary assets should still be within the long-term growth and income section as a hedge against inflation. If inflation is expected to increase, interest rates can also be expected to move up. A good fixed-income strategy would be to put funds into short-term, highest-available-coupon, money market instruments such as T-bills, short-term CDs, or money market funds. As interest rates trend downward, it's logical to go to longer-term fixed-income instruments and move additional assets into the equity side of the portfolio.

3. Varying Investment Objectives *Pyramid I* could represent an investment strategy trying to achieve long-term funding for retirement or for a child's education. Pyramids II, III, and IV would be appropriate for the same objectives with a shorter time frame. Growth and speculation would be the investment terms most closely correlated with this shape.

Pyramid II would be appropriate for a balanced approach with an emphasis on growth. A goal of long-term wealth accumulation could be represented by this shape.

Pyramid III has a greater safety orientation and is appropriate for a total return portfolios, as well as long-term growth.

Pyramid IV is oriented toward preservation of capital and safety.

The comments on the various pyramid structures are certainly not exact, or totally comprehensive. Alternative interpretations can be made, usually based on a slightly different investment philosophies. Also, the needs of the client would shift the interpretations. However, it does give the idea about how different personal needs, economic/market directions, and investment objectives cause the structure and the asset mix to be modified. We also find that *these illustrations are an excellent sales tool when explaining investment philosophies and strategies with a client.* Finally, it begins to show that the dynamic investment and resource pyramid is a "living" document that must be periodically updated based upon changes in any of the previously mentioned conditions.

Applying the Investment and Resource Pyramid to Smaller Portfolios

Resource apportionment and coordination tasks becomes more difficult for smaller portfolios. In many cases the specific product may be doing a "double duty" by working on two investment objectives simultaneously. For example, any excess income beyond a certain amount required for safety might be allocated to fund a vacation home or some other special project. Investments exceeding their growth expectations might have some of the additional income transferred to fund a child's education.

When working with clients with smaller portfolios, it is extremely important to avoid "borrowing from Peter to pay Paul" within the same portfolio. People have an unfortunate tendency to mentally have "double-duty money" where the same funds are expected to magically fulfill two separate, mutually exclusive goals. For example, a $50,000 investment may be expected to provide retirement income and fund an Ivy League education. While this is an unreasonable expectation, many clients unconsciously view what may be for them a large sum of money as able to accomplish these goals.

In essence, they feel richer than they actually are. Clients with smaller amounts of income occasionally think that all their investment dreams can be achieved with the one sum. Here, your unfortunate, but necessary, task is to disillusion the client of their unrealistic expectations. Occasionally, a married couple may each have the money earmarked for a different goal and never let their spouse know. Such miscommunications can be easily avoided within the profiling meeting.

LIFE CHANGES

In working with your clients, it is important to keep in mind that their lives are certainly not static. Most people experience a number of life-cycle changes that create new and different investment needs and objectives. As a broker, it is essential for you to understand the major life-cycle events that represent key change—what they are and how they can influence financial needs and buying decisions.

The following life changes will each create a need for different financial products and services. In some cases you will be able to make simple modifications in the portfolio. However, some of these events may require a massive restructuring. Consider each of the life-cycle events and think about how you would be able to assist the client for each. For example, marriage might entail the need for a new joint account, merged portfolios, new checking account, an updated will, and insurance policies on each other.

Life-Cycle Event	Possible Financial Need(s)
• Marriage	
• Birth of child	
• Divorce	
• Inheritance/bonus	
• Death of spouse	
• Death of business partner	
• Layoff	
• Job change	
• Retirement	
• Illness	

Each of these events may also modify the resource apportionment within the dynamic investment and resource pyramid. It is vitally important to your clients and to yourself that you keep appraised of these extremely important events. Clients should tell you as soon as they know. Of course, you cannot rely on people to remember to inform you of these changes. Therefore, as part of your responsibilities, we believe that you should contact each client at least every three to six months. There are some people that you contact daily or weekly. Many brokers, we've unfortunately found, contact some of their "inactive" clients about once a year, and there are many clients who are not contacted at all.

Within the banking industry this problem is also widespread. Many investment reps don't call their clients after the first trade. There are untold opportunities for cross-selling and referrals to other bank officers and departments—if only they coordinated their efforts more efficiently and initiated the necessary cultural shifts. In our work with banks we've found that many bank reps do not fully appreciate the potential that each client has to offer their bank. Even more important, these reps fail to appreciate how much benefit they can be to their clients if they go beyond the first sale to the fourth, sixth, and eighth sales.

If you are a banker, broker, or insurance agent, we believe that it is in everyone's best interest to periodically call each client. Check for changes in their personal situation while you simultaneously comment on their portfolio. During this call you can also use the referral technique described in Chapter 20. The important point is that you cannot help your clients if you don't know what's going on. The brokers we've worked with were amazed at how many additional assets, referrals, and sales they obtained when they went back to their clients and updated the client's financial profile. Leading producers throughout the industry use a variety of methods to contact their clients regularly.

While the investment and resource pyramid may be modified due to the personal, economic/market, objectives changes previously described, there is an additional strategy that has not been introduced—the logic of *re*-Apportionment.

REAPPORTIONMENT: SPREADING THE GAINS

Assume that you have carefully helped a person create a pyramid appropriate for their needs. For the sake of the discussion, assume that it is a

$100,000 portfolio in a pyramid II configuration, with the assets/resources divided in the following manner: 40 percent safety; 30 percent long-term growth and income; 20 percent speculation; and 10 percent high risk as shown here.

Because of brilliant selection techniques on your part, the speculative area appreciates by 50 percent. The speculative segment of the pyramid is now worth $30,000, representing 27 percent (not the agreed-upon 20 percent) of the portfolio. (Had you doubled the clients' money, the speculative segment would represent 33.3 percent of portfolio value.) Graphically, the pyramid changed its shape to

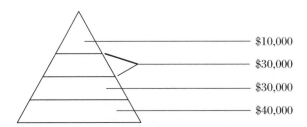

Most people would reinvest the entire $30,000 into another speculative stock. Perhaps they'd do well again; perhaps not. This tendency to "let the profits ride" (a term typically used in a casino, but a poor choice of words for investments) would be inappropriate from the point of view of maintaining the correct portfolio percentages. (Depending upon the sum involved, allowing the money to ride might constitute a shift in investment objectives, which must be noted on your account forms.) In this example, the pyramid II structure (originally deemed optimum for the client) has essentially modified its shape/structure toward the more speculative pyramid I posture. This client should probably take the $10,000 (or whatever) gain and spread the money throughout the pyramid to reattain the appropriate portfolio weightings, as follows:

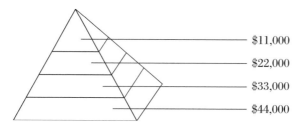

The concept remains the same regardless of portfolio size. The numbers are more impressive with a $1,000,000 portfolio, and additional diversification is easier to achieve. The numbers almost seem insignificant when applied to smaller portfolios such as the one in our example.

Regardless of the size or the pyramid shape, the logic remains the same: Take some of the profits and put the money into something safe. After a series of profits, you have created a nice "nest egg" for the client. A market truism is that *those who let it ride will eventually lose it all.*

The dynamic investment and resource allocation method introduced in this chapter can be used to develop and explain your investment philosophy. Of course, it can be introduced to the prospect/client during the profiling interview in the manner suggested in Chapter 11. It's usefulness lies in graphically illustrating the need to take different investment approaches based on a variety of changes. Once certain changes occur, including profits, a reapportionment may be warranted. The logic behind the reapportionment demonstrates to your client your level of professionalism and shows that you care.

Remember that consultative selling is not a one-time deal. Consultative selling must continue throughout the relationship.

We recommend that you contact your active and inactive clients and educate them to this process, or whatever process you currently employ. We're sure you'll be surprised at how much interest this creates. Although we've only presented the gist of our approach, you will find yourself doing increased business and getting more referrals as a result. We wish you success with this challenge.

CHAPTER

24

Consider Your "Options"

We asked Alex Jacobson of the CBOE Institute to contribute a chapter on option strategies because too many brokers automatically discount options as being too risky, too difficult, too time consuming, and so on. In our opinion, this doesn't have to be true. Like anything else, the results of investing in options depend upon the broker, the market, and the option strategy.

Consultative selling requires you to be able to introduce all the appropriate tools that may help a person achieve investment success. It also requires you to have different strategies for different markets—strategies that will allow you to maximize your rates of return and to do comparatively better for your clients than they might otherwise have done either by themselves or with one of your competitors.

Virtually anyone can make money in a bull market. Throw a few darts and you will probably ride the upward wave. But what about the vast majority of the time when the markets are essentially flat? *How do you manage risk in a downward market* (something which most new brokers haven't really experienced)? *How do you increase the overall portfolio returns in a bull market?* Options products provide opportunities that will allow you to differentiate yourself from your competition.

OPTIONS: A TOOL FOR INVESTMENT FLEXIBILITY [1]

The trading of listed options in the United States is now over 20 years old (since April 1973). Options trade on five exchanges:

- Chicago Board of Options Exchange
- New York Stock Exchange
- American Stock Exchange
- Philadelphia Stock Exchange
- Pacific Stock Exchange

The options markets are the only securities exchanges in the United States where individual investors represent the majority of the trading volume. More than 50 percent of the customer volume directed to the options market on a daily basis originates with brokers representing individual investors—unlike the stock exchanges where the lion's share of volume represents institutional trading. The pioneer options exchange was the CBOE, which currently executes about 60 percent of all options volume. The monetary value of options traded on the CBOE exceeds the monetary value of all stocks traded at the NYSE.

Prior to the advent of listed options trading in April 1973, equity investors only had three alternatives: to buy (go long) stock, to short stock, and to be in cash (which included any debt instrument.) *The options markets were created to give equity investors the ability to manage, reallocate, and adjust stock risk.* The listed options market now gives an investor a virtually unlimited choice of payoffs.

Option Buyers

Investors who purchase options outright, without any offsetting stock position, gain the benefit of leverage and limited risk. The easiest way to view an option buyer is as an investor whose belief is that stock price volatility will be greater than the current view of volatility in the marketplace. In short, option buyers are hoping for unexpected events which will change the price of the stock (and underlying option). That is, buyers of options are hoping for unexpected events. The current price of an option has imbedded

---

[1] This discussion has been contributed by Alex Jacobson of The Options Institute, the Educational Division of the Chicago Board Options Exchange.

within it the current view of overall price volatility. The option buyer's view of volatility is greater than the stock buyer's view of volatility. (Depending upon his or her view, a speculator will buy a stock or an option. The greater the expected movement, the more one leans toward options.) The benefits to the option buyer are straightforward:

- The buyer gains leverage.
- The buyer has a limited risk position.
- The buyer has the potential for large upside appreciation.
- The buyer has the challenge of managing the daily time erosion.

Options buyers will be profitable less frequently than option sellers (writers), but the trade-off is that buyers can earn higher rates of return than sellers and buyers are subject to finite risk. A well-informed option buyer is one who creates a good balance between the leverage inherent in the option and the challenge of daily time erosion. (There is technology readily available which allows both buyers/speculators and investors to easily access selection and information screens. This information is of great benefit to the option buyer.)

An additional choice for option buyers is the innovation created by LEAPS® (Long Term Equity Anticipation Securities) options. LEAPS are options with expiration dates extending out up to three years. The major benefit of LEAPS to the option buyer is the fact that for purchased LEAPS "time erosion occurs at a much slower rate than conventional options." The purchase of LEAPS, especially in-the-money LEAPS calls, provide investors with a very viable alternative to stock ownership. Investors who buy stock on margin will generally find far superior risk-reward economics through the purchase of LEAPS. Investors who short stock will find the purchase of in-the-money LEAPS puts a far superior alternative to outright shorting.

Purchased options can also provide hedge payoffs not available in the equity markets. Put options, when held in conjunction with a position in the underlying stock, provide a form of "term insurance" against the stock. The lower the strike price of the put, the larger the insurance deductible. Take a $75 stock as an example. If you purchase the $75 strike put, that could be viewed as a "0" deductible insurance trade for the life of the put. If, instead of a $75 strike put, an investor chooses to assume a greater portion of the downside risk themselves, they might choose to purchase a $70 strike put. The lower strike put—$5 out of the money—could be viewed as an insurance trade with a $5 deductible. The further out of the money a put is, the less the protection costs and the higher the deductible. From the standpoint of port-folio asset allocation, a purchased put essentially causes a stock position to perform like cash at or below the put's strike for the duration of the put.

LEAPS puts provide longer duration protection for individual stock positions. *Index LEAPS provide long-term protection for entire portfolios.* Be certain to select an index whose performance characteristics most closely match your customer's portfolio. Using far out-of-the-money puts is often a form of "disaster" insurance. Investors find LEAPS disaster protection highly desirable because it allows them to put a long-term disaster hedge.

Option Sellers

Investors who sell equity options are essentially doing the purest form of asset allocation. The seller of an equity call option against a position in the underlying stock (a covered call writer) is agreeing to trade his stock for cash upon assignment. The seller of an equity put option against cash or margin is agreeing to trade stock for their cash or margin on assignment. *The call seller agrees to sell high—at the call's strike price. The put seller agrees to buy low—at the put's strike price.*

One of the greatest misconceptions in the investment community is the perception of the risk related to put writing. The economics of covered call writing and put writing are identical (excluding transaction costs). An important distinction should be made between the leverage available to each strategy under current, generally accepted, margin rules (firms may set margin requirements in excess of regulatory minimums). An investor might be able to obtain greater leverage selling puts than buying calls. The economics of put writing and covered call writing are similar only if the collateral required are the same. Accordingly, a "cash secured" put and a "fully paid for" covered write have identical economics and payoffs.

Why Write Options?

Much of the community, both investors and brokers, view the writing of options as an income strategy. *It's far more than that.* In addition, the evaluation of option writing based on rates of return tends to drive investors to higher-volatility stocks. Higher-volatility stocks yield higher possible rates of return, but bear higher risk.

Criteria for Writing Options

Criterion 1: Select a stock you can be comfortable owning—literally, a stock you can sleep nights owning. The purpose of the options market is to give investors the ability to manage the risks associated with that equity.

Criterion 2: Identify a current comfort level of overall investment risk. In other words, what is the investor's current asset allocation for equities and for cash? For purpose of our examples, we'll assume a two-asset world—equities and cash.

Assume an investor whose current asset allocation is 50 percent long stock and 50 percent cash. We will also assume a multiposition portfolio and recent events that have led to a $60,000 cash balance as a result of an option assignment or maturity of a cash investment.

The investor's profile is straightforward. They are willing to assume equity risk. Their target is to outperform the market in flat, trendless markets; to earn an attractive rate of return in upward trending markets; and, last, to use down markets as a buying opportunity, during which they could accumulate good-quality issues. Consider the following example:

$60,000 to invest

ABC stock at 59 7/8.

50% Long/50% Cash asset allocation.

Dividends and commission excluded.

Buy 500 ABC at 59 7/8.

(Now 50% long with this purchase.)

Invest balance to cash instruments.

Objective: Earn more on the equity portion in flat/trendless markets than you would if you just owned equities.

Strategy: Lighten the equity portion on advances (commonly referred to as *sell high*). Add to the position on declines. Acquire additional stock you're comfortable with at attractive levels (commonly referred to as *buy low*).

Recap: Earn a better return on the equity portion if the stock is unchanged. Lighten up and earn an attractive return if the stock advances.

To accomplish this against our initial 500-share position, sell 5 of the $65 strike call options (as a covered write), and sell 5 of the $55 strike put options. Each of the options are 120 days in duration. The call is bid $2. The put is bid $1 1/2.

In summary thus far, the investor with $60,000 for this trade is about 50% long (long 500 shares at 59 7/8, short (written) 5 $65 calls, and short

5 $55 puts. The calls are covered by the long stock. The puts are secured by the fact that the investor is 50% in cash. Total premiums received are $3.50 per share for a total of $1,750.

Three possible outcomes exist:

1. The stock remains between $55 and $65. The options will probably expire worthless. The $1,750 in premium income adds to the investor's cash flow from the portfolio.

2. The stock rises to a price over $65. The calls are exercised. The effective selling price for our shares is 68 1/2. (We bought stock at 59 7/8 and sold it at 65 strike plus 3 1/2 total option premium—sell high.)

3. The stock declines below $55. We purchase an additional 500 shares at an effective price of $51 1/2 (55 strike minus 3 1/2 total option premium—buy low).

Buy Low, Sell High—Get Paid

What is the key to making this strategy work? Good stock selection. Are we comfortable owning a 50 percent position now selling at 68 1/2 or adding to the position at 51 1/2?

What about the traditional measurement of rate of return. You can still calculate it for the trade, but the driving factor isn't the rate of return. If the investor is comfortable with the stock, if the buy points and sell points feel right, the overall rate of return should, in the long run, be superior to merely owning stock.

In conclusion, options are a valuable tool for you to consider. They can provide significant investment flexibility and allow the investor to buy low and sell high. More important, you gain additional flexibility within the stock and debt markets. While options may not be for everyone, they are appropriate for some. Large portfolios should employ option strategies during certain market scenarios. Sophisticated investors expect you to be aware of the basic strategies or to be able to refer them to someone who is aware.

25

Doing the Right Thing

We felt that a book promoting consultative selling would be lacking if it did not deal with the regulatory environment and basic compliance issues. Obviously, from everything that has been written thus far, the primary message is, "Do the right thing for your clients."

We live in a litigious society. Attorneys advertise in local newspapers that they can get people's money back from their brokers. Clients sometimes rely on the advice of brokers who

- May not have adequate product knowledge.
- Did not fully describe the risks.
- Did not determine suitability.
- May have overtraded—accidentally or on purpose.
- May have made an honest mistake.

The rules of thumb provided within this chapter follow a different format from our previous chapters. The chapter starts with a poem entitled " 'Owed' to the Compliance Director," which makes many points reinforced by two checklists, a newspaper article, and some commentary.

COMPLIANCE

Every firm trading and/or dealing with securities most have a compliance officer. In our opinion, these people have among the most difficult jobs in the entire business because they must ensure that "everyone" follows the rules, and spend the majority of their time dealing with situations in which the rules were not followed. (Perhaps the only job more difficult is that of the branch office manager, who is responsible for *everything* that happens, or fails to happen, within the branch.)

Compliance with both industry and your firm's rules is mandatory. These rules are fair and logical and are often the result of past abuses by financial salespeople who put their own interests before those of their clients. It can be easily said that if you are truly consultative you will abide by the vast majority of the rules; and, if you run into a compliance problem, the chances are that you did not follow consultative selling principles.

Here is a great poem that has been around for a number of years. We think you'll appreciate it.

"OWED" TO THE COMPLIANCE DIRECTOR

Compliance is bothersome, that much is clear.
But sometimes it helps remove the fear
Of hearings and depos and responses we're sending
To all those awful lawsuits pending.
It's an ugly way to spend your time
When you could be working on making a dime
And increasing production, that's languished so sadly
To buy the Mercedes you need so badly.

The first part is simple; it's easy, you'll find,
Put the client's best interest in the front of your mind.
And if you want to be truly compliant,
First and foremost, "Know Your Customer!

The New Account Form is the first of your tasks,
That wonderful form and the questions it asks.
So grab that form promptly and get down to cases,
Check the right boxes and fill in the spaces
Of net worth and income and taxation bracket,
And ask about risk: Can the man really hack it?
You need a home address to buy bonds and stocks,
For few people live in a post office box.

Now finish up quickly and get on with the buying,
But check with the bank to make sure he's not lying.

And don't take the easy way out my friend,
(Who may think the form stinks from beginning to end;)
Who may say, "Not my job! let my SA complete
This silly old form, with such detail replete.
As for me, I'm a broker, don't bother my kind
With meaningless information that a SA can find."
No; the profile is helpful, so don't pass the buck.
And the next test is coming, so don't press your luck!

Your client develops a strong, sudden yearning
For some speculation, and to do some learning.
He thinks that Options and Futures are nifty,
So he rolls the dice and stops being thrifty.
It's probably best to favor the wealthy,
Keep away from the elderly and stick with the healthy
To avoid all those awkward courtroom scenes,
With clients in wheelchairs who have no means.
Even spacious courtrooms can seem mighty close
When one of your clients is comatose.

Above all, know your client; that's the warning we sport,
Ignore it too often, and we'll see you in court!

Adapted from the original.
Author Unknown

While this poem is humorous, it does make a series of key points, the most important of which *Know Your Customer*. You are a financial physician and must be able to prescribe reasonable solutions to a client's problem. Saying "I didn't know" or "I just assumed that" are not satisfactory excuses. It's a bit more complicated than that.

The brokerage, banking, and insurance communities are each governed by different sets of regulators. It is important to realize that the financial services industry is slowly moving toward a consistent set of rules and regulations, but this will probably not occur in the immediate future. The banking industry is entering into the mutual fund and annuity business with speed. The Office of the Comptroller of the Currency has been issuing numerous mandates suggesting how bank investment representatives must carefully explain all of the risks involved in these traditionally nonbank products to ensure that the clients understand that many of the products are not FDIC insured. This has been a challenge for the banking industry, which has not gone through the same compliance-maturation process that the brokerage industry has. (Additional comments taken from Jim Fridl's address to the Association of Banks in Insurance conference will shed additional light on this issue. These are presented in the final segment of this chapter.)

It has been said that "happiness is a stock that's going up," but that's not always so. Clients have actually sued on the basis of their stocks not going up enough, and occasionally won. If a stock (or any investment) doesn't perform as expected, the clients friends, family, and associates will often ask, "How could you have listened to that broker?" Someone may have added, "Maybe you should see a lawyer." Fortunately, on a percentage basis, this is a relatively rare occurrence. The vast majority of people appreciate the risks involved and willingly accept them. The vast majority of brokers are honestly trying to do the best job that they know how to do. However, as the adage indicates, "A falling bridge makes more noise than a thousand standing ones." When something goes somewhat wrong (such as the "1987 readjustment"), or when a mistake is made, the media may publicize the story and the entire profession gets a black eye.

Clients also may bring suit when they are dissatisfied or do not feel they were given appropriate recommendations. Consider the following story, which appeared in the business section of a major newspaper.[1] (We've changed the names, but not the essential details.)

Saver Turns into Unhappy Investor

Having built his savings through decades of hard work and frugality, customer Mike Smith says he was not inclined to take any risks. Yet, like millions of retirees, he was searching for higher yields than the 3 percent or less he was getting on his savings accounts and certificates of deposit.

He moved $164,000 (more than half his life savings) from bank CDs to an annuity that guaranteed him a fixed rate of 5 percent. Bank representatives began to recommend that he consider annuities and mutual funds available through the bank affiliate for the remaining $164,000.

Smith, 63, joins what securities regulators say is a legion of American consumers confused about the risks and costs of uninsured investments sold at bank branches. His case can serve as a reminder of how investors—whether they're investing at a

---

[1]*On Personal Finance*, by Craig Stock, *Philadelphia Inquirer*, July 12, 1994.

bank, brokerage firm or mutual fund—should take the time to investigate and truly understand what they're buying. For many
people, that means taking days or weeks, not hours, to consider
an investment decision.

Smith had spent less than an hour with a broker before agreeing
to invest $9,226 in a tax-exempt bond fund, despite the fact that
he was in the 15 percent tax bracket. Twenty-eight percent is, at
the time of writing, the break point between taxable and nontaxable investments. The broker did not supply that information, according to Smith.

Smith invested an additional $40,000 into mutual funds offering
"growth" as well as "capital preservation." So far, because of
commission costs and a slump in bond and stock prices, the investments have not met either objective—his capital has neither
appreciated nor been preserved.

He insists that he told the bank manager as well as the investment representative that he wanted no loss of principle. While
he admits that he was told of risks, he claims he had neither
the time nor the sophistication to understand those risks—he
"trusted" the representative and the manager.

Smith signed disclosure documents. "They didn't say, 'Read it
over.' They said, 'Put your signature here.'" . . .

After making additional investments (in mutual funds), he lost a
net of 7.4 percent on his investment ($3,000) over a 7 month time
frame. Although Smith is down a relatively small amount, (now
only 5.1 percent) he is still angry and frightened. . . .

Can you imagine being the broker whose name was prominently mentioned in this article or being one of the many brokers mentioned in similar
articles? By most industry standards, we would consider the $3,000 a
"minor loss" and, as brokers, perhaps be proud that we had made such a
wise choice in funds (after all, the market was down substantially more). Unfortunately, the client didn't quite see it that way and didn't have "a sense
of humor." Who was right? Even if the broker wins the suit, he still loses.

WHAT CAN YOU DO?

We believe that one of the best ways to simultaneously do the appropriate
thing and avoid compliance problems is to imagine that every aspect of a

particular transaction will be reviewed on the front page of *The Wall Street Journal*. The question is: Would you feel proud of the story? If "Yes," then you probably did everything correctly. However, if you get a bad feeling in your stomach, or if you would prefer that the world does not know of some aspect of the transaction, then you probably violated some legal or ethical rule. Is this test always accurate? Of course not. There are things, such as a market crash, that are outside of your control. However, this simple questionnaire help determine if you took as many factors into account as you could.

Generally, "do the right thing by your clients, and your clients will do the right thing by you" according most industry experts.

QUESTIONS TO CONSIDER[2]

There are many rules of thumb you can follow. Among the best ways we've found to avoid compliance problems is to ask yourself a series of questions. While the list that follows is certainly not complete, it should give you some ideas.

DID I

1. Get an estimate, guesstimate, or actual dollar figure on income?

2. Ask what made up the net worth and liquid net worth?

3. Get the full business address, telephone number, position with the firm, and length of time employed?

4. Get the account number or branch office where another brokerage account is maintained?

5. Ask for the specific branch and the name of a person to contact at the bank reference given?

6. Ask the person if he or she was married, and, if so, how many dependents does he or she have?

7. Discuss the short- and long-term investment objectives and write them down with the date?

8. Review in detail any investment concepts with him, and, if so, review the basic suitability requirements?

[2]Derived from compliance lectures made to Merrill Lynch training classes by Mike Golden and George Janos of the Merrill Lynch Compliance Department. They gave extremely interesting and enjoyable trainings and had significant influence on thousands of brokers, as well as the authors.

9. Feel at ease with the prospective client personally?

10. Get the feeling that I was being told the complete truth about all we discussed?

11. Mention that I'm required to do some basic check on this information as routine (did it seem to upset the prospective client)?

12. Ask for a deposit on the first transaction (buy) or receipt of the security deposit (sell) in good deliverable form (proof of ownership and further check needed if a bearer security or bond)?

13. Review all the documents that would be required to sign, and the reasons why?

14. Check with the employer, bank, and other brokerage firm as I told him I would? (Note: This requirement varies from firm to firm.)

15. Do all I said I'd do and still feel comfortable with this perspective client?

If "yes," then by all means, open the account and good luck, because you are a broker who is aware.

IS THERE A TIME TO SAY "STOP"?[3]

Is there a time to stop? If you ask your friendly regulator or jury, the answer will most certainly be Yes!

When you do physical exercise beyond the extremes of what your body can absorb, a little bell rings sending a message to your brain saying "Stop." The same message should hold true when you see your client is about to commit "economic suicide." You should, and must, say "stop!" It's not very pleasant, and most certainly, a very difficult decision to be made.

Your professional responsibilities extend far beyond the boundaries of what the "Know Your Customer" Rule (405) is intended to imply. You must now add the dimension of the ethical, moral, and professional responsibility to the client, your office, the firm—and, of course, yourself.

A medical doctor has a responsibility to provide the best of which she is capable and not participate in treatments that are inappropriate to the pa-

---

[3]Originally presented by Mike Golden and George Janos. Authorship is unknown. Original notes are modified for this book.

tient. Even if the patient signs a letter releasing the doctor from any responsibility for a course of treatment, the doctor is still under an obligation to do what she (the physician) thinks best, not what the patient thinks best. If a doctor accedes to a patient's request, and the patient becomes ill or dies, the doctor will certainly lose the ensuing lawsuit.

In almost every sense of the word, you are a "financial physician." You have a fiduciary responsibility to give competent advice, based upon full knowledge of your client's circumstances. If your client wishes to do something that is inappropriate, your legal, moral, and ethical responsibility is to say "No." (Although the last sentence may seem strong or dogmatic, it is the way juries and arbitrators generally view the situation.) If the client insists, bring the situation to the attention of your manager. Your manager may place specific limits on the client's investment and may even refuse the trade. If limits are imposed, make sure that you make a notation on your holding page (customer record) and then be sure that you follow those limits. If, for example, a client's limit is set at $30,000 for options, and the client makes a $10,000 profit, you should withdraw $10,000 and place it in a safe investment and limit his options to the original $30,000.

Clients are known, at times, to assert extreme pressure on their brokers to execute transactions that may eventually prove to be inappropriate—especially at an arbitration or courtroom hearing. Always review the type of transaction you suggest to your client, or which he requests, relative to the amount of money at risk, age, income, net worth, and most important, suitability. In essence, you must take into account the various factors discussed in Chapter 22. *If you are uncomfortable, or have a bad feeling about any part of a transaction, bring it to your manager's attention—don't go it alone.* Once a client has already retained an attorney whose sole purpose will be to prove that you, your manager, and the firm failed in their responsibility of properly supervising the clients' best interests, it will be too late. What's at risk? Your career, reputation, self-respect, community standing, and so on. The impact of a suit, especially one that goes to trial or in any other way receives publicity, is impossible to imagine and, we hope, one you'll never have to experience.

Remember: The client will be the first one to tell you not to worry. "I can afford the loss," "It's my idea," "It's absolutely suitable for me." As long as things are in their favor, all seems well. But you do have to worry. Beyond the client there lies other interested parties, including any heirs. Only you are truly capable to making the determination of when to say "Stop."

The following article discusses issues facing the banking community as banks expand their product lines. There are important comments for all readers.

Bank Programs[4]

There is an old adage that states that the role of a salesman is not to make sales, but to make customers. Not a bad thought, especially if you consider it takes less effort and cost to keep an old customer satisfied than it does to get a new customer relationship started. Offering these financial products involving risk of principle as a new bank service can easily result in customers turning their backs on banks if their investments go bad, and they were not appropriate or suitable. In the bank environment, the alternative adage, "Go for the big order" will only get you in trouble. . . .

. . . Making the leap from representing FDIC-backed deposits and insurance company-backed annuities to investment products with no guarantees, representations, or warranties requires a fundamental shift in how customers are handled. . . . The Office of the Comptroller of the Currency issued Circular No. B274 to address the investment sales process in banks in the interest of ensuring that the customer has all the information necessary to make informed and responsible decisions. . . . The directive issued states that "banks must develop programs and procedures addressing their investment sales activities to apprise customers fully in the nature of these investments."

"Suitability" has become an industry watchword for the sale of nondeposit products to bank customers. The OCC has directed that the NASD Rules of Fair Practice will be the benchmark for the treatment of your customers in the investing process.

There isn't a salesperson on this planet who hasn't heard, "But you didn't tell me that," if a customer is dissatisfied. Oftentimes the truth is a breakdown in communication: either the salesperson failed to make his points clearly, or the customer has experienced selective hearing. The OCC is aware of the weaknesses in the sales process and requires that responses to inquiries be documented, and that disclosures be made and countersigned to protect the consumer, the bank, and the registered representative.

The only way to determine if an investment is suitable is by getting to know your customer. You must focus on areas such as:

[4]These comments were given by James J. Fridl, president, Cross Marketing, Inc. (Peapack, NJ) in an address to the ABI Conference, October 4, 1993. Selected comments from his speech are reprinted within this book. LifeCycle is a registered trademark of AEGON.

- Financial status/ability to invest.
- Tax status.
- Investment objectives.
- Tolerance for risk.
- Personal information for sales and tax documents.

Everyone likes to make a quick dollar. Cashing in CDs to buy a hot stock for a retired couple could mean a luxury sedan on the upside, or the loss of their emergency fund on the downside. *"What does the customer have?" does not equate to "What does the customer need?"*

"Hand-in-hand with suitability comes the responsibility of helping the customer understand the difference between depository products of the bank and investment products. While disclosures are essential, the setting for interviewing and selling to the customer leaves a more lasting impression. Customers have strong affinities to their banks and believe with their hearts rather than with their intellects that everything a bank has to offer them is safe. The OCC requires that the investment program be established separately and distinctly from depository activities to help draw the separation for the customer between the bank-vault image and the risks inherent in investing in the market. Distinguishing the selling area, business cards, signage and collateral material from the rest of the bank is one way to draw the distinction.

Detailed knowledge of customer's financial position, risk tolerances and objectives is a sure fire way to success in predicting customer suitability and whether that customer will buy. However, financial planning "per se" takes too long in a platform sales or even a dedicated branch representative program. The banking environment requires that service be provided in minutes that builds and sustains loyalty....Financial profiling programs such as the LifeCycle™ program establishes rapport and creates the condition for a sale by identifying how well current investments meet tangible investment objectives. It works to simplify the management of investments, easing customer apprehensions so that, as major changes or events in their life occur, they turn to the bank to update their personal profile, investments, and objectives.

As a banker [or any other financial professional], you have customer trust, perceived objectivity and a distribution system that
can be trained to reach a broad base of customer relationships.
A properly trained sales force is the first step in a sales culture
and a primary source of productivity gains when marketing programs are put in place that cement the customer relationship. I
encourage you all to develop relationship marketing tools that
integrate compliance, control, and consistency into your sales
process.

*Compliance is not a dark spectre. It's a marketing opportunity
to learn more about your customer and to develop a long-term
relationship.*

An important part of compliance and of consultative selling also
includes ongoing professional development.

Ongoing Professional Development

Times are changing and we must change with them. Ongoing education and
personal and professional development is a hallmark of leading producers
throughout the nation. You must continue to "grow" professionally. This final
segment discusses new requirements that will be mandatory continuing education requirements, and ways to increase your own professional knowledge with resultant gains in productivity and effectiveness.

Continuing Education Requirements for Bankers and Brokers

Paul Weisman,[5] a member of the NASD task force for continuing education
in the brokerage industry, indicates that brokers will be required to complete continuing education requirements (like most other professions) on a
regular basis in order to maintain their licenses. Commenting on continuing
education requirements for the securities industry for publication within this
book, Mr. Weisman wrote:[6]

"In May 1993, a task force sponsored by the NASD, NYSE, and North
American Securities Administrators Association (NASAA) was formed to research the need for a continuing education program for the securities industry. The members of this task force were selected by the regulators and have

[5]Paul Weisman is President of Securities Training Corporation. Continuing education requirements for
most/all brokers should go into effect by mid-1995.

[6]Letter to Drozdeck & Gretz dated June 29, 1994.

extensive securities industry experience. The task force published its findings in September 1993. The report indicated that there was a need to man-
date an industry-wide program for continuing education. This was reinforced
in early 1994 in a letter to member firms by SEC Chairman Arthur Levitt. The
goal of the task force is '...to design a truly beneficial program to transmit
meaningful information to appropriate industry personnel while satisfying
wide variations in the specific needs of individuals and their firms.'

"The task force reviewed continuing education programs currently in
place in other industries and professions. Many of these programs are based
on a specific number of classroom hours in approved courses. In some cases,
it is very difficult to verify attendance and proficiency. The task force determined that the program for the securities industry should *not* be modeled
on that of another industry.

"The proposed program for the securities industry consists of a regulatory element and a firm element. The regulatory element would be uni-
formly administered to all registered securities industry personnel with less
than 10 years of experience. Individuals with more than 10 years of experience are exempt from this requirement provided that they have an unblem-
ished regulatory history. The element of the continuing education program
is intended to be delivered via computer-based training and is designed to
teach and assess, but not to test, an individual's proficiency in various areas
of regulatory concern (such as issues regarding qualification of customers
and sales practices). Member firms will be given reports as to the performance of their personnel in this element. Deficiencies may require the firm
to adjust its internal training practices. *Persons who do not partake in this
required training must cease doing business until the requirement is met.*
[emphasis added]

"The firm element is to be delivered by the firm or by [3rd party]
providers on behalf of the firm. This training should address product knowledge and ethical sales practices in keeping with the specific job functions
and products of the member. *Each firm must create a plan that provides for
the ongoing training of its personnel to meet the need of the various segments
of their business.* [emphasis added] Failure to comply with the firm element
standards will result in the initiation of disciplinary proceedings by the regulatory authorities."

We applaud the work of the industry leaders, such as Paul Weisman
and Frank McAuliffee of the NASD (who has spent years coordinating these
efforts and helping to establish the standards which will apply throughout
the industry). Continuing education requirements, we believe, will add substantial value to our profession.

As we wrote in *The Effective Manager: Being the Best in Financial Sales Management*, the financial services industry has changed so much in the last ten years that it has become almost a different industry for many people. The players have changed. The proliferation of products and services, alone, is enough to require constant updating of training if one is to stay current. And, finally, the market has changed. We believe that the changes will accelerate in the years ahead.

Today's market is made up of individuals and companies that are far better informed about their financial needs than ever before. They expect, and demand, service. For brokers, old methods of selling and product knowledge that is not up to date will no longer bring success and could even lead to lawsuits.

However, the domestic market is not the only one that is changing. More and more firms and their brokers are becoming involved with foreign customers. As we approach the twenty-first century, and the new global marketplace, we must be ready to serve the world-wide community or lose our competitive edge. It therefore becomes vital that we constantly (whether or not it is mandated) improve our level of product knowledge and levels of sophistication.

A

Resources for the Financial Services Industry

EDUCATIONAL SERVICES

Securities Training Corp.
17 Battery Place, New York, NY 10004
212-425-7255 / 800-STC-1223
(Paul Weisman, president)

Securities Training Corporation (STC) successfully prepares individuals for the various securities and financial industry examinations. Serving the financial services industry since 1969, STC has been a part of more than 350,000 individual success stories. Their exceptionally high first-time pass rates have earned them a solid reputation among their 3,000 corporate clients worldwide.

STC offers training programs for the qualifications exams required by the NASD, NYSE, MSRB, NFA, and NASAA. Their study materials are complete, current, and comprehensive. They are designed to be easily understood regardless of a student's previous experience or knowledge of the securities industry. Course formats include classroom instruction, correspondence courses, computer-based training, audio cassettes, and videotapes.

Other Educational Resources[1]

The American Institute of Banking, associated with the ABA, is the principal resource for bankers. Its BEN-line (Banker's Educational Network) can be particularly useful. The number is (202) 663-5430.

On the general level, the **New York Institute of Finance** has been training Wall Street professionals for more than a half century.

Their programs are given in the classroom (New York City only), in tailor-made programs that will be developed for individual firms, and in correspondence courses. The New York Institute of Finance, which is a subsidiary of Simon & Schuster, also has an extensive library of professional books for the continuing education of both securities and commodities brokerage employees. They also develop specialized programs for individual companies and associations, providing them with programs on a wide range of business and industry topics. Call (212) 361-1500.

For securities brokerage professionals who are interested in certification as financial planners, you may consider the **College for Financial Planning** located in Denver, Colorado. Call (303) 220-1200.

The College of Insurance, located in New York City, provides professional development courses and both a graduate and undergraduate degree program for resident and non-resident students. Call (212) 962-4111.

We have provided the names and telephone numbers of four institutions that provide ongoing courses. There are many other organizations, some of which may be in your area, that offer excellent professional development courses. No slight is intended.

MOTIVATIONAL SPEAKERS

Art Mortell
Systematic Achievement Corp.
P.O. Box 721, Malibu, CA 90265
(310) 457-2551

One of the most dynamic speakers in the United States, Art Mortell's talks have a powerful impact and produce lasting results. His audio cassette tape series, with accompanying workbook, is a valuable resource.

---

[1]Taken from "Going Back to School" by Joseph Ross, Ph.D., as written in *The Effective Manager: Being the Best in Financial Sales Management*.

SPECIAL INDUSTRY MAGAZINES WORTH OBTAINING

Research
P.O. Box 77905
San Francisco, CA 94107
(800) 458-2700

Bank Investment Representative
P.O. Box 4364
Logan, UT 84323
(801) 752-1173

BANK AND BROKERAGE RESOURCES

Cross Marketing Inc.
87 Main Street
Peapack, NJ 07977
(908) 781-2006
(James J. Fridl, president)

CMI's Cross Track is an innovative database marketing and sales management program that monitors and evaluates all aspects of bank and brokerage marketing programs. This includes registration of personnel, lead tracking, sales tracking and analysis, and word processing with mail merge capabilities, in addition to providing a host of other functions that would be useful in the implementation of any sales effort. CMI also provides training, sales, and marketing support for the delivery of fixed and variable annuities, mutual funds, UIT's, personal lines, and life insurance products through financial institutions and banking associations.

Kray Management Corp.
180 Alan Road
202 South Bldg.
Atlanta, GA 30328
(404) 250-9094

Kray Management specializes in precision streamlining or restructuring of the marketing and sales function. Key to Kray's unique approach are

- A mapping tool that identifies the thinking strategies of those involved
- State-of-the-art assessment instruments to ensure right "job fit"
- Training and coaching tools for providing the skills and know-how

Jay Associates, Inc.
2300 Computer Avenue, #J-54
Willow Grove, PA 19090
(215) 830-9725
(Walt Wiesenhutter, president)

Jay Associates provides published books and reference materials (individually or in bulk) to the financial services industry.

B

Recommended Reading

Carnegie, Dale. *How to Win Friends and Influence People*. New York: Simon & Schuster, 1936.

Drozdeck, Steven, Joseph Yeager, and Linda Sommer. *What They DON'T Teach You in Sales 101*. New York: McGraw-Hill, 1991.

Gayed, Michael E. S. *Intermarket Analysis and Investing: Integrating Economic, Fundamental, and Technical Trends*. New York: Simon & Schuster/New York Institute of Finance, 1990.

Gretz, Karl F. and Steven R. Drozdeck. *Consultative Selling Techniques for Financial Professional*. New York: Simon & Schuster/New York Institute of Finance, 1990.

Gretz, Karl F. and Steven R. Drozdeck. *The Effective Manager: Being the Best in Financial Sales Management*. New York: Simon & Schuster/New York Institute of Finance, 1991.

Gretz, Karl F. and Steven R. Drozdeck. *Empowering Innovative People: How Managers Challenge, Channel and Control the Truly Creative and Talented*. Chicago: Probus Publishing, 1992.

Kelly, Eugene A. *For What It's Worth*. Thomasville, GA: Marshwinds Advisory Company, 1984.

Lorayne, Harry and Jerry Lucas. *The Memory Book*. New York: Stein and Day, 1974.

Mortell, Art. *The Courage to Fail: Art Mortell's Secrets for Business Success*. New York: McGraw-Hill, 1993.

Mortell, Art. *World Class Selling: How to Turn Adversity into Success*. Dearborn: Dearborn Financial Publishing, 1991.

Murray, Nick. *Serious Money: The Art of Marketing Mutual Funds*. New Jersey: Robert A. Stanger, 1992.

Pessin, Allan H. and Joseph A. Ross. *More Words of Wall Street: 2000 More Investment Terms Defined*. Homewood, IL: Dow Jones-Irwin, 1986.

Pessin, Allan H. and Joseph A. Ross. *Words of Wall Street: 2000 Investment Terms Defined*. Homewood, IL: Dow Jones-Irwin, 1983.

Peters, Thomas J. and Robert H. Waterman, Jr. *In Search of Excellence*. New York: Warner Books, 1982.

Stanley, Dr. Thomas J. *Marketing to the Affluent*. Homewood: Dow-Jones Irwin, 1988.

Stanley, Dr. Thomas J. *Selling to the Affluent*. Homewood: Business One Irwin, 1991.

About the Authors

Steven R. Drozdeck and Karl F. Gretz are the managing directors of Training Groups International, an organization which specializes in increasing personal/personnel performance and productivity. Training Groups International offers courses in many formats and levels of sophistication. Courses include: Consultative Selling Techniques for Financial Professionals; Motivating Representatives to Higher Performance; Look To Your Book; Market Strategies; Stress Management for Increased Productivity; and Building Effective Sales Teams and Organizations. Both authors were brokers with Merrill Lynch. They have been featured at numerous financial industry conferences and have presented their ideas through television shows, articles, books and training sessions. Both have worked with many corporations in the brokerage, banking and insurance industries and have trained more than 35,000 sales professionals and managers in effectively selling financial products and services.

Steven R. Drozdeck has over 20 years of experience in the financial services industry, medicine, and education. He was a stockbroker for 6 years before becoming the manager of professional development for Merrill Lynch. He has personally trained over 25,000 financial professionals in sales and stock selection techniques. Drozdeck is listed in numerous *Who's Who* publications and is a leading expert in neuro linguistic programming (NLP). He is also the author of *What They DON'T Teach You in Sales 101* (with Yeager and Sommer).

Karl F. Gretz, Ph.D., has more than 16 years experience in training professionals in the financial services industry, medicine, education, and the military. Dr. Gretz was also with Merrill Lynch, first as a successful broker and later as senior training consultant. He has trained over 16,000 executives, medical professionals, military officials, sales professionals and their managers in the psychology of sales, management, and leadership. He has also helped them to increase sales productivity and lower staff turnover by providing easy, effective methods for managing stress.

Other books by Gretz and Drozdeck:

Consultative Selling Techniques for Financial Professionals
The Effective Manager: Being the Best in Financial Sales Management
Empowering Innovative People

For additional information regarding other books, tapes, lectures, courses and materials, contact:

Training Groups International
PO Box 996
Newtown, PA 18940
Phones: (215) 579-2149 or (215) 639-1922

INDEX